Scientific Database and Programming Examples

Using PHP, MySQL, XML, MATLAB, PYTHON, PERL

Scientific Database and Programming Examples

Using PHP, MySQL, XML, MATLAB, PYTHON, PERL

K.Y. Cheung

Library of Congress Control Number:		2011916422
ISBN:	Hardcover	978-1-4653-6444-9
	Softcover	978-1-4653-6443-2
	Ebook	978-1-4653-6445-6

This book was printed in the United States of America.

To order additional copies of this book, contact:
Xlibris Corporation
1-888-795-4274
www.Xlibris.com
Orders@Xlibris.com
105001

CONTENTS

Chapter 1

INTRODUCTION

This book deals with, but is not limited to, the following:

(1) A collection of typical computer programs written in Python and Matlab for scientific computations and their comparisons;
(2) Interfaces of Php, Python, Perl with Matlab and vice versa;
(3) Use of MySQL tables and XML for storing and transmitting scientific and economic data in scientific programming with Matlab, Python and Perl;
(4) Converting from XML to MySQL tables and vice versa using Php;
(5) Creating XML and MySQL tables and retrieving data from them for inputting to Matlab and to Python, using Php.

It is assumed that the reader has had some knowledge of Php, Matlab, Python, Perl, MySQL and XML. As this book is written with Matlab programmers in mind, the following books are highly recommended for understanding the details of computer programs in this book:

(1) Julie C. Meloni, PHP, MySQL and Apache,All in One, 4th ed.
(2) Hans Petter Langstangen, A Primer on Scientific Programming with Python.
(3) Robin Nixon, PHP, MySQL & JavaScript.

The sections in the book have been organized as independent units. For example, Chapter 14.3 has Appendix 14.3 and computer_files 14.3. All the computer program files used in the section are included in this computer_files 14.3, as if the section is completely a stand-alone unit, with all the data needed to run the computer programs of that section provided. In principle, the reader can just click and paste the computer files to run the computer programs, provided that he/she uses the same setup of paths as described in Chapter2, Chapter 3 and Chapter 4.

All the computer files may be downloaded from xlibrisbook.com. For example type http://www.xlibrisbook.com/downloads/book105001/computer_files_10.1/create_basicdata1.py.txt to download the computer file "create_basicdata1.py.txt".

Chapter 2

SETTING UP XAMPP ON WINDOWS

2.1 INSTALLING PHP, MYSQL AND PERL.

The website for downloading and installing XAMPP is http://www.apachefriends.org/en/xampp-windows.html

Current version of XAMPP installs Apache 2.2.1, MySQL 5.5.8, PHP 5.3.5, phpMyAdmin 3.3.9 and Perl 5.10.1. Apache is a webserver which makes the users' computer as "localhost". The phpMyAdmin is a PHP script to give users the ability to interact with their MySQL databases. For most cases, we need to choose XAMPP using Method A with installer. Perl will be installed automatically. There is no need to do Perl add-on separately. Follow the instruction to download and install the package. For most of the applications, we need to click the "start" buttons for Apache and MySQL on the XAMPP Control Panel Application. Make sure to check the security setting in phpMyAdmin. The default user name is "root". But the password must be set or else the MySQL table cannot be accessed with Php script.

With this installation, the Php files for execution are to be placed in the subfolders after C:\xampp\htdocs\; the Perl files for execution are placed in the subfolders after C:\xampp\cgi-bin\. For example, if the Php script "XXX.php" is in C:\xampp\htdocs\new_sci2\XXX.php, where "new_sci2" is one of the subfolders after C:\xampp\htdocs\, then, to run this Php script, we type http://localhost/new_sci2/XXX.php. If the Perl script "YYY.pl" is in C:\xampp\cgi-bin\xampp_perl\YYY.pl, where "xampp_perl" is one of the subfolders after C:\xampp\cgi-bin\, then to run this Perl script, we type http://localhost/cgi-bin/xampp_perl/YYY.pl.

To access MySQL directly, we go to http://localhost/phpmyadmin/index.php. After logging on with user name ("root" for example) and password, go to the toolbar to select "SQL". This will allow the user to type in the MySQL commands (one at a time). Highlight the command and click "go" to execute the MySQL command.

Chapter 3

Setting Up Python Scientific Application on Windows

3.1 Installing Python

The following is the recommended way to download and install Python and other programs associated with scientific application of Python:

Go to http://www.enthought.com/products/epddownload.php

Select "Academic" and give an academic email address if you are qualified. You will be given a link by email to download and install the package. The file to be downloaded is big. so—depending on your internet connection—this step may take a while.

Once the process is completed, you should find that you have the new software installed under Start->All Programs->Enthought. The program we will use usually is labelled IDLE (Python GUI).

The default installation location is C:\Python27. The current package contains:

python version 2.7.1
numpy version 1.5.1
matplotlib version 1.0.1 which is pylab
scipy version 0.9.0rc2

SciTools is a Python package containing lots of useful tools for scientific computing in Python. The package is built on top of other widely used packages such as NumPy, SciPy, ScientificPython, Gnuplot, etc. See http://pypi.python.org/pypi/SciTools.

The download URL is http://scitools.googlecode.com/files/scitools-0.8.tar.gz

Its home page is http://scitools.googlecode.com. The current version is SciTools 0.8. SciTool is installed in C:\Python27\Lib\site-packages\folder. For convenience, a copy of SciTools is in "computer_files_3.1". After installing the Enthought package,simply place the attached SciTools folder in C:\Python27\Lib\site-packages\.

We shall also need "MySQLdb", a module for Python to interface with MySQL. The exe files for MySQLdb are: MySQL-python-1.2.3.win32-py2.7.exe (1023.1 KiB) and MySQL-python-1.2.3.win-amd64-py2.7.exe (1.0MiB). They are in http://www.codegood.com/archive/129. Download whichever is appropriate, double-click it to install. A copy of MySQLdb is included in "computer-files_3.1".

3.2 Installing GNUPLOT.

GNUPLOT is by itself an independent program for plotting. (There is a version of GNUPLOT which can be called directly from Python, but with reduced capability.) See http://gnuplot-py.sourceforge.net/.

To install it, download either gnuplot-py-1.8.tar.gz or Gnuplot-1.8.zip from http://sourceforge.net/projects/gnuplot-py/files/ Untar or unzip it, which will create a directory to be placed in C:\Python27\gnuplot. To execute GNUPLOTas an independent program, (with data generated by Python, or Matlab, manually input to GNUPLOT), go to C:\Python27\gnuplot\binary\ and click on the gnuplot icon to begin execution. A copy of "gnuplot" is included in "computer_file_3.2".

There is a brief but useful users' manual of GNUPLOT in http://www.duke.edu/~hpgavin/gnuplot.html.

Chapter 4

Installing Matlab and Some Additional Capabilities

Installing Matlab is easy because Mathsoft provides all the instructions of installation. However, in order to have the interfaces of Matlab with Python, with MySQL and with XML, we may need to do the following:

(1) Interface with Python: Place "python.m" in the "\MATLAB" folder. See Section 13.2.
(2) Interface with MySQL: Place "mysql.dll" in the "\MATLAB" folder and "libmysql.dll" in the "\WINDOWS\System32" folder. See Section 8.1.
(3) Interface with XML: Place the "xmltree" package in the "\MATLAB" folder. See Chapter 12.

All these files: "python.m", "mysql.dll", "libmysql.dll" and the entire "xmltree" package have been included in "computer_files_4.1".

Chapter 5

PHP AND MYSQL

5.1 CREATING MYSQL DATABASE TABLES.

Example 1

We shall go through the process of creating a MySQL table named "basicdata1" and populate data in it. We shall use two approaches: (1) directly type in commands on the MySQL window; (2) use Php programs. The data in this table are properties and labels of some chemical elements, taken from a text book. They are used for demonstration only.

Go to http://localhost/phpmyadmin/index.php to create database "science". Click on SQL on the toolbar and type in the commands:

```
CREATE TABLE science.basicdata1 (
id INT NOT NULL PRIMARY KEY AUTO_INCREMENT,
element VARCHAR(15) NOT NULL,
atomic_number SMALLINT(15) NOT NULL,
symbol VARCHAR(8) NOT NULL,
atomic_weight FLOAT NOT NULL,
absorption FLOAT NOT NULL,
scattering FLOAT NOT NULL
);

INSERT INTO science.basicdata1
(id,element,atomic_number,symbol,atomic_weight,absorption,scattering)
VALUES('1','Hydrogen','1','H',1.0080,0.33,80.0);

INSERT INTO science.basicdata1
```

```
(id,element,atomic_number,symbol,atomic_weight,absorption,scattering)
VALUES('2','Deuterium','1','D',2.015,0.00046,5.4);

INSERT INTO science.basicdata1
(id,element,atomic_number,symbol,atomic_weight,absorption,scattering)
VALUES('3','Helium','2','He',4.003,0.0,0.8);

INSERT INTO science.basicdata1
(id,element,atomic_number,symbol,atomic_weight,absorption,scattering)
VALUES('4','Lithium','3','Li',6.94,70.0,1.4);

INSERT INTO science.basicdata1
(id,element,atomic_number,symbol,atomic_weight,absorption,scattering)
VALUES('5','Berylium','4','Be',9.01,0.009,7.0);

INSERT INTO science.basicdata1
(id,element,atomic_number,symbol,atomic_weight,absorption,scattering)
VALUES('6','Boron','5','B',10.82,750.0,4.0);

INSERT INTO science.basicdata1
(id,element,atomic_number,symbol,atomic_weight,absorption,scattering)
VALUES('7','Carbon','6','C',12.01,0.0045,4.8);
```

The following Php program is to insert more data into the MySQL database table "basicdata1":

```
<?php
//—http://localhost/new_sci2/to_insert_in_basicdata1.php
//*******
// To log in
$db_hostname = 'localhost';
$db_database = 'science';
$db_username = 'root';
$db_password = 'xxxxxxxx';
// To connect to MySQL
$db_server = mysql_connect($db_hostname, $db_username, $db_password);
if (!$db_server) die("Unable to connect to MySQL: " . mysql_error());
// To select a database
mysql_select_db($db_database,$db_server)
        or die("Unable to select database: " . mysql_error());
// To query a database
```

```
//$query = "INSERT INTO basicdata1 VALUES('NULL','Nitrogen','7','N',14.008,1.
8,10.0)";
//$query = "INSERT INTO basicdata1 VALUES('NULL','Oxygen','8','O',16.000,0.0
002,4.2)";
//$query = "INSERT INTO basicdata1 VALUES('NULL','Fluorine','9','F',19.00,0.00
9,4.1)";
//$query = "INSERT INTO basicdata1 VALUES('NULL','Neon','10','Ne',20.18,2.8,
2.4)";
$query = "INSERT INTO basicdata1 VALUES('NULL','Sodium','11','Na',22.997,0.
50,4.0)";
$result = mysql_query($query);
if($result){
echo "One row of data has been inserted.";
}else{
echo "Database access failed: " . mysql_error();
}

?>
```

Example 2

We shall create another MySQL table "science.rare_earth", and then slightly modify it by adding a new column on the table. The Php program to create table "science.rare_earth" is:

```
<?php
//—http://localhost/new_sci2/to_create_rare_earth.php
//
$db_hostname = 'localhost';
$db_database = 'science';
$db_username = 'root';
$db_password = 'xxxxxxxx';
// To connect to MySQL
$db_server = mysql_connect($db_hostname, $db_username, $db_password);
if (!$db_server) die("Unable to connect to MySQL: " . mysql_error());
// to select a database
mysql_select_db($db_database, $db_server)
        or die("Unable to select database: " . mysql_error());
//
```

```
$query = "CREATE TABLE rare_earth (
                    id SMALLINT NOT NULL AUTO_INCREMENT,
                    element VARCHAR(15) NOT NULL,
                    uses VARCHAR(50) NOT NULL,
                    oxide_price_USD_per_kg VARCHAR(25) NOT NULL,
                    PRIMARY KEY (id)
                    )";

$result = mysql_query($query,$db_server);
if($result){
        echo "Table rare_earth has been created";
        }else{
        echo "Failed to create table: " . mysql_error();
        }
?>
```

To populate the table "science.rare_earth", we shall use the following commands:

```
INSERT INTO science.rare_earth
(id,element,uses,oxide_price_USD_per_kg)
VALUES('NULL','Lanthanum','Batteries\,Catalyst\,Lasers','40'),
('NULL','Yttrium','Lasers\,Superconductors','50'),
('NULL','Neodymium','Lasers\,Magnets\,Computers','60'),
('NULL','Cerium','Catalyst\,Fuel addititive\,Optical polish','65'),
('NULL','Praseodymium','Lasers\,Magnets\,Lighting\,Alloys','75'),
('NULL','Gadolinium','Lasers\,Magnets\,Computers\,X-rays','150'),
('NULL','Dysprosium','Lasers\,Magnets\,Cars','160'),
('NULL','Erbium','Lasers\,Alloys\,Photography','165'),
('NULL','Samarium','Lasers\,Magnets\,Neutron absorption','350'),
('NULL','Ytterbium','Lasers\,Alloys\,Gamma rays','450'),
('NULL','Holmium','Lasers\,Magnets\,Optics','750'),
('NULL','Terbium','Lasers\,Phosphors\,Lighting','850'),
('NULL','Europium','Lasers\,Phosphors\,Lighting','1200'),
('NULL','Thulium','Lasers\,X-rays','2500'),
('NULL','Lutetium','Catalyst\,Medicine','3500'),
('NULL','Scandium','Lasers\,Lighting\,Aerospace','14000'),
('NULL','Promethium','Nuclear batteries','No price');
```

Note that the "\"s are to tell MySQL to ignore the symbol immediately following it otherwise syntax errors will result.

We now modify this table by adding a column "atomic_number" in it. Before making the changes, we shall duplicate the table "rare_earth" as "rare_earth_1" and then make the changes in "rare_earth_1":

```
CREATE TABLE science.rare_earth_1 LIKE science.rare_earth;
INSERT science.rare_earth_1 SELECT * FROM science.rare_earth;

ALTER TABLE science.rare_earth_1 ADD atomic_number SMALLINT UNSIGNED;

UPDATE science.rare_earth_1 SET atomic_number='57' WHERE id='1';
UPDATE science.rare_earth_1 SET atomic_number='39' WHERE id='2';
UPDATE science.rare_earth_1 SET atomic_number='60' WHERE id='3';
UPDATE science.rare_earth_1 SET atomic_number='58' WHERE id='4';
UPDATE science.rare_earth_1 SET atomic_number='59' WHERE id='5';

UPDATE science.rare_earth_1 SET atomic_number='64' WHERE id='6';
UPDATE science.rare_earth_1 SET atomic_number='66' WHERE id='7';
UPDATE science.rare_earth_1 SET atomic_number='68' WHERE id='8';
UPDATE science.rare_earth_1 SET atomic_number='62' WHERE id='9';
UPDATE science.rare_earth_1 SET atomic_number='70' WHERE id='10';

UPDATE science.rare_earth_1 SET atomic_number='67' WHERE id='11';
UPDATE science.rare_earth_1 SET atomic_number='65' WHERE id='12';
UPDATE science.rare_earth_1 SET atomic_number='63' WHERE id='13';
UPDATE science.rare_earth_1 SET atomic_number='69' WHERE id='14';
UPDATE science.rare_earth_1 SET atomic_number='71' WHERE id='15';

UPDATE science.rare_earth_1 SET atomic_number='21' WHERE id='16';
UPDATE science.rare_earth_1 SET atomic_number='61' WHERE id='17';
```

5.2 Retrieving data from MySQL database tables.

It is more natural to retrieve data by rows from MySQL tables, than by columns. Example 1, Example 2 and Example 3 are three different Php codes to extract data by rows, using three different ways to connect to the MySQL server. They achieve the same goal. Example 4 and Example 5 are the modified versions of Example 1 to write the results by columns on files which will later on be read by another computer program. Example 1,2,3,4 refer to database table "basicdata1" discussed in Section 5.1. Example 5 refers to database "GE" discussed in Section 14.8. For convenience, database tables used in this section are also shown in Appendix 5.2 and computer_files_5.2.

Example 1

```
<?php
//—http://localhost/new_sci2/to_retrieve_basicdata1.php
//*******
// To log in
$db_hostname = 'localhost';
$db_database = 'science';
$db_username = 'root';
$db_password = 'xxxxxxxx';
// To connect to MySQL
$db_server = mysql_connect($db_hostname, $db_username, $db_password);
if (!$db_server) die("Unable to connect to MySQL: " . mysql_error());
// To select a database
mysql_select_db($db_database,$db_server)
        or die("Unable to select database: " . mysql_error());
// To query a database
$query = "SELECT * FROM basicdata1";
$result = mysql_query($query,$db_server);
if (!$result) die ("Database access failed: " . mysql_error());
$rows=mysql_num_rows($result);
// To fetch results one row at a time
for ($j = 0 ; $j < $rows ; ++$j)
{
        $row = mysql_fetch_row($result);
        echo 'id: ' .         $row[0] . '<br />';
        echo 'element: ' .$row[1] . '<br />';
        echo 'atomic_number: ' .  $row[2] . '<br />';
        echo 'symbol: ' .         $row[3] . '<br />';
        echo 'atomic_weight: ' .          $row[4] . '<br />';
        echo 'absorption: ' .             $row[5] . '<br />';
        echo 'scattering: ' .             $row[6] . '<br /><br />';
}
// To close the database connection
mysql_close($db_server);
?>
```

Example 2

```
<?php
//—http://localhost/new_sci2/to_retrieve_basicdata1A.php
//*************
// To log in
$db_hostname = 'localhost';
$db_database = 'science';
$db_username = 'root';
$db_password = 'xxxxxxxx';
// To connect to MySQL
$db_server = mysqli_connect($db_hostname, $db_username, $db_password,
$db_database);
if (!$db_server) die("Unable to connect to MySQL: " . mysqli_connect_error());
//
$query = "SELECT * FROM basicdata1";
$result = mysqli_query($db_server,$query);
if (!$result) die ("Database access failed: " . mysqli_error($db_server));
// To fetch an array
while($newArray=mysqli_fetch_array($result,MYSQLI_ASSOC)){
$element=$newArray['element'];
$atomic_number=$newArray['atomic_number'];
$symbol=$newArray['symbol'];
$atomic_weight=$newArray['atomic_weight'];
$absorption=$newArray['absorption'];
$scattering=$newArray['scattering'];
echo 'element:'.$element.'<br />';
echo 'atomic_number:'.$atomic_number.'<br />';
echo 'symbol:'.$symbol.'<br />';
echo 'atomic_weight:'.$atomic_weight.'<br />';
echo 'absorption:'.$absorption.'<br />';
echo 'scattering:'.$scattering.'<br />'.'<br />';
}
// To close the database connection
mysqli_free_result($result);
mysqli_close($db_server);
?>
```

Example 3

```
<?php
//—http://localhost/new_sci2/to_retrieve_basicdata1B.php
// To log in
$db_hostname = 'localhost';
$db_database = 'science';
$db_username = 'root';
$db_password = 'xxxxxxxx';
try {
   $db_server = new PDO("mysql:host=$db_hostname;dbname=$db_database",
$db_username, $db_password);
   /*** echo a message saying we have connected ***/
   echo 'Connected to database'. '<br />';
   $query = "SELECT * FROM basicdata1";
   foreach ($db_server->query($query) as $row)
      {
      print $row['id'] . '<br />';
      print $row['element'] . '<br />';
      print $row['atomic_number'] . '<br />';
      print $row['symbol'] . '<br />';
      print $row['atomic_weight'] . '<br />';
      print $row['absorption'] . '<br />';
      print $row['scattering'] . '<br />'. '<br />';
      }
   /*** close the database connection ***/
   $db_server = null;
}
catch(PDOException $e)
   {
   echo $e->getMessage();
   }
?>
```

Example 4

```
<?php
//—http://localhost/new_sci2/to_retrieve_column.php
//*******
// To log in
$db_hostname = 'localhost';
$db_database = 'science';
$db_username = 'root';
$db_password = 'xxxxxxxx';
// To connect to MySQL
$db_server = mysql_connect($db_hostname, $db_username, $db_password);
if (!$db_server) die("Unable to connect to MySQL: " . mysql_error());
// To select a database
mysql_select_db($db_database,$db_server)
        or die("Unable to select database: " . mysql_error());
// To query a database
$query = "SELECT * FROM basicdata1";
$result = mysql_query($query,$db_server);
if (!$result) die ("Database access failed: " . mysql_error());
$rows=mysql_num_rows($result);
// To fetch results one row at a time
// To write the results to a file
$fpA=fopen("file_basicdata1A.txt","w");
$fpB=fopen("file_basicdata1B.txt","w");
$fpC=fopen("file_basicdata1C.txt","w");
$fpD=fopen("file_basicdata1D.txt","w");
for ($j = 0 ; $j < $rows ; ++$j)
{
        $row = mysql_fetch_row($result);
        echo 'id: ' .       $row[0] . '<br />';

        echo 'element: ' .$row[1] . '<br />';

        echo 'atomic_number: ' . $row[2] . '<br />';
        fwrite($fpA,$row[2]);
        fwrite($fpA,"\n");
        echo 'symbol: ' .           $row[3] . '<br />';

        echo 'atomic_weight: ' .            $row[4] . '<br />';
        fwrite($fpB,$row[4]);
        fwrite($fpB,"\n");
```

```
        echo 'absorption: ' .              $row[5] . '<br />';
        fwrite($fpC,$row[5]);
        fwrite($fpC,"\n");
        echo 'scattering: ' .              $row[6] . '<br /><br />';
        fwrite($fpD,$row[6]);
        fwrite($fpD,"\n");
}
fclose($fpA);
fclose($fpB);
fclose($fpC);
fclose($fpD);

// To close the database connection
mysql_close($db_server);
?>
```

Example 5

```
<?php
//—http://localhost/new_sci2/to_retrieve_column_1.php
//*******
// To log in
$db_hostname = 'localhost';
$db_database = 'stocks';
$db_username = 'root1';
$db_password = 'xxxxxxxx';
// To connect to MySQL
$db_server = mysql_connect($db_hostname, $db_username, $db_password);
if (!$db_server) die("Unable to connect to MySQL: " . mysql_error());
// To select a database
mysql_select_db($db_database,$db_server)
        or die("Unable to select database: " . mysql_error());
// To query a database
$query = "SELECT * FROM GE";
$result = mysql_query($query,$db_server);
if (!$result) die ("Database access failed: " . mysql_error());
$rows=mysql_num_rows($result);
// To fetch results one row at a time
// To write the results to a file
$fpA=fopen("file_GE_A.txt","w");
$fpB=fopen("file_GE_B.txt","w");
```

```
for ($j = 0 ; $j < $rows ; ++$j)
{
        $row = mysql_fetch_row($result);
        echo 'id: ' .       $row[0] . '<br />';

        echo 'date: ' .     $row[1] . '<br />';
        fwrite($fpA,$row[1]);
        fwrite($fpA,"\n");
        echo 'open: ' .     $row[2] . '<br />';

        echo 'high: ' .             $row[3] . '<br />';

        echo 'low: ' .              $row[4] . '<br />';

        echo 'close: ' .            $row[5] . '<br />';

        echo 'volume: ' .           $row[6] . '<br />';

        echo 'adj_close: ' .                $row[7] . '<br /><br />';
        fwrite($fpB,$row[7]);
        fwrite($fpB,"\n");


}
fclose($fpA);
fclose($fpB);

// To close the database connection
mysql_close($db_server);
?>
```

5.3 Manipulations of MySQL database tables

Example 1 shows how to join two tables ("basicdata1" and "rare_earth_1" developed in Section 5.1) together. Example 2 shows how to add two columns of "basicdata1" as in a spreadsheet.

Example 1

In MySQL command window, type (one command at a time):

CREATE TABLE science.basicdata2 SELECT symbol,uses FROM science.basicdata1 AS a,science.rare_earth_1 AS b WHERE a.atomic_number=b.atomic_number;

ALTER TABLE science.basicdata2 CHANGE symbol element_symbol VARCHAR(15);

SELECT * FROM science.basicdata2;

Then click "Export" on the toolbar.

The result is the MySQL table "basicdata2" as shown in Appendix 5.3 and computer_files_5.3.

Example 2

In Section 5.2, we have extracted four columns of data from table "basicdata1", two of which are the "absorption" and "scattering" columns. They are in the files "file_basicdata1C" and "file_basicdata1D" respectively. Suppose that it is desired to create a new table called "basicdata3" which will have an additional column called "total" which is the sum of absorption and scattering data, based on the previously created table "basicdata1", we can proceed as follows:

For convenience, the files "file_basicdata1C" and "file_basicdata1D" are shown in computer_files_5.3.

First, we create "basicdata3" as a copy of "bascidata1":

CREATE TABLE science.basicdata3 LIKE science.basicdata1;
INSERT science.basicdata3 SELECT * FROM science.basicdata1;

Second, we add one column called "total" to "basicdata3". Column "total" is blank:

ALTER TABLE science.basicdata3 ADD total FLOAT NOT NULL;

Then, third, we use the following script:

```
<?php
//—http://localhost/new_sci2/to_add_2_columns.php
//*******
// To log in
$db_hostname = 'localhost';
$db_database = 'science';
$db_username = 'root';
$db_password = 'xxxxxxxx';
// To connect to MySQL
$db_server = mysql_connect($db_hostname, $db_username, $db_password);
if (!$db_server) die("Unable to connect to MySQL: " . mysql_error());
// To select a database
mysql_select_db($db_database,$db_server)
         or die("Unable to select database: " . mysql_error());
//
$filename1 = "file_basicdata1C.txt";
$fp1= fopen($filename1, "r") or die("Couldn't open $filename1");
$j=0;
while (!feof($fp1)) {
  $ab[$j] = fgets($fp1, 1024);
         echo $ab[$j]."<br/>";
         $j=$j+1;
}
fclose($fp1);
echo "<br />";
//
$filename2 = "file_basicdata1D.txt";
$fp2= fopen($filename2, "r") or die("Couldn't open $filename2");
$k=0;
while (!feof($fp2)) {
         $sc[$k] = fgets($fp2, 1024);
         echo $sc[$k]."<br/>";
         $k=$k+1;
}
fclose($fp2);
echo "<br/>";
//
// To query a database
$query = "SELECT * FROM basicdata3";
$result = mysql_query($query,$db_server);
```

```
if (!$result) die ("Database access failed: " . mysql_error());
$rows=mysql_num_rows($result);
echo "number of rows= ".$rows."<br />";
//
for($count=0; $count<=$rows-1; $count++){
$tl[$count]=$ab[$count]+$sc[$count];
echo $tl[$count]."<br />";
}
echo "<br />";
$query1= "UPDATE basicdata3 SET total='$tl[0]' WHERE id='1'";
$result1 = mysql_query($query1,$db_server);
if (!$result1) die ("Database access failed: " . mysql_error());
$query2= "UPDATE basicdata3 SET total='$tl[1]' WHERE id='2'";
$result2 = mysql_query($query2,$db_server);
if (!$result2) die ("Database access failed: " . mysql_error());
$query3= "UPDATE basicdata3 SET total='$tl[2]' WHERE id='3'";
$result3 = mysql_query($query3,$db_server);
if (!$result3) die ("Database access failed: " . mysql_error());
$query4= "UPDATE basicdata3 SET total='$tl[3]' WHERE id='4'";
$result4 = mysql_query($query4,$db_server);
if (!$result4) die ("Database access failed: " . mysql_error());
$query5= "UPDATE basicdata3 SET total='$tl[4]' WHERE id='5'";
$result5 = mysql_query($query5,$db_server);
if (!$result5) die ("Database access failed: " . mysql_error());
$query6= "UPDATE basicdata3 SET total='$tl[5]' WHERE id='6'";
$result6 = mysql_query($query6,$db_server);
if (!$result6) die ("Database access failed: " . mysql_error());
$query7= "UPDATE basicdata3 SET total='$tl[6]' WHERE id='7'";
$result7 = mysql_query($query7,$db_server);
if (!$result7) die ("Database access failed: " . mysql_error());
$query8= "UPDATE basicdata3 SET total='$tl[7]' WHERE id='8'";
$result8 = mysql_query($query8,$db_server);
if (!$result8) die ("Database access failed: " . mysql_error());
$query9= "UPDATE basicdata3 SET total='$tl[8]' WHERE id='9'";
$result9 = mysql_query($query9,$db_server);
if (!$result9) die ("Database access failed: " . mysql_error());
$query10= "UPDATE basicdata3 SET total='$tl[9]' WHERE id='10'";
$result10 = mysql_query($query10,$db_server);
if (!$result10) die ("Database access failed: " . mysql_error());
$query11= "UPDATE basicdata3 SET total='$tl[10]' WHERE id='11'";
$result11 = mysql_query($query11,$db_server);
if (!$result11) die ("Database access failed: " . mysql_error());
```

```
$query12= "UPDATE basicdata3 SET total='$tl[11]' WHERE id='12'";
$result12 = mysql_query($query12,$db_server);
if (!$result12) die ("Database access failed: " . mysql_error());
$query13= "UPDATE basicdata3 SET total='$tl[12]' WHERE id='13'";
$result13 = mysql_query($query13,$db_server);
if (!$result13) die ("Database access failed: " . mysql_error());
$query14= "UPDATE basicdata3 SET total='$tl[13]' WHERE id='14'";
$result14 = mysql_query($query14,$db_server);
if (!$result14) die ("Database access failed: " . mysql_error());
$query15= "UPDATE basicdata3 SET total='$tl[14]' WHERE id='15'";
$result15 = mysql_query($query15,$db_server);
if (!$result15) die ("Database access failed: " . mysql_error());
$query16= "UPDATE basicdata3 SET total='$tl[15]' WHERE id='16'";
$result16 = mysql_query($query16,$db_server);
if (!$result16) die ("Database access failed: " . mysql_error());
$query17= "UPDATE basicdata3 SET total='$tl[16]' WHERE id='17'";
$result17 = mysql_query($query17,$db_server);
if (!$result17) die ("Database access failed: " . mysql_error());
$query18= "UPDATE basicdata3 SET total='$tl[17]' WHERE id='18'";
$result18 = mysql_query($query18,$db_server);
if (!$result18) die ("Database access failed: " . mysql_error());
$query19= "UPDATE basicdata3 SET total='$tl[18]' WHERE id='19'";
$result19 = mysql_query($query19,$db_server);
if (!$result19) die ("Database access failed: " . mysql_error());
$query20= "UPDATE basicdata3 SET total='$tl[19]' WHERE id='20'";
$result20 = mysql_query($query20,$db_server);
if (!$result20) die ("Database access failed: " . mysql_error());
$query21= "UPDATE basicdata3 SET total='$tl[20]' WHERE id='21'";
$result21 = mysql_query($query21,$db_server);
if (!$result21) die ("Database access failed: " . mysql_error());
$query22= "UPDATE basicdata3 SET total='$tl[21]' WHERE id='22'";
$result22 = mysql_query($query22,$db_server);
if (!$result22) die ("Database access failed: " . mysql_error());
$query23= "UPDATE basicdata3 SET total='$tl[22]' WHERE id='23'";
$result23 = mysql_query($query23,$db_server);
if (!$result23) die ("Database access failed: " . mysql_error());
$query24= "UPDATE basicdata3 SET total='$tl[23]' WHERE id='24'";
$result24 = mysql_query($query24,$db_server);
if (!$result24) die ("Database access failed: " . mysql_error());
$query25= "UPDATE basicdata3 SET total='$tl[24]' WHERE id='25'";
$result25 = mysql_query($query25,$db_server);
if (!$result25) die ("Database access failed: " . mysql_error());
```

```
$query26= "UPDATE basicdata3 SET total='$tl[25]' WHERE id='26'";
$result26 = mysql_query($query26,$db_server);
if (!$result26) die ("Database access failed: " . mysql_error());
$query27= "UPDATE basicdata3 SET total='$tl[26]' WHERE id='27'";
$result27 = mysql_query($query27,$db_server);
if (!$result27) die ("Database access failed: " . mysql_error());
$query28= "UPDATE basicdata3 SET total='$tl[27]' WHERE id='28'";
$result28 = mysql_query($query28,$db_server);
if (!$result28) die ("Database access failed: " . mysql_error());
$query29= "UPDATE basicdata3 SET total='$tl[28]' WHERE id='29'";
$result29 = mysql_query($query29,$db_server);
if (!$result29) die ("Database access failed: " . mysql_error());
$query30= "UPDATE basicdata3 SET total='$tl[29]' WHERE id='30'";
$result30 = mysql_query($query30,$db_server);
if (!$result30) die ("Database access failed: " . mysql_error());
$query31= "UPDATE basicdata3 SET total='$tl[30]' WHERE id='31'";
$result31 = mysql_query($query31,$db_server);
if (!$result31) die ("Database access failed: " . mysql_error());
$query32= "UPDATE basicdata3 SET total='$tl[31]' WHERE id='32'";
$result32 = mysql_query($query32,$db_server);
if (!$result32) die ("Database access failed: " . mysql_error());
$query33= "UPDATE basicdata3 SET total='$tl[32]' WHERE id='33'";
$result33 = mysql_query($query33,$db_server);
if (!$result33) die ("Database access failed: " . mysql_error());
$query34= "UPDATE basicdata3 SET total='$tl[33]' WHERE id='34'";
$result34 = mysql_query($query34,$db_server);
if (!$result34) die ("Database access failed: " . mysql_error());
$query35= "UPDATE basicdata3 SET total='$tl[34]' WHERE id='35'";
$result35 = mysql_query($query35,$db_server);
if (!$result35) die ("Database access failed: " . mysql_error());
$query36= "UPDATE basicdata3 SET total='$tl[35]' WHERE id='36'";
$result36 = mysql_query($query36,$db_server);
if (!$result36) die ("Database access failed: " . mysql_error());
$query37= "UPDATE basicdata3 SET total='$tl[36]' WHERE id='37'";
$result37 = mysql_query($query37,$db_server);
if (!$result37) die ("Database access failed: " . mysql_error());
$query38= "UPDATE basicdata3 SET total='$tl[37]' WHERE id='38'";
$result38 = mysql_query($query38,$db_server);
if (!$result38) die ("Database access failed: " . mysql_error());
$query39= "UPDATE basicdata3 SET total='$tl[38]' WHERE id='39'";
$result39 = mysql_query($query39,$db_server);
if (!$result39) die ("Database access failed: " . mysql_error());
```

```
$query40= "UPDATE basicdata3 SET total='$tl[39]' WHERE id='40'";
$result40 = mysql_query($query40,$db_server);
if (!$result40) die ("Database access failed: " . mysql_error());
$query41= "UPDATE basicdata3 SET total='$tl[40]' WHERE id='41'";
$result41 = mysql_query($query41,$db_server);
if (!$result41) die ("Database access failed: " . mysql_error());
$query42= "UPDATE basicdata3 SET total='$tl[41]' WHERE id='42'";
$result42 = mysql_query($query42,$db_server);
if (!$result42) die ("Database access failed: " . mysql_error());
$query43= "UPDATE basicdata3 SET total='$tl[42]' WHERE id='43'";
$result43 = mysql_query($query43,$db_server);
if (!$result43) die ("Database access failed: " . mysql_error());
$query44= "UPDATE basicdata3 SET total='$tl[43]' WHERE id='44'";
$result44 = mysql_query($query44,$db_server);
if (!$result44) die ("Database access failed: " . mysql_error());
$query45= "UPDATE basicdata3 SET total='$tl[44]' WHERE id='45'";
$result45 = mysql_query($query45,$db_server);
if (!$result45) die ("Database access failed: " . mysql_error());
$query46= "UPDATE basicdata3 SET total='$tl[45]' WHERE id='46'";
$result46 = mysql_query($query46,$db_server);
if (!$result46) die ("Database access failed: " . mysql_error());
$query47= "UPDATE basicdata3 SET total='$tl[46]' WHERE id='47'";
$result47 = mysql_query($query47,$db_server);
if (!$result47) die ("Database access failed: " . mysql_error());
$query48= "UPDATE basicdata3 SET total='$tl[47]' WHERE id='48'";
$result48 = mysql_query($query48,$db_server);
if (!$result48) die ("Database access failed: " . mysql_error());
$query49= "UPDATE basicdata3 SET total='$tl[48]' WHERE id='49'";
$result49 = mysql_query($query49,$db_server);
if (!$result49) die ("Database access failed: " . mysql_error());
$query50= "UPDATE basicdata3 SET total='$tl[49]' WHERE id='50'";
$result50 = mysql_query($query50,$db_server);
if (!$result50) die ("Database access failed: " . mysql_error());
$query51= "UPDATE basicdata3 SET total='$tl[50]' WHERE id='51'";
$result51 = mysql_query($query51,$db_server);
if (!$result51) die ("Database access failed: " . mysql_error());

// To close the database connection
mysql_close($db_server);
?>
```

5.4 Smarty

As we have seen from previous sections of this chapter, if we want to add or delete a row in the MySQL table, we have to do it one at a time. If a table is frequently used and frequently modified, it will be desirable to customize it for easy add and delete records.

One method based on the technology called "Smarty" is used in this section. Smarty is a Php template engine. Originally it was developed to separate the html and the Php portions of the web page, and to rearrange the execution sequence. But in the present application, we are interested in just setting up an input form for adding and deleting data easily, to a MySQL table.

The MySQL table used is "basicdata5" which is just a copy of "basicdata1" discussed earlier. But it has now 52 rows, because a few rows have been added to it. All the computer files needed are included in "computer_files_5.4". First we shall click and paste the entire folder "mysmartysite" to C:\xampp\htdocs\. Appendix 5.4 shows the output after executing the program

http://localhost/mysmartysite/to_insert_in_basicdata5.php

Chapter 6

Perl and MySQL

6.1 Perl scripts to retrieve data from and insert data to MySQL database table.

Example 1

The Perl script to retrieve data from MySQL table "rare_earth" is as follows:

```
#!"C:\xampp\perl\bin\perl.exe"

# http://localhost/cgi-bin/xampp_perl/perl2mysql.pl

# PERL MODULES WE WILL BE USING
use DBI;
use DBD::mysql;

# HTTP HEADER
print "Content-type: text/html \n\n";

# CONFIG VARIABLES
$platform = "mysql";
$database = "science";
$host = "localhost";
$port = "3306";
$tablename = "rare_earth";
$user = "root";
$pw = "xxxxxxxx";
```

```
# DATA SOURCE NAME
$dsn = "dbi:$platform:$database:$host:$port";

# PERL DBI CONNECT
$connect = DBI->connect($dsn, $user, $pw);

# PREPARE THE QUERY
$query = "SELECT * FROM rare_earth ORDER BY id";
$query_handle = $connect->prepare($query);

# EXECUTE THE QUERY
$query_handle->execute();

# BIND TABLE COLUMNS TO VARIABLES
$query_handle->bind_columns(undef, \$id, \$element, \$uses,
\$oxide_price_USD_per_kg);

# LOOP THROUGH RESULTS
while($query_handle->fetch()) {
  print "$id, $element, $uses, $oxide_price_USD_per_kg <br />";
}
```

Example 2

The Perl script to retrieve data from MySQL table “basicdata1” is as follows:

```
#!"C:\xampp\perl\bin\perl.exe"

# http://localhost/cgi-bin/xampp_perl/perl2mysql_1.pl

# PERL MODULES WE WILL BE USING
use DBI;
use DBD::mysql;

# HTTP HEADER
print "Content-type: text/html \n\n";

# CONFIG VARIABLES
$platform = "mysql";
$database = "science";
$host = "localhost";
```

```
$port = "3306";
$tablename = "basicdata1";
$user = "root";
$pw = "xxxxxxxx";

# DATA SOURCE NAME
$dsn = "dbi:$platform:$database:$host:$port";

# PERL DBI CONNECT
$connect = DBI->connect($dsn, $user, $pw);

# PREPARE THE QUERY
$query = "SELECT * FROM basicdata1 ORDER BY id";
$query_handle = $connect->prepare($query);

# EXECUTE THE QUERY
$query_handle->execute();

# BIND TABLE COLUMNS TO VARIABLES
$query_handle->bind_columns(undef, \$id, \$element, \$atomic_number,
\$symbol, \$atomic_weight, \$absorption, \$scattering);

# LOOP THROUGH RESULTS
while($query_handle->fetch()) {
  print "$id, $element, $atomic_number, $symbol, $atomic_weight, $absorption,
$scattering <br />";
}
```

Example 3

We first create a new table “basicdata4” by duplicating table “basicdata1”. On the MySQL command window, type:

```
CREATE TABLE science.basicdata4 LIKE science.basicdata1;
INSERT science.basicdata4 SELECT * FROM science.basicdata1;
```

Then we execute the following Perl script to insert a new row onto table “basicdata4”:

```
#!"C:\xampp\perl\bin\perl.exe"
```

```
# http://localhost/cgi-bin/xampp_perl/perl2mysql_2.pl

# PERL MODULES WE WILL BE USING
use DBI;
use DBD::mysql;

# HTTP HEADER
print "Content-type: text/html \n\n";

# CONFIG VARIABLES
$platform = "mysql";
$database = "science";
$host = "localhost";
$port = "3306";
$tablename = "basicdata4";
$user = "root";
$pw = "xxxxxxxx";

# DATA SOURCE NAME
$dsn = "dbi:$platform:$database:$host:$port";

# PERL DBI CONNECT
$connect = DBI->connect($dsn, $user, $pw);

# PREPARE THE QUERY
$query = "INSERT INTO basicdata4(id,element,atomic_number,symbol,atomic_
weight,absorption,scattering)VALUES('NULL','Hafnium','72','Hf','178.6','115','0')";
$query_handle = $connect->prepare($query);

# EXECUTE THE QUERY
$query_handle->execute();
```

Chapter 7

PYTHON AND MYSQL

The interface of Python with MySQL is through MySQLdb. The latest versions "MySQL-python-1.2.3.win32-py2.7.exe" and "MySQL-python-1.2.3.win-amd64-py2.7.exe" are available at http://www.codegood.com/archive/129. Depending on the computer system, a version of MySQLdb has to be installed before interfacing with MySQL.

Example 1

The following Python program is to print out the data in the MySQL table "basicdata1":

```
# to_retrieve_basicdata1.py
import sys
import MySQLdb
import string
dbmod = MySQLdb
conn = MySQLdb.connect (host = "localhost",user="root",passwd="xxxxxxxx",db
="science")
cursor = conn.cursor ()
cursor.execute ("SELECT * FROM basicdata1")
rows = cursor.fetchall()
numrows = cursor.rowcount
print numrows
import pprint
pprint.pprint(rows)
for record in rows:
   print record[1],"-->",record[4]
```

Example 2

This example is to demonstrate how to create a MySQL table, named "science. measurement" with Python. It will be a table of recording measurements of some properties (A,B,C and D); each property is measured 6 times. The properties are to be displayed as columns "A", "B", "C" and "D"; the six measurements are to be displayed as six rows, "1", "2",..."6".

```
# to_create_measurement.py
import sys
import MySQLdb
import string
dbmod = MySQLdb
conn = MySQLdb.connect (host = "localhost",user="root",passwd="xxxxxxxx",db
="science")
cursor = conn.cursor ()
cursor.execute ("CREATE TABLE measurement(id INT NOT NULL PRIMARY
KEY AUTO_INCREMENT,A VARCHAR(15) NOT NULL,B VARCHAR(15) NOT
NULL,C VARCHAR(15) NOT NULL,D VARCHAR(15) NOT NULL)")
cursor.close()
conn.close()
```

Example 3

The following Python program is for inserting data into the table "measurement":

```
# to_insert_measurement.py
import sys
import MySQLdb
import string
dbmod = MySQLdb
conn = MySQLdb.connect (host = "localhost",user="root",passwd="xxxxxxxx",db
="science")
cursor = conn.cursor ()
#cursor.execute ("INSERT INTO measurement(id,A,B,C,D)VALUES('1','11.7','0.0
35','2017','99.1')")
cursor.execute ("INSERT INTO measurement(id,A,B,C,D)VALUES('2','9.2','0.037
','2019','101.2')")
#cursor.execute ("INSERT INTO measurement(id,A,B,C,D)VALUES('3','12.2','no'
,'no','105.2')")
```

```
#cursor.execute ("INSERT INTO measurement(id,A,B,C,D)VALUES('4','10.1','0.0
31','no','102.1')")
#cursor.execute ("INSERT INTOmeasurement(id,A,B,C,D)VALUES('5','9.1','0.033
','2009','103.3')")
#cursor.execute ("INSERT INTOmeasurement(id,A,B,C,D)VALUES('6','8.7','0.036
','2015','101.9')")
cursor.close()
conn.close()
```

Example 4

The Python script to calculate the mean value of each property and to display the table is “to_parse_measurement.py”:

```
import sys
import MySQLdb
import string
dbmod = MySQLdb
conn = MySQLdb.connect (host = "localhost",user="root",passwd="xxxxxxxx",db
="science")
cursor = conn.cursor ()
cursor.execute ("SELECT * FROM measurement")
rows = cursor.fetchall()
numrows = cursor.rowcount
print numrows

sum=0
for record in rows:
   sum=sum+float(record[1])
A_mean=sum/numrows
print 'Mean value of property A = %g' % A_mean

sum=0
i=0
for record in rows:
   if i==2:
      sum=sum
   else:
      sum=sum+float(record[2])
   i=i+1
B_mean=sum/(numrows-1)
```

```
print 'Mean value of property B = %g' % B_mean

sum=0
i=0
for record in rows:
   if (i==2) or (i==3):
      sum=sum
   else:
      sum=sum+float(record[3])
   i=i+1
C_mean=sum/(numrows-2)
print 'Mean value of property C = %g' % C_mean

sum=0
for record in rows:
   sum=sum+float(record[4])
D_mean=sum/numrows
print 'Mean value of property D = %g' % D_mean

import pprint
pprint.pprint(rows)

cursor.close()
conn.close()
```

Chapter 8

MATLAB AND MYSQL

8.1 PARSING A MYSQL TABLE WITH MATLAB.

The Matlab's interface with MySQL database is discussed in Robert Almgren's web page : http://www.mmf.utoronto.ca/resrchres/mysql/. For Windows application, the user will need to download three files: mysql.m which is an M-file containing help text; mysql.dll which is a binary file to be placed in Matlab's home directory folder; and libmysql.dll which is a binary file to be put into C:\WINDOWS\system32 folder. These files are included in the computer_files8.1

The following shows the commands and responses on the Matlab command window for parsing "stocks.GE" table: (Make sure that XAMPP server is on, in order to use "localhost")

```
>> mysql('status')
Warning: Calling MEX-file 'C:\Documents and Settings\Compaq_Administrator\
My Documents\MATLAB\mysql.dll'.
MEX-files with .dll extensions will not execute in a future version of MATLAB.
Not connected
>> mysql('open','localhost','root','xxxxxxxx')
Connecting to  host=localhost  user=root  password=xxxxxxxx
Uptime: 1334  Threads: 1  Questions: 293  Slow queries: 0  Opens: 39  Flush
tables: 1  Open tables: 31  Queries per second avg: 0.219
>> mysql('use','stocks')
Current database is "stocks"
>> mysql('SELECT * FROM stocks.GE')
id    date        open    high    low     close   volume     adj_close
+---+ +----------+ +------+ +------+ +------+ +------+ +---------+ +---------+
1     2011-07-01  18.86   19.45   18.29   18.41   52463100   18.41
2     2011-06-01  19.47   19.6    17.97   18.86   53953900   18.86
```

```
3    2011-05-02  20.7    20.71   18.97   19.64   45910500  19.48
4    2011-04-01  20.14   20.85   19.51   20.45   56260900  20.28
5    2011-03-01  21.12   21.17   18.6    20.05   63914200  19.89
6    2011-02-01  20.38   21.65   20.08   20.92   52895600  20.75
7    2011-01-03  18.49   20.74   18.12   20.14   76413100  19.84
8    2010-12-01  16.03   18.49   16.03   18.29   57131500  18.02
9    2010-11-01  16.09   16.86   15.63   15.83   55387200  15.47
10   2010-10-01  16.4    17.49   15.88   16.02   64676100  15.66
...  ...         ...     ...     ...     ...     ...       ...
130  2000-10-02  58      59.94   49      54.81   20282300  39.55
131  2000-09-01  59.25   60.06   55      57.81   12225400  41.71
132  2000-08-01  51.94   60.5    51.19   58.63   11558800  42.21
133  2000-07-03  52.5    54.75   49.5    51.69   13163300  37.21
134  2000-06-01  52.06   54      47.94   53      12857500  38.05
135  2000-05-01  159     162     48.75   52.63   14351800  37.79
136  2000-04-03  155.25  167.94  143.06  157.25  21992900  37.64
137  2000-03-01  133.5   164.88  126.25  155.63  25483700  37.25
138  2000-02-01  134.25  143.13  124.94  132.38  23404600  31.59
139  2000-01-03  153     154.94  133.06  134     22127500  31.98
(139 rows total)
>> mysql('close')
```

8.2 Creating MySQL table with Matlab

In this section, we shall discuss three examples to create table "science.steam_table4"; to insert data to the table; and then to retrieve data from the table, all with Matlab, with the method of Robert Almgren, as discussed in the previous section (Section 8.1).

Example 1. To create MySQL table "science.steam_table4".

```
% create_steam_table4
%
clear; help create_steam_table4;
%
mysql('open','localhost','root','xxxxxxxx');
mysql('use','science');
mysql('CREATE TABLE steam_table4(id INT NOT NULL PRIMARY KEY AUTO_INCREMENT,t FLOAT NOT NULL,p FLOAT NOT NULL,hf FLOAT NOT NULL,hg FLOAT NOT NULL,sf FLOAT NOT NULL,sg FLOAT NOT NULL)');
```

In this table, t=temperature, p=pressure, hf and hg=specific enthalpy for fluid and gas respectively, sf and sg=specific entropy for fluid and gas respectively, for water, in English units.

Example 2. To insert data into MySQL table "science.steam_table4".

```
% insert_steam_table4
%
clear; help insert_steam_table4;
%
mysql('open','localhost','root','xxxxxxxx');
mysql('use','science');
mysql('INSERT INTO steam_table4(id,t,p,hf,hg,sf,sg)VALUES("1","450","422.1","
430.2","1205.6","0.6282","1.4806")');
mysql('INSERT INTO steam_table4(id,t,p,hf,hg,sf,sg)VALUES("2","475","539.3","
458.5","1204.9","0.6586","1.4571")');
mysql('INSERT INTO steam_table4(id,t,p,hf,hg,sf,sg)VALUES("3","500","680.0","
487.7","1202.5","0.6888","1.4335")');
mysql('INSERT INTO steam_table4(id,t,p,hf,hg,sf,sg)VALUES("4","525","847.1","
517.8","1197.8","0.7191","1.4097")');
mysql('INSERT INTO steam_table4(id,t,p,hf,hg,sf,sg)VALUES("5","550","1044.0",
"549.1","1190.6","0.7497","1.3851")');
mysql('INSERT INTO steam_table4(id,t,p,hf,hg,sf,sg)VALUES("6","575","1274.0",
"581.9","1180.4","0.7808","1.3593")');
mysql('INSERT INTO steam_table4(id,t,p,hf,hg,sf,sg)VALUES("7","600","1541.0",
"616.7","1166.4","0.8130","1.3317")');
mysql('INSERT INTO steam_table4(id,t,p,hf,hg,sf,sg)VALUES("8","625","1849.7",
"654.2","1147.0","0.8467","1.3010")');
mysql('INSERT INTO steam_table4(id,t,p,hf,hg,sf,sg)VALUES("9","650","2205.0",
"695.9","1119.8","0.8831","1.2651")');
mysql('INSERT INTO steam_table4(id,t,p,hf,hg,sf,sg)VALUES("10","675","2616.0
","745.3","1078.2","0.9252","1.2186")');
mysql('INSERT INTO steam_table4(id,t,p,hf,hg,sf,sg)VALUES("11","700","3090.0
","822.7","990.2","0.9902","1.1346")');
mysql('SELECT * FROM steam_table4');
```

Example 3. To fetch data from MySQL table "science.steam_table4".

```
% fetch_steam_table4
%
clear; help fetch_steam_table4;
%
mysql('open','localhost','root','xxxxxxxx');
mysql('use','science');
mysql('SELECT * FROM steam_table4');

temp=zeros(11,1);

temp(1)=mysql('SELECT t FROM steam_table4 WHERE id="1"');
temp(2)=mysql('SELECT t FROM steam_table4 WHERE id="2"');
temp(3)=mysql('SELECT t FROM steam_table4 WHERE id="3"');
temp(4)=mysql('SELECT t FROM steam_table4 WHERE id="4"');
temp(5)=mysql('SELECT t FROM steam_table4 WHERE id="5"');
temp(6)=mysql('SELECT t FROM steam_table4 WHERE id="6"');
temp(7)=mysql('SELECT t FROM steam_table4 WHERE id="7"');
temp(8)=mysql('SELECT t FROM steam_table4 WHERE id="8"');
temp(9)=mysql('SELECT t FROM steam_table4 WHERE id="9"');
temp(10)=mysql('SELECT t FROM steam_table4 WHERE id="10"');
temp(11)=mysql('SELECT t FROM steam_table4 WHERE id="11"');

HF=zeros(11,1);

HF(1)=mysql('SELECT hf FROM steam_table4 WHERE id="1"');
HF(2)=mysql('SELECT hf FROM steam_table4 WHERE id="2"');
HF(3)=mysql('SELECT hf FROM steam_table4 WHERE id="3"');
HF(4)=mysql('SELECT hf FROM steam_table4 WHERE id="4"');
HF(5)=mysql('SELECT hf FROM steam_table4 WHERE id="5"');
HF(6)=mysql('SELECT hf FROM steam_table4 WHERE id="6"');
HF(7)=mysql('SELECT hf FROM steam_table4 WHERE id="7"');
HF(8)=mysql('SELECT hf FROM steam_table4 WHERE id="8"');
HF(9)=mysql('SELECT hf FROM steam_table4 WHERE id="9"');
HF(10)=mysql('SELECT hf FROM steam_table4 WHERE id="10"');
HF(11)=mysql('SELECT hf FROM steam_table4 WHERE id="11"');

plot(temp,HF,'r-');
xlabel('Temperature(F)');
ylabel('Specific enthalpy (Btu/lb)');
title('Enthalpy vs. Temperature for Saturated Water');
```

The sequence of events in the Matlab command window is as follows:

```
>> create_steam_table4
 create_steam_table4


Connecting to  host=localhost  user=root  password=xxxxxxxx
Uptime: 7568  Threads: 1  Questions: 296  Slow queries: 0  Opens: 40  Flush
tables: 1  Open tables: 0  Queries per second avg: 0.39
Current database is "science"
0 rows affected
>> insert_steam_table4
 insert_steam_table4


Connecting to  host=localhost  user=root  password=xxxxxxxx
Uptime: 7621  Threads: 2  Questions: 298  Slow queries: 0  Opens: 41  Flush
tables: 1  Open tables: 0  Queries per second avg: 0.39
Current database is "science"
1 rows affected
1 rows affected
1 rows affected
1 rows affected
1 rows affected
1 rows affected
1 rows affected
1 rows affected
1 rows affected
1 rows affected
1 rows affected

id    t      p        hf      hg       sf       sg
+--+  +---+  +------+ +-----+ +------+ +------+ +------+
1     450    422.1    430.2   1205.6   0.6282   1.4806
2     475    539.3    458.5   1204.9   0.6586   1.4571
3     500    680      487.7   1202.5   0.6888   1.4335
4     525    847.1    517.8   1197.8   0.7191   1.4097
5     550    1044     549.1   1190.6   0.7497   1.3851
6     575    1274     581.9   1180.4   0.7808   1.3593
7     600    1541     616.7   1166.4   0.813    1.3317
8     625    1849.7   654.2   1147     0.8467   1.301
9     650    2205     695.9   1119.8   0.8831   1.2651
10    675    2616     745.3   1078.2   0.9252   1.2186
11    700    3090     822.7   990.2    0.9902   1.1346
```

```
>> fetch_steam_table4
 fetch_steam_table4


Connecting to  host=localhost  user=root  password=xxxxxxxx
Uptime: 7848  Threads: 3  Questions: 311  Slow queries: 0  Opens: 42  Flush
tables: 1  Open tables: 1  Queries per second avg: 0.39
Current database is "science"

id    t      p        hf      hg       sf       sg
+--+  +---+  +------+ +-----+ +------+ +------+ +------+
1     450    422.1    430.2   1205.6   0.6282   1.4806
2     475    539.3    458.5   1204.9   0.6586   1.4571
3     500    680      487.7   1202.5   0.6888   1.4335
4     525    847.1    517.8   1197.8   0.7191   1.4097
5     550    1044     549.1   1190.6   0.7497   1.3851
6     575    1274     581.9   1180.4   0.7808   1.3593
7     600    1541     616.7   1166.4   0.813    1.3317
8     625    1849.7   654.2   1147     0.8467   1.301
9     650    2205     695.9   1119.8   0.8831   1.2651
10    675    2616     745.3   1078.2   0.9252   1.2186
11    700    3090     822.7   990.2    0.9902   1.1346

>>
```

The computer files in this section are in computer_files_8.2.

Chapter 9

PHP AND XML

9.1 CREATING XML FROM MYSQL TABLE.

The Extensible Markup Language, or XML, has been widely used in the web mainly as a means to store and to transmit data. (However, the use of XML in scientific programming is still very limited. This may change in the future.)

In this book, we shall only deal with the simplest form of XML without the complexities of "attributes", "namespace", etc. In this section, we shall demonstrate how to convert a MySQL table to an XML file. This is not the usual way to create an XML file. It is to demonstrate here that, in their simplest forms, XML and MySQL table are closely related.

The starting point is that we have a MySQL table called "stocks.GE" which is shown in Appendix 14.8. It is assumed known here. We are interested in how to convert it to an XML file.

Step 1.

Use the following Php program "table_GE_to_str.php" to convert the MySQL table "stocks.GE" into a long string "test_file_GE.txt". In this long string, the Php program inserts a separator symbol "|" between items, and another separator "#" at the end of each row in the original table. The Php program is:

```
<?php
// ....http://localhost/new_sci2/table_GE_to_str.php
//*************
// To log in
```

```
$db_hostname = 'localhost';
$db_database = 'stocks';
$db_username = 'root1';
$db_password = 'xxxxxxxx';
// To connect to MySQL
$db_server = mysqli_connect($db_hostname, $db_username, $db_password,
$db_database);
if (mysqli_connect_errno()){
printf("Connection failed: %s\n",mysqli_connect_error());
exit();
}else{

$query = "SELECT * FROM GE";
$result = mysqli_query($db_server, $query);
if ($result) {
while ($newArray=mysqli_fetch_array($result, MYSQLI_ASSOC)){
$id=$newArray['id'];
$date=$newArray['date'];
$open=$newArray['open'];
$high=$newArray['high'];
$low=$newArray['low'];
$close=$newArray['close'];
$volume=$newArray['volume'];
$adj_close=$newArray['adj_close'];

$fp=fopen("test_file_GE.txt","a");
$str2=$id."|".$date."|".$open."|".$high."|".$low."|".$close."|".$volume."|".$a
dj_close."|"."#";
fputs($fp,$str2);
fclose($fp);

}
}else {
printf("Could not retrieve records: %s\n", mysqli_error($db_server));
}
mysqli_free_result($result);
mysqli_close($db_server);
echo "<center><br><br>The MySQL connection has been closed.</center>";
}
?>
```

Step 2.

Use the following Php program (str_to_xml_GE.php) to convert the long string "test_file_GE.txt" created in Step 1 into GE.xml:

```
<?php
//—http://localhost/new_sci2/str_to_xml_GE.php

$filename = "test_file_GE.txt";
$fp = fopen($filename, "r") or die("Couldn't open $filename");
while (!feof($fp)) {
        $chunk = fread($fp, 12000);
//      echo $chunk."<br/>";
}
fclose($fp);
$delims = "#";
$Row_array=explode($delims,$chunk,-1);
//echo "Number of elements in Row_array=".sizeof($Row_array)."<br/>";
//print_r($Row_array);
//echo $Row_array[0]."<br/>";
//echo $Row_array[1]."<br/>";
//
//echo $Row_array[138];
$subarray_0=explode('|',$Row_array[0],-1);
//echo "Number of elements in subarray_0=".sizeof($subarray_0)."<br/>";
//echo $subarray_0[0]."<br/>";
//echo $subarray_0[1]."<br/>";
//echo $subarray_0[2]."<br/>";
//echo $subarray_0[3]."<br/>";
//echo $subarray_0[4]."<br/>";
//echo $subarray_0[5]."<br/>";
//echo $subarray_0[6]."<br/>";
//echo $subarray_0[7]."<br/>";
$subarray_1=explode('|',$Row_array[1],-1);
//echo "Number of elements in subarray_1=".sizeof($subarray_1)."<br/>";
//echo $subarray_1[0]."<br/>";
//echo $subarray_1[1]."<br/>";
//echo $subarray_1[2]."<br/>";
//echo $subarray_1[3]."<br/>";
//echo $subarray_1[4]."<br/>";
//echo $subarray_1[5]."<br/>";
//echo $subarray_1[6]."<br/>";
```

```
//echo $subarray_1[7]."<br/>";

$subarray_2=explode('|',$Row_array[2],-1);
$subarray_3=explode('|',$Row_array[3],-1);
$subarray_4=explode('|',$Row_array[4],-1);
$subarray_5=explode('|',$Row_array[5],-1);
$subarray_6=explode('|',$Row_array[6],-1);
$subarray_7=explode('|',$Row_array[7],-1);
$subarray_8=explode('|',$Row_array[8],-1);
$subarray_9=explode('|',$Row_array[9],-1);
$subarray_10=explode('|',$Row_array[10],-1);
$subarray_11=explode('|',$Row_array[11],-1);
$subarray_12=explode('|',$Row_array[12],-1);
$subarray_13=explode('|',$Row_array[13],-1);
$subarray_14=explode('|',$Row_array[14],-1);
$subarray_15=explode('|',$Row_array[15],-1);
$subarray_16=explode('|',$Row_array[16],-1);
$subarray_17=explode('|',$Row_array[17],-1);
$subarray_18=explode('|',$Row_array[18],-1);
$subarray_19=explode('|',$Row_array[19],-1);
$subarray_20=explode('|',$Row_array[20],-1);
$subarray_21=explode('|',$Row_array[21],-1);
$subarray_22=explode('|',$Row_array[22],-1);
$subarray_23=explode('|',$Row_array[23],-1);
$subarray_24=explode('|',$Row_array[24],-1);
$subarray_25=explode('|',$Row_array[25],-1);
$subarray_26=explode('|',$Row_array[26],-1);
$subarray_27=explode('|',$Row_array[27],-1);
$subarray_28=explode('|',$Row_array[28],-1);
$subarray_29=explode('|',$Row_array[29],-1);
$subarray_30=explode('|',$Row_array[30],-1);
$subarray_31=explode('|',$Row_array[31],-1);
$subarray_32=explode('|',$Row_array[32],-1);
$subarray_33=explode('|',$Row_array[33],-1);
$subarray_34=explode('|',$Row_array[34],-1);
$subarray_35=explode('|',$Row_array[35],-1);
$subarray_36=explode('|',$Row_array[36],-1);
$subarray_37=explode('|',$Row_array[37],-1);
$subarray_38=explode('|',$Row_array[38],-1);
$subarray_39=explode('|',$Row_array[39],-1);
$subarray_40=explode('|',$Row_array[40],-1);
$subarray_41=explode('|',$Row_array[41],-1);
```

```
$subarray_42=explode('|',$Row_array[42],-1);
$subarray_43=explode('|',$Row_array[43],-1);
$subarray_44=explode('|',$Row_array[44],-1);
$subarray_45=explode('|',$Row_array[45],-1);
$subarray_46=explode('|',$Row_array[46],-1);
$subarray_47=explode('|',$Row_array[47],-1);
$subarray_48=explode('|',$Row_array[48],-1);
$subarray_49=explode('|',$Row_array[49],-1);
$subarray_50=explode('|',$Row_array[50],-1);
$subarray_51=explode('|',$Row_array[51],-1);
$subarray_52=explode('|',$Row_array[52],-1);
$subarray_53=explode('|',$Row_array[53],-1);
$subarray_54=explode('|',$Row_array[54],-1);
$subarray_55=explode('|',$Row_array[55],-1);
$subarray_56=explode('|',$Row_array[56],-1);
$subarray_57=explode('|',$Row_array[57],-1);
$subarray_58=explode('|',$Row_array[58],-1);
$subarray_59=explode('|',$Row_array[59],-1);
$subarray_60=explode('|',$Row_array[60],-1);
$subarray_61=explode('|',$Row_array[61],-1);
$subarray_62=explode('|',$Row_array[62],-1);
$subarray_63=explode('|',$Row_array[63],-1);
$subarray_64=explode('|',$Row_array[64],-1);
$subarray_65=explode('|',$Row_array[65],-1);
$subarray_66=explode('|',$Row_array[66],-1);
$subarray_67=explode('|',$Row_array[67],-1);
$subarray_68=explode('|',$Row_array[68],-1);
$subarray_69=explode('|',$Row_array[69],-1);
$subarray_70=explode('|',$Row_array[70],-1);
$subarray_71=explode('|',$Row_array[71],-1);
$subarray_72=explode('|',$Row_array[72],-1);
$subarray_73=explode('|',$Row_array[73],-1);
$subarray_74=explode('|',$Row_array[74],-1);
$subarray_75=explode('|',$Row_array[75],-1);
$subarray_76=explode('|',$Row_array[76],-1);
$subarray_77=explode('|',$Row_array[77],-1);
$subarray_78=explode('|',$Row_array[78],-1);
$subarray_79=explode('|',$Row_array[79],-1);
$subarray_80=explode('|',$Row_array[80],-1);
$subarray_81=explode('|',$Row_array[81],-1);
$subarray_82=explode('|',$Row_array[82],-1);
$subarray_83=explode('|',$Row_array[83],-1);
```

```
$subarray_84=explode('|',$Row_array[84],-1);
$subarray_85=explode('|',$Row_array[85],-1);
$subarray_86=explode('|',$Row_array[86],-1);
$subarray_87=explode('|',$Row_array[87],-1);
$subarray_88=explode('|',$Row_array[88],-1);
$subarray_89=explode('|',$Row_array[89],-1);
$subarray_90=explode('|',$Row_array[90],-1);
$subarray_91=explode('|',$Row_array[91],-1);
$subarray_92=explode('|',$Row_array[92],-1);
$subarray_93=explode('|',$Row_array[93],-1);
$subarray_94=explode('|',$Row_array[94],-1);
$subarray_95=explode('|',$Row_array[95],-1);
$subarray_96=explode('|',$Row_array[96],-1);
$subarray_97=explode('|',$Row_array[97],-1);
$subarray_98=explode('|',$Row_array[98],-1);
$subarray_99=explode('|',$Row_array[99],-1);
$subarray_100=explode('|',$Row_array[100],-1);
$subarray_101=explode('|',$Row_array[101],-1);
$subarray_102=explode('|',$Row_array[102],-1);
$subarray_103=explode('|',$Row_array[103],-1);
$subarray_104=explode('|',$Row_array[104],-1);
$subarray_105=explode('|',$Row_array[105],-1);
$subarray_106=explode('|',$Row_array[106],-1);
$subarray_107=explode('|',$Row_array[107],-1);
$subarray_108=explode('|',$Row_array[108],-1);
$subarray_109=explode('|',$Row_array[109],-1);
$subarray_110=explode('|',$Row_array[110],-1);
$subarray_111=explode('|',$Row_array[111],-1);
$subarray_112=explode('|',$Row_array[112],-1);
$subarray_113=explode('|',$Row_array[113],-1);
$subarray_114=explode('|',$Row_array[114],-1);
$subarray_115=explode('|',$Row_array[115],-1);
$subarray_116=explode('|',$Row_array[116],-1);
$subarray_117=explode('|',$Row_array[117],-1);
$subarray_118=explode('|',$Row_array[118],-1);
$subarray_119=explode('|',$Row_array[119],-1);
$subarray_120=explode('|',$Row_array[120],-1);
$subarray_121=explode('|',$Row_array[121],-1);
$subarray_122=explode('|',$Row_array[122],-1);
$subarray_123=explode('|',$Row_array[123],-1);
$subarray_124=explode('|',$Row_array[124],-1);
$subarray_125=explode('|',$Row_array[125],-1);
```

```
$subarray_126=explode('|',$Row_array[126],-1);
$subarray_127=explode('|',$Row_array[127],-1);
$subarray_128=explode('|',$Row_array[128],-1);
$subarray_129=explode('|',$Row_array[129],-1);
$subarray_130=explode('|',$Row_array[130],-1);
$subarray_131=explode('|',$Row_array[131],-1);
$subarray_132=explode('|',$Row_array[132],-1);
$subarray_133=explode('|',$Row_array[133],-1);
$subarray_134=explode('|',$Row_array[134],-1);
$subarray_135=explode('|',$Row_array[135],-1);
$subarray_136=explode('|',$Row_array[136],-1);
$subarray_137=explode('|',$Row_array[137],-1);
$subarray_138=explode('|',$Row_array[138],-1);

$Big_array=array(
        array(
                                "id"=>$subarray_0[0],
                                        "date"=>$subarray_0[1],
    "open"=>$subarray_0[2],
                                        "high"=>$subarray_0[3],
                                        "low"=>$subarray_0[4],
                                        "close"=>$subarray_0[5],
                                        "volume"=>$subarray_0[6],
                                        "adj_close"=>$subarray_0[7]
                                        ),
                                        array(
                                "id"=>$subarray_1[0],
                                        "date"=>$subarray_1[1],
    "open"=>$subarray_1[2],
                                        "high"=>$subarray_1[3],
                                        "low"=>$subarray_1[4],
                                        "close"=>$subarray_1[5],
                                        "volume"=>$subarray_1[6],
                                        "adj_close"=>$subarray_1[7]
                                        ),
                                            array(
                                "id"=>$subarray_2[0],
                                        "date"=>$subarray_2[1],
    "open"=>$subarray_2[2],
                                        "high"=>$subarray_2[3],
                                        "low"=>$subarray_2[4],
                                        "close"=>$subarray_2[5],
```

```
                                        "volume"=>$subarray_2[6],
                                        "adj_close"=>$subarray_2[7]
                                        ),
                                        array(
                                "id"=>$subarray_3[0],
                                        "date"=>$subarray_3[1],
"open"=>$subarray_3[2],
                                        "high"=>$subarray_3[3],
                                        "low"=>$subarray_3[4],
                                        "close"=>$subarray_3[5],
                                        "volume"=>$subarray_3[6],
                                        "adj_close"=>$subarray_3[7]
                                        ),
                                            array(
                                "id"=>$subarray_4[0],
                                        "date"=>$subarray_4[1],
"open"=>$subarray_4[2],
                                        "high"=>$subarray_4[3],
                                        "low"=>$subarray_4[4],
                                        "close"=>$subarray_4[5],
                                        "volume"=>$subarray_4[6],
                                        "adj_close"=>$subarray_4[7]
                                        ),
                                        array(
                                "id"=>$subarray_5[0],
                                        "date"=>$subarray_5[1],
"open"=>$subarray_5[2],
                                        "high"=>$subarray_5[3],
                                        "low"=>$subarray_5[4],
                                        "close"=>$subarray_5[5],
                                        "volume"=>$subarray_5[6],
                                        "adj_close"=>$subarray_5[7]
                                        ),
                                           array(
                                "id"=>$subarray_6[0],
                                        "date"=>$subarray_6[1],
"open"=>$subarray_6[2],
                                        "high"=>$subarray_6[3],
                                        "low"=>$subarray_6[4],
                                        "close"=>$subarray_6[5],
                                        "volume"=>$subarray_6[6],
                                        "adj_close"=>$subarray_6[7]
```

```
                                ),
                                array(
                        "id"=>$subarray_7[0],
                                "date"=>$subarray_7[1],
"open"=>$subarray_7[2],
                                "high"=>$subarray_7[3],
                                "low"=>$subarray_7[4],
                                "close"=>$subarray_7[5],
                                "volume"=>$subarray_7[6],
                                "adj_close"=>$subarray_7[7]
                                ),
                                  array(
                        "id"=>$subarray_8[0],
                                "date"=>$subarray_8[1],
"open"=>$subarray_8[2],
                                "high"=>$subarray_8[3],
                                "low"=>$subarray_8[4],
                                "close"=>$subarray_8[5],
                                "volume"=>$subarray_8[6],
                                "adj_close"=>$subarray_8[7]
                                ),
                                array(
                        "id"=>$subarray_9[0],
                                "date"=>$subarray_9[1],
"open"=>$subarray_9[2],
                                "high"=>$subarray_9[3],
                                "low"=>$subarray_9[4],
                                "close"=>$subarray_9[5],
                                "volume"=>$subarray_9[6],
                                "adj_close"=>$subarray_9[7]
                                ),
                                    array(
                        "id"=>$subarray_10[0],
                                "date"=>$subarray_10[1],
"open"=>$subarray_10[2],
                                "high"=>$subarray_10[3],
                                "low"=>$subarray_10[4],
                                "close"=>$subarray_10[5],
                                "volume"=>$subarray_10[6],
                                "adj_close"=>$subarray_10[7]
                                ),
                                array(
```

```
                    "id"=>$subarray_11[0],
                         "date"=>$subarray_11[1],
"open"=>$subarray_11[2],
                         "high"=>$subarray_11[3],
                         "low"=>$subarray_11[4],
                         "close"=>$subarray_11[5],
                         "volume"=>$subarray_11[6],
                         "adj_close"=>$subarray_11[7]
                         ),
                            array(
                    "id"=>$subarray_12[0],
                         "date"=>$subarray_12[1],
"open"=>$subarray_12[2],
                         "high"=>$subarray_12[3],
                         "low"=>$subarray_12[4],
                         "close"=>$subarray_12[5],
                         "volume"=>$subarray_12[6],
                         "adj_close"=>$subarray_12[7]
                         ),
                         array(
                    "id"=>$subarray_13[0],
                         "date"=>$subarray_13[1],
"open"=>$subarray_13[2],
                         "high"=>$subarray_13[3],
                         "low"=>$subarray_13[4],
                         "close"=>$subarray_13[5],
                         "volume"=>$subarray_13[6],
                         "adj_close"=>$subarray_13[7]
                         ),
                           array(
                    "id"=>$subarray_14[0],
                         "date"=>$subarray_14[1],
"open"=>$subarray_14[2],
                         "high"=>$subarray_14[3],
                         "low"=>$subarray_14[4],
                         "close"=>$subarray_14[5],
                         "volume"=>$subarray_14[6],
                         "adj_close"=>$subarray_14[7]
                         ),
                         array(
                    "id"=>$subarray_15[0],
                         "date"=>$subarray_15[1],
```

```
"open"=>$subarray_15[2],
                                "high"=>$subarray_15[3],
                                "low"=>$subarray_15[4],
                                "close"=>$subarray_15[5],
                                "volume"=>$subarray_15[6],
                                "adj_close"=>$subarray_15[7]
                                ),

                                    array(
                          "id"=>$subarray_16[0],
                                "date"=>$subarray_16[1],
"open"=>$subarray_16[2],
                                "high"=>$subarray_16[3],
                                "low"=>$subarray_16[4],
                                "close"=>$subarray_16[5],
                                "volume"=>$subarray_16[6],
                                "adj_close"=>$subarray_16[7]
                                ),
                                array(
                          "id"=>$subarray_17[0],
                                "date"=>$subarray_17[1],
"open"=>$subarray_17[2],
                                "high"=>$subarray_17[3],
                                "low"=>$subarray_17[4],
                                "close"=>$subarray_17[5],
                                "volume"=>$subarray_17[6],
                                "adj_close"=>$subarray_17[7]
                                ),
                                   array(
                          "id"=>$subarray_18[0],
                                "date"=>$subarray_18[1],
"open"=>$subarray_18[2],
                                "high"=>$subarray_18[3],
                                "low"=>$subarray_18[4],
                                "close"=>$subarray_18[5],
                                "volume"=>$subarray_18[6],
                                "adj_close"=>$subarray_18[7]
                                ),
                                array(
                          "id"=>$subarray_19[0],
                                "date"=>$subarray_19[1],
"open"=>$subarray_19[2],
```

```
"high"=>$subarray_19[3],
"low"=>$subarray_19[4],
"close"=>$subarray_19[5],
"volume"=>$subarray_19[6],
"adj_close"=>$subarray_19[7]
),
array(
"id"=>$subarray_20[0],
"date"=>$subarray_20[1],
"open"=>$subarray_20[2],
"high"=>$subarray_20[3],
"low"=>$subarray_20[4],
"close"=>$subarray_20[5],
"volume"=>$subarray_20[6],
"adj_close"=>$subarray_20[7]
),
array(
"id"=>$subarray_21[0],
"date"=>$subarray_21[1],
"open"=>$subarray_21[2],
"high"=>$subarray_21[3],
"low"=>$subarray_21[4],
"close"=>$subarray_21[5],
"volume"=>$subarray_21[6],
"adj_close"=>$subarray_21[7]
),
array(
"id"=>$subarray_22[0],
"date"=>$subarray_22[1],
"open"=>$subarray_22[2],
"high"=>$subarray_22[3],
"low"=>$subarray_22[4],
"close"=>$subarray_22[5],
"volume"=>$subarray_22[6],
"adj_close"=>$subarray_22[7]
),
array(
"id"=>$subarray_23[0],
"date"=>$subarray_23[1],
"open"=>$subarray_23[2],
"high"=>$subarray_23[3],
"low"=>$subarray_23[4],
```

```
                                "close"=>$subarray_23[5],
                                "volume"=>$subarray_23[6],
                                "adj_close"=>$subarray_23[7]
                                ),
                                  array(
                        "id"=>$subarray_24[0],
                                "date"=>$subarray_24[1],
"open"=>$subarray_24[2],
                                "high"=>$subarray_24[3],
                                "low"=>$subarray_24[4],
                                "close"=>$subarray_24[5],
                                "volume"=>$subarray_24[6],
                                "adj_close"=>$subarray_24[7]
                                ),
                                array(
                        "id"=>$subarray_25[0],
                                "date"=>$subarray_25[1],
"open"=>$subarray_25[2],
                                "high"=>$subarray_25[3],
                                "low"=>$subarray_25[4],
                                "close"=>$subarray_25[5],
                                "volume"=>$subarray_25[6],
                                "adj_close"=>$subarray_25[7]
                                ),
                                   array(
                        "id"=>$subarray_26[0],
                                "date"=>$subarray_26[1],
"open"=>$subarray_26[2],
                                "high"=>$subarray_26[3],
                                "low"=>$subarray_26[4],
                                "close"=>$subarray_26[5],
                                "volume"=>$subarray_26[6],
                                "adj_close"=>$subarray_26[7]
                                ),
                                array(
                        "id"=>$subarray_27[0],
                                "date"=>$subarray_27[1],
"open"=>$subarray_27[2],
                                "high"=>$subarray_27[3],
                                "low"=>$subarray_27[4],
                                "close"=>$subarray_27[5],
                                "volume"=>$subarray_27[6],
```

```
                    "adj_close"=>$subarray_27[7]
                    ),
                        array(
                "id"=>$subarray_28[0],
                    "date"=>$subarray_28[1],
"open"=>$subarray_28[2],
                    "high"=>$subarray_28[3],
                    "low"=>$subarray_28[4],
                    "close"=>$subarray_28[5],
                    "volume"=>$subarray_28[6],
                    "adj_close"=>$subarray_28[7]
                    ),
                    array(
                "id"=>$subarray_29[0],
                    "date"=>$subarray_29[1],
"open"=>$subarray_29[2],
                    "high"=>$subarray_29[3],
                    "low"=>$subarray_29[4],
                    "close"=>$subarray_29[5],
                    "volume"=>$subarray_29[6],
                    "adj_close"=>$subarray_29[7]
                    ),
                        array(
                "id"=>$subarray_30[0],
                    "date"=>$subarray_30[1],
"open"=>$subarray_30[2],
                    "high"=>$subarray_30[3],
                    "low"=>$subarray_30[4],
                    "close"=>$subarray_30[5],
                    "volume"=>$subarray_30[6],
                    "adj_close"=>$subarray_30[7]
                    ),
                    array(
                "id"=>$subarray_31[0],
                    "date"=>$subarray_31[1],
"open"=>$subarray_31[2],
                    "high"=>$subarray_31[3],
                    "low"=>$subarray_31[4],
                    "close"=>$subarray_31[5],
                    "volume"=>$subarray_31[6],
                    "adj_close"=>$subarray_31[7]
                    ),
```

```
array(
"id"=>$subarray_32[0],
"date"=>$subarray_32[1],
"open"=>$subarray_32[2],
"high"=>$subarray_32[3],
"low"=>$subarray_32[4],
"close"=>$subarray_32[5],
"volume"=>$subarray_32[6],
"adj_close"=>$subarray_32[7]
),
array(
"id"=>$subarray_33[0],
"date"=>$subarray_33[1],
"open"=>$subarray_33[2],
"high"=>$subarray_33[3],
"low"=>$subarray_33[4],
"close"=>$subarray_33[5],
"volume"=>$subarray_33[6],
"adj_close"=>$subarray_33[7]
),
array(
"id"=>$subarray_34[0],
"date"=>$subarray_34[1],
"open"=>$subarray_34[2],
"high"=>$subarray_34[3],
"low"=>$subarray_34[4],
"close"=>$subarray_34[5],
"volume"=>$subarray_34[6],
"adj_close"=>$subarray_34[7]
),
array(
"id"=>$subarray_35[0],
"date"=>$subarray_35[1],
"open"=>$subarray_35[2],
"high"=>$subarray_35[3],
"low"=>$subarray_35[4],
"close"=>$subarray_35[5],
"volume"=>$subarray_35[6],
"adj_close"=>$subarray_35[7]
),
array(
"id"=>$subarray_36[0],
```

```
                                "date"=>$subarray_36[1],
"open"=>$subarray_36[2],
                                "high"=>$subarray_36[3],
                                "low"=>$subarray_36[4],
                                "close"=>$subarray_36[5],
                                "volume"=>$subarray_36[6],
                                "adj_close"=>$subarray_36[7]
                                ),
                                array(
                          "id"=>$subarray_37[0],
                                "date"=>$subarray_37[1],
"open"=>$subarray_37[2],
                                "high"=>$subarray_37[3],
                                "low"=>$subarray_37[4],
                                "close"=>$subarray_37[5],
                                "volume"=>$subarray_37[6],
                                "adj_close"=>$subarray_37[7]
                                ),
                                   array(
                          "id"=>$subarray_38[0],
                                "date"=>$subarray_38[1],
"open"=>$subarray_38[2],
                                "high"=>$subarray_38[3],
                                "low"=>$subarray_38[4],
                                "close"=>$subarray_38[5],
                                "volume"=>$subarray_38[6],
                                "adj_close"=>$subarray_38[7]
                                ),
                                array(
                          "id"=>$subarray_39[0],
                                "date"=>$subarray_39[1],
"open"=>$subarray_39[2],
                                "high"=>$subarray_39[3],
                                "low"=>$subarray_39[4],
                                "close"=>$subarray_39[5],
                                "volume"=>$subarray_39[6],
                                "adj_close"=>$subarray_39[7]
                                ),
                                  array(
                          "id"=>$subarray_40[0],
                                "date"=>$subarray_40[1],
"open"=>$subarray_40[2],
```

```
                    "high"=>$subarray_40[3],
                    "low"=>$subarray_40[4],
                    "close"=>$subarray_40[5],
                    "volume"=>$subarray_40[6],
                    "adj_close"=>$subarray_40[7]
                    ),
                    array(
                "id"=>$subarray_41[0],
                    "date"=>$subarray_41[1],
"open"=>$subarray_41[2],
                    "high"=>$subarray_41[3],
                    "low"=>$subarray_41[4],
                    "close"=>$subarray_41[5],
                    "volume"=>$subarray_41[6],
                    "adj_close"=>$subarray_41[7]
                    ),
                      array(
                "id"=>$subarray_42[0],
                    "date"=>$subarray_42[1],
"open"=>$subarray_42[2],
                    "high"=>$subarray_42[3],
                    "low"=>$subarray_42[4],
                    "close"=>$subarray_42[5],
                    "volume"=>$subarray_42[6],
                    "adj_close"=>$subarray_42[7]
                    ),
                    array(
                "id"=>$subarray_43[0],
                    "date"=>$subarray_43[1],
"open"=>$subarray_43[2],
                    "high"=>$subarray_43[3],
                    "low"=>$subarray_43[4],
                    "close"=>$subarray_43[5],
                    "volume"=>$subarray_43[6],
                    "adj_close"=>$subarray_43[7]
                    ),
                      array(
                "id"=>$subarray_44[0],
                    "date"=>$subarray_44[1],
"open"=>$subarray_44[2],
                    "high"=>$subarray_44[3],
                    "low"=>$subarray_44[4],
```

```
                    "close"=>$subarray_44[5],
                    "volume"=>$subarray_44[6],
                    "adj_close"=>$subarray_44[7]
                    ),
                    array(
                "id"=>$subarray_45[0],
                    "date"=>$subarray_45[1],
"open"=>$subarray_45[2],
                    "high"=>$subarray_45[3],
                    "low"=>$subarray_45[4],
                    "close"=>$subarray_45[5],
                    "volume"=>$subarray_45[6],
                    "adj_close"=>$subarray_45[7]
                    ),
                      array(
                "id"=>$subarray_46[0],
                    "date"=>$subarray_46[1],
"open"=>$subarray_46[2],
                    "high"=>$subarray_46[3],
                    "low"=>$subarray_46[4],
                    "close"=>$subarray_46[5],
                    "volume"=>$subarray_46[6],
                    "adj_close"=>$subarray_46[7]
                    ),
                    array(
                "id"=>$subarray_47[0],
                    "date"=>$subarray_47[1],
"open"=>$subarray_47[2],
                    "high"=>$subarray_47[3],
                    "low"=>$subarray_47[4],
                    "close"=>$subarray_47[5],
                    "volume"=>$subarray_47[6],
                    "adj_close"=>$subarray_47[7]
                    ),

                      array(
                "id"=>$subarray_48[0],
                    "date"=>$subarray_48[1],
"open"=>$subarray_48[2],
                    "high"=>$subarray_48[3],
                    "low"=>$subarray_48[4],
                    "close"=>$subarray_48[5],
```

```
                        "volume"=>$subarray_48[6],
                        "adj_close"=>$subarray_48[7]
                        ),
                        array(
                    "id"=>$subarray_49[0],
                        "date"=>$subarray_49[1],
"open"=>$subarray_49[2],
                        "high"=>$subarray_49[3],
                        "low"=>$subarray_49[4],
                        "close"=>$subarray_49[5],
                        "volume"=>$subarray_49[6],
                        "adj_close"=>$subarray_49[7]
                        ),
                          array(
                    "id"=>$subarray_50[0],
                        "date"=>$subarray_50[1],
"open"=>$subarray_50[2],
                        "high"=>$subarray_50[3],
                        "low"=>$subarray_50[4],
                        "close"=>$subarray_50[5],
                        "volume"=>$subarray_50[6],
                        "adj_close"=>$subarray_50[7]
                        ),
                        array(
                    "id"=>$subarray_51[0],
                        "date"=>$subarray_51[1],
"open"=>$subarray_51[2],
                        "high"=>$subarray_51[3],
                        "low"=>$subarray_51[4],
                        "close"=>$subarray_51[5],
                        "volume"=>$subarray_51[6],
                        "adj_close"=>$subarray_51[7]
                        ),
                          array(
                    "id"=>$subarray_52[0],
                        "date"=>$subarray_52[1],
"open"=>$subarray_52[2],
                        "high"=>$subarray_52[3],
                        "low"=>$subarray_52[4],
                        "close"=>$subarray_52[5],
                        "volume"=>$subarray_52[6],
                        "adj_close"=>$subarray_52[7]
```

```
                    ),
                    array(
                "id"=>$subarray_53[0],
                    "date"=>$subarray_53[1],
"open"=>$subarray_53[2],
                    "high"=>$subarray_53[3],
                    "low"=>$subarray_53[4],
                    "close"=>$subarray_53[5],
                    "volume"=>$subarray_53[6],
                    "adj_close"=>$subarray_53[7]
                    ),
                      array(
                "id"=>$subarray_54[0],
                    "date"=>$subarray_54[1],
"open"=>$subarray_54[2],
                    "high"=>$subarray_54[3],
                    "low"=>$subarray_54[4],
                    "close"=>$subarray_54[5],
                    "volume"=>$subarray_54[6],
                    "adj_close"=>$subarray_54[7]
                    ),
                    array(
                "id"=>$subarray_55[0],
                    "date"=>$subarray_55[1],
"open"=>$subarray_55[2],
                    "high"=>$subarray_55[3],
                    "low"=>$subarray_55[4],
                    "close"=>$subarray_55[5],
                    "volume"=>$subarray_55[6],
                    "adj_close"=>$subarray_55[7]
                    ),
                     array(
                "id"=>$subarray_56[0],
                    "date"=>$subarray_56[1],
"open"=>$subarray_56[2],
                    "high"=>$subarray_56[3],
                    "low"=>$subarray_56[4],
                    "close"=>$subarray_56[5],
                    "volume"=>$subarray_56[6],
                    "adj_close"=>$subarray_56[7]
                    ),
                    array(
```

```
                "id"=>$subarray_57[0],
                      "date"=>$subarray_57[1],
"open"=>$subarray_57[2],
                      "high"=>$subarray_57[3],
                      "low"=>$subarray_57[4],
                      "close"=>$subarray_57[5],
                      "volume"=>$subarray_57[6],
                      "adj_close"=>$subarray_57[7]
                      ),
                          array(
                "id"=>$subarray_58[0],
                      "date"=>$subarray_58[1],
"open"=>$subarray_58[2],
                      "high"=>$subarray_58[3],
                      "low"=>$subarray_58[4],
                      "close"=>$subarray_58[5],
                      "volume"=>$subarray_58[6],
                      "adj_close"=>$subarray_58[7]
                      ),
                      array(
                "id"=>$subarray_59[0],
                      "date"=>$subarray_59[1],
"open"=>$subarray_59[2],
                      "high"=>$subarray_59[3],
                      "low"=>$subarray_59[4],
                      "close"=>$subarray_59[5],
                      "volume"=>$subarray_59[6],
                      "adj_close"=>$subarray_59[7]
                      ),
                          array(
                "id"=>$subarray_60[0],
                      "date"=>$subarray_60[1],
"open"=>$subarray_60[2],
                      "high"=>$subarray_60[3],
                      "low"=>$subarray_60[4],
                      "close"=>$subarray_60[5],
                      "volume"=>$subarray_60[6],
                      "adj_close"=>$subarray_60[7]
                      ),
                      array(
                "id"=>$subarray_61[0],
                      "date"=>$subarray_61[1],
```

```
"open"=>$subarray_61[2],
                                  "high"=>$subarray_61[3],
                                  "low"=>$subarray_61[4],
                                  "close"=>$subarray_61[5],
                                  "volume"=>$subarray_61[6],
                                  "adj_close"=>$subarray_61[7]
                                  ),
                                     array(
                           "id"=>$subarray_62[0],
                                  "date"=>$subarray_62[1],
"open"=>$subarray_62[2],
                                  "high"=>$subarray_62[3],
                                  "low"=>$subarray_62[4],
                                  "close"=>$subarray_62[5],
                                  "volume"=>$subarray_62[6],
                                  "adj_close"=>$subarray_62[7]
                                  ),
                                  array(
                           "id"=>$subarray_63[0],
                                  "date"=>$subarray_63[1],
"open"=>$subarray_63[2],
                                  "high"=>$subarray_63[3],
                                  "low"=>$subarray_63[4],
                                  "close"=>$subarray_63[5],
                                  "volume"=>$subarray_63[6],
                                  "adj_close"=>$subarray_63[7]
                                  ),

                                    array(
                           "id"=>$subarray_64[0],
                                  "date"=>$subarray_64[1],
"open"=>$subarray_64[2],
                                  "high"=>$subarray_64[3],
                                  "low"=>$subarray_64[4],
                                  "close"=>$subarray_64[5],
                                  "volume"=>$subarray_64[6],
                                  "adj_close"=>$subarray_64[7]
                                  ),
                                  array(
                           "id"=>$subarray_65[0],
                                  "date"=>$subarray_65[1],
"open"=>$subarray_65[2],
```

```
"high"=>$subarray_65[3],
"low"=>$subarray_65[4],
"close"=>$subarray_65[5],
"volume"=>$subarray_65[6],
"adj_close"=>$subarray_65[7]
),
array(
"id"=>$subarray_66[0],
"date"=>$subarray_66[1],
"open"=>$subarray_66[2],
"high"=>$subarray_66[3],
"low"=>$subarray_66[4],
"close"=>$subarray_66[5],
"volume"=>$subarray_66[6],
"adj_close"=>$subarray_66[7]
),
array(
"id"=>$subarray_67[0],
"date"=>$subarray_67[1],
"open"=>$subarray_67[2],
"high"=>$subarray_67[3],
"low"=>$subarray_67[4],
"close"=>$subarray_67[5],
"volume"=>$subarray_67[6],
"adj_close"=>$subarray_67[7]
),
array(
"id"=>$subarray_68[0],
"date"=>$subarray_68[1],
"open"=>$subarray_68[2],
"high"=>$subarray_68[3],
"low"=>$subarray_68[4],
"close"=>$subarray_68[5],
"volume"=>$subarray_68[6],
"adj_close"=>$subarray_68[7]
),
array(
"id"=>$subarray_69[0],
"date"=>$subarray_69[1],
"open"=>$subarray_69[2],
"high"=>$subarray_69[3],
"low"=>$subarray_69[4],
```

```
                    "close"=>$subarray_69[5],
                    "volume"=>$subarray_69[6],
                    "adj_close"=>$subarray_69[7]
                    ),
                       array(
                "id"=>$subarray_70[0],
                    "date"=>$subarray_70[1],
"open"=>$subarray_70[2],
                    "high"=>$subarray_70[3],
                    "low"=>$subarray_70[4],
                    "close"=>$subarray_70[5],
                    "volume"=>$subarray_70[6],
                    "adj_close"=>$subarray_70[7]
                    ),
                    array(
                "id"=>$subarray_71[0],
                    "date"=>$subarray_71[1],
"open"=>$subarray_71[2],
                    "high"=>$subarray_71[3],
                    "low"=>$subarray_71[4],
                    "close"=>$subarray_71[5],
                    "volume"=>$subarray_71[6],
                    "adj_close"=>$subarray_71[7]
                    ),
                      array(
                "id"=>$subarray_72[0],
                    "date"=>$subarray_72[1],
"open"=>$subarray_72[2],
                    "high"=>$subarray_72[3],
                    "low"=>$subarray_72[4],
                    "close"=>$subarray_72[5],
                    "volume"=>$subarray_72[6],
                    "adj_close"=>$subarray_72[7]
                    ),
                    array(
                "id"=>$subarray_73[0],
                    "date"=>$subarray_73[1],
"open"=>$subarray_73[2],
                    "high"=>$subarray_73[3],
                    "low"=>$subarray_73[4],
                    "close"=>$subarray_73[5],
                    "volume"=>$subarray_73[6],
```

```
                    "adj_close"=>$subarray_73[7]
                    ),
                        array(
                "id"=>$subarray_74[0],
                    "date"=>$subarray_74[1],
"open"=>$subarray_74[2],
                    "high"=>$subarray_74[3],
                    "low"=>$subarray_74[4],
                    "close"=>$subarray_74[5],
                    "volume"=>$subarray_74[6],
                    "adj_close"=>$subarray_74[7]
                    ),
                    array(
                "id"=>$subarray_75[0],
                    "date"=>$subarray_75[1],
"open"=>$subarray_75[2],
                    "high"=>$subarray_75[3],
                    "low"=>$subarray_75[4],
                    "close"=>$subarray_75[5],
                    "volume"=>$subarray_75[6],
                    "adj_close"=>$subarray_75[7]
                    ),
                        array(
                "id"=>$subarray_76[0],
                    "date"=>$subarray_76[1],
"open"=>$subarray_76[2],
                    "high"=>$subarray_76[3],
                    "low"=>$subarray_76[4],
                    "close"=>$subarray_76[5],
                    "volume"=>$subarray_76[6],
                    "adj_close"=>$subarray_76[7]
                    ),
                    array(
                "id"=>$subarray_77[0],
                    "date"=>$subarray_77[1],
"open"=>$subarray_77[2],
                    "high"=>$subarray_77[3],
                    "low"=>$subarray_77[4],
                    "close"=>$subarray_77[5],
                    "volume"=>$subarray_77[6],
                    "adj_close"=>$subarray_77[7]
                    ),
```

```
                        array(
                "id"=>$subarray_78[0],
                    "date"=>$subarray_78[1],
"open"=>$subarray_78[2],
                    "high"=>$subarray_78[3],
                    "low"=>$subarray_78[4],
                    "close"=>$subarray_78[5],
                    "volume"=>$subarray_78[6],
                    "adj_close"=>$subarray_78[7]
                    ),
                    array(
                "id"=>$subarray_79[0],
                    "date"=>$subarray_79[1],
"open"=>$subarray_79[2],
                    "high"=>$subarray_79[3],
                    "low"=>$subarray_79[4],
                    "close"=>$subarray_79[5],
                    "volume"=>$subarray_79[6],
                    "adj_close"=>$subarray_79[7]
                    ),

                        array(
                "id"=>$subarray_80[0],
                    "date"=>$subarray_80[1],
"open"=>$subarray_80[2],
                    "high"=>$subarray_80[3],
                    "low"=>$subarray_80[4],
                    "close"=>$subarray_80[5],
                    "volume"=>$subarray_80[6],
                    "adj_close"=>$subarray_80[7]
                    ),
                    array(
                "id"=>$subarray_81[0],
                    "date"=>$subarray_81[1],
"open"=>$subarray_81[2],
                    "high"=>$subarray_81[3],
                    "low"=>$subarray_81[4],
                    "close"=>$subarray_81[5],
                    "volume"=>$subarray_81[6],
                    "adj_close"=>$subarray_81[7]
                    ),
                        array(
```

```
                    "id"=>$subarray_82[0],
                        "date"=>$subarray_82[1],
"open"=>$subarray_82[2],
                        "high"=>$subarray_82[3],
                        "low"=>$subarray_82[4],
                        "close"=>$subarray_82[5],
                        "volume"=>$subarray_82[6],
                        "adj_close"=>$subarray_82[7]
                        ),
                        array(
                    "id"=>$subarray_83[0],
                        "date"=>$subarray_83[1],
"open"=>$subarray_83[2],
                        "high"=>$subarray_83[3],
                        "low"=>$subarray_83[4],
                        "close"=>$subarray_83[5],
                        "volume"=>$subarray_83[6],
                        "adj_close"=>$subarray_83[7]
                        ),
                            array(
                    "id"=>$subarray_84[0],
                        "date"=>$subarray_84[1],
"open"=>$subarray_84[2],
                        "high"=>$subarray_84[3],
                        "low"=>$subarray_84[4],
                        "close"=>$subarray_84[5],
                        "volume"=>$subarray_84[6],
                        "adj_close"=>$subarray_84[7]
                        ),
                        array(
                    "id"=>$subarray_85[0],
                        "date"=>$subarray_85[1],
"open"=>$subarray_85[2],
                        "high"=>$subarray_85[3],
                        "low"=>$subarray_85[4],
                        "close"=>$subarray_85[5],
                        "volume"=>$subarray_85[6],
                        "adj_close"=>$subarray_85[7]
                        ),
                           array(
                    "id"=>$subarray_86[0],
                        "date"=>$subarray_86[1],
```

```
"open"=>$subarray_86[2],
                                    "high"=>$subarray_86[3],
                                    "low"=>$subarray_86[4],
                                    "close"=>$subarray_86[5],
                                    "volume"=>$subarray_86[6],
                                    "adj_close"=>$subarray_86[7]
                                    ),
                                    array(
                              "id"=>$subarray_87[0],
                                    "date"=>$subarray_87[1],
"open"=>$subarray_87[2],
                                    "high"=>$subarray_87[3],
                                    "low"=>$subarray_87[4],
                                    "close"=>$subarray_87[5],
                                    "volume"=>$subarray_87[6],
                                    "adj_close"=>$subarray_87[7]
                                    ),
                                      array(
                              "id"=>$subarray_88[0],
                                    "date"=>$subarray_88[1],
"open"=>$subarray_88[2],
                                    "high"=>$subarray_88[3],
                                    "low"=>$subarray_88[4],
                                    "close"=>$subarray_88[5],
                                    "volume"=>$subarray_88[6],
                                    "adj_close"=>$subarray_88[7]
                                    ),
                                    array(
                              "id"=>$subarray_89[0],
                                    "date"=>$subarray_89[1],
"open"=>$subarray_89[2],
                                    "high"=>$subarray_89[3],
                                    "low"=>$subarray_89[4],
                                    "close"=>$subarray_89[5],
                                    "volume"=>$subarray_89[6],
                                    "adj_close"=>$subarray_89[7]
                                    ),
                                       array(
                              "id"=>$subarray_90[0],
                                    "date"=>$subarray_90[1],
"open"=>$subarray_90[2],
                                    "high"=>$subarray_90[3],
```

```
                    "low"=>$subarray_90[4],
                    "close"=>$subarray_90[5],
                    "volume"=>$subarray_90[6],
                    "adj_close"=>$subarray_90[7]
                    ),
                    array(
                "id"=>$subarray_91[0],
                    "date"=>$subarray_91[1],
"open"=>$subarray_91[2],
                    "high"=>$subarray_91[3],
                    "low"=>$subarray_91[4],
                    "close"=>$subarray_91[5],
                    "volume"=>$subarray_91[6],
                    "adj_close"=>$subarray_91[7]
                    ),
                      array(
                "id"=>$subarray_92[0],
                    "date"=>$subarray_92[1],
"open"=>$subarray_92[2],
                    "high"=>$subarray_92[3],
                    "low"=>$subarray_92[4],
                    "close"=>$subarray_92[5],
                    "volume"=>$subarray_92[6],
                    "adj_close"=>$subarray_92[7]
                    ),
                    array(
                "id"=>$subarray_93[0],
                    "date"=>$subarray_93[1],
"open"=>$subarray_93[2],
                    "high"=>$subarray_93[3],
                    "low"=>$subarray_93[4],
                    "close"=>$subarray_93[5],
                    "volume"=>$subarray_93[6],
                    "adj_close"=>$subarray_93[7]
                    ),
                      array(
                "id"=>$subarray_94[0],
                    "date"=>$subarray_94[1],
"open"=>$subarray_94[2],
                    "high"=>$subarray_94[3],
                    "low"=>$subarray_94[4],
                    "close"=>$subarray_94[5],
```

```
                    "volume"=>$subarray_94[6],
                    "adj_close"=>$subarray_94[7]
                    ),
                    array(
                "id"=>$subarray_95[0],
                    "date"=>$subarray_95[1],
"open"=>$subarray_95[2],
                    "high"=>$subarray_95[3],
                    "low"=>$subarray_95[4],
                    "close"=>$subarray_95[5],
                    "volume"=>$subarray_95[6],
                    "adj_close"=>$subarray_95[7]
                    ),
                      array(
                "id"=>$subarray_96[0],
                    "date"=>$subarray_96[1],
"open"=>$subarray_96[2],
                    "high"=>$subarray_96[3],
                    "low"=>$subarray_96[4],
                    "close"=>$subarray_96[5],
                    "volume"=>$subarray_96[6],
                    "adj_close"=>$subarray_96[7]
                    ),
                    array(
                "id"=>$subarray_97[0],
                    "date"=>$subarray_97[1],
"open"=>$subarray_97[2],
                    "high"=>$subarray_97[3],
                    "low"=>$subarray_97[4],
                    "close"=>$subarray_97[5],
                    "volume"=>$subarray_97[6],
                    "adj_close"=>$subarray_97[7]
                    ),
                      array(
                "id"=>$subarray_98[0],
                    "date"=>$subarray_98[1],
"open"=>$subarray_98[2],
                    "high"=>$subarray_98[3],
                    "low"=>$subarray_98[4],
                    "close"=>$subarray_98[5],
                    "volume"=>$subarray_98[6],
                    "adj_close"=>$subarray_98[7]
```

```
                        ),
                        array(
                "id"=>$subarray_99[0],
                        "date"=>$subarray_99[1],
"open"=>$subarray_99[2],
                        "high"=>$subarray_99[3],
                        "low"=>$subarray_99[4],
                        "close"=>$subarray_99[5],
                        "volume"=>$subarray_99[6],
                        "adj_close"=>$subarray_99[7]
                        ),
                            array(
                "id"=>$subarray_100[0],
                        "date"=>$subarray_100[1],
"open"=>$subarray_100[2],
                        "high"=>$subarray_100[3],
                        "low"=>$subarray_100[4],
                        "close"=>$subarray_100[5],
                        "volume"=>$subarray_100[6],
                        "adj_close"=>$subarray_100[7]
                        ),
                        array(
                "id"=>$subarray_101[0],
                        "date"=>$subarray_101[1],
"open"=>$subarray_101[2],
                        "high"=>$subarray_101[3],
                        "low"=>$subarray_101[4],
                        "close"=>$subarray_101[5],
                        "volume"=>$subarray_101[6],
                        "adj_close"=>$subarray_101[7]
                        ),
                           array(
                "id"=>$subarray_102[0],
                        "date"=>$subarray_102[1],
"open"=>$subarray_102[2],
                        "high"=>$subarray_102[3],
                        "low"=>$subarray_102[4],
                        "close"=>$subarray_102[5],
                        "volume"=>$subarray_102[6],
                        "adj_close"=>$subarray_102[7]
                        ),
                        array(
```

```
"id"=>$subarray_103[0],
        "date"=>$subarray_103[1],
"open"=>$subarray_103[2],
        "high"=>$subarray_103[3],
        "low"=>$subarray_103[4],
        "close"=>$subarray_103[5],
        "volume"=>$subarray_103[6],
        "adj_close"=>$subarray_103[7]
        ),
            array(
"id"=>$subarray_104[0],
        "date"=>$subarray_104[1],
"open"=>$subarray_104[2],
        "high"=>$subarray_104[3],
        "low"=>$subarray_104[4],
        "close"=>$subarray_104[5],
        "volume"=>$subarray_104[6],
        "adj_close"=>$subarray_104[7]
        ),
        array(
"id"=>$subarray_105[0],
        "date"=>$subarray_105[1],
"open"=>$subarray_105[2],
        "high"=>$subarray_105[3],
        "low"=>$subarray_105[4],
        "close"=>$subarray_105[5],
        "volume"=>$subarray_105[6],
        "adj_close"=>$subarray_105[7]
        ),
            array(
"id"=>$subarray_106[0],
        "date"=>$subarray_106[1],
"open"=>$subarray_106[2],
        "high"=>$subarray_106[3],
        "low"=>$subarray_106[4],
        "close"=>$subarray_106[5],
        "volume"=>$subarray_106[6],
        "adj_close"=>$subarray_106[7]
        ),
        array(
"id"=>$subarray_107[0],
        "date"=>$subarray_107[1],
```

```
"open"=>$subarray_107[2],
                    "high"=>$subarray_107[3],
                    "low"=>$subarray_107[4],
                    "close"=>$subarray_107[5],
                    "volume"=>$subarray_107[6],
                    "adj_close"=>$subarray_107[7]
                    ),
                      array(
                "id"=>$subarray_108[0],
                    "date"=>$subarray_108[1],
"open"=>$subarray_108[2],
                    "high"=>$subarray_108[3],
                    "low"=>$subarray_108[4],
                    "close"=>$subarray_108[5],
                    "volume"=>$subarray_108[6],
                    "adj_close"=>$subarray_108[7]
                    ),
                    array(
                "id"=>$subarray_109[0],
                    "date"=>$subarray_109[1],
"open"=>$subarray_109[2],
                    "high"=>$subarray_109[3],
                    "low"=>$subarray_109[4],
                    "close"=>$subarray_109[5],
                    "volume"=>$subarray_109[6],
                    "adj_close"=>$subarray_109[7]
                    ),
                        array(
                "id"=>$subarray_110[0],
                    "date"=>$subarray_110[1],
"open"=>$subarray_110[2],
                    "high"=>$subarray_110[3],
                    "low"=>$subarray_110[4],
                    "close"=>$subarray_110[5],
                    "volume"=>$subarray_110[6],
                    "adj_close"=>$subarray_110[7]
                    ),
                    array(
                "id"=>$subarray_111[0],
                    "date"=>$subarray_111[1],
"open"=>$subarray_111[2],
                    "high"=>$subarray_111[3],
```

```
                "low"=>$subarray_111[4],
                "close"=>$subarray_111[5],
                "volume"=>$subarray_111[6],
                "adj_close"=>$subarray_111[7]
                ),
                    array(
            "id"=>$subarray_112[0],
                "date"=>$subarray_112[1],
"open"=>$subarray_112[2],
                "high"=>$subarray_112[3],
                "low"=>$subarray_112[4],
                "close"=>$subarray_112[5],
                "volume"=>$subarray_112[6],
                "adj_close"=>$subarray_112[7]
                ),
                array(
            "id"=>$subarray_113[0],
                "date"=>$subarray_113[1],
"open"=>$subarray_113[2],
                "high"=>$subarray_113[3],
                "low"=>$subarray_113[4],
                "close"=>$subarray_113[5],
                "volume"=>$subarray_113[6],
                "adj_close"=>$subarray_113[7]
                ),
                    array(
            "id"=>$subarray_114[0],
                "date"=>$subarray_114[1],
"open"=>$subarray_114[2],
                "high"=>$subarray_114[3],
                "low"=>$subarray_114[4],
                "close"=>$subarray_114[5],
                "volume"=>$subarray_114[6],
                "adj_close"=>$subarray_114[7]
                ),
                array(
            "id"=>$subarray_115[0],
                "date"=>$subarray_115[1],
"open"=>$subarray_115[2],
                "high"=>$subarray_115[3],
                "low"=>$subarray_115[4],
                "close"=>$subarray_115[5],
```

```
                    "volume"=>$subarray_115[6],
                    "adj_close"=>$subarray_115[7]
                    ),

                        array(
                "id"=>$subarray_116[0],
                    "date"=>$subarray_116[1],
"open"=>$subarray_116[2],
                    "high"=>$subarray_116[3],
                    "low"=>$subarray_116[4],
                    "close"=>$subarray_116[5],
                    "volume"=>$subarray_116[6],
                    "adj_close"=>$subarray_116[7]
                    ),
                    array(
                "id"=>$subarray_117[0],
                    "date"=>$subarray_117[1],
"open"=>$subarray_117[2],
                    "high"=>$subarray_117[3],
                    "low"=>$subarray_117[4],
                    "close"=>$subarray_117[5],
                    "volume"=>$subarray_117[6],
                    "adj_close"=>$subarray_117[7]
                    ),
                      array(
                "id"=>$subarray_118[0],
                    "date"=>$subarray_118[1],
"open"=>$subarray_118[2],
                    "high"=>$subarray_118[3],
                    "low"=>$subarray_118[4],
                    "close"=>$subarray_118[5],
                    "volume"=>$subarray_118[6],
                    "adj_close"=>$subarray_118[7]
                    ),
                    array(
                "id"=>$subarray_119[0],
                    "date"=>$subarray_119[1],
"open"=>$subarray_119[2],
                    "high"=>$subarray_119[3],
                    "low"=>$subarray_119[4],
                    "close"=>$subarray_119[5],
                    "volume"=>$subarray_119[6],
```

```
"adj_close"=>$subarray_119[7]
),
array(
"id"=>$subarray_120[0],
"date"=>$subarray_120[1],
"open"=>$subarray_120[2],
"high"=>$subarray_120[3],
"low"=>$subarray_120[4],
"close"=>$subarray_120[5],
"volume"=>$subarray_120[6],
"adj_close"=>$subarray_120[7]
),
array(
"id"=>$subarray_121[0],
"date"=>$subarray_121[1],
"open"=>$subarray_121[2],
"high"=>$subarray_121[3],
"low"=>$subarray_121[4],
"close"=>$subarray_121[5],
"volume"=>$subarray_121[6],
"adj_close"=>$subarray_121[7]
),
array(
"id"=>$subarray_122[0],
"date"=>$subarray_122[1],
"open"=>$subarray_122[2],
"high"=>$subarray_122[3],
"low"=>$subarray_122[4],
"close"=>$subarray_122[5],
"volume"=>$subarray_122[6],
"adj_close"=>$subarray_122[7]
),
array(
"id"=>$subarray_123[0],
"date"=>$subarray_123[1],
"open"=>$subarray_123[2],
"high"=>$subarray_123[3],
"low"=>$subarray_123[4],
"close"=>$subarray_123[5],
"volume"=>$subarray_123[6],
"adj_close"=>$subarray_123[7]
),
```

```
array(
"id"=>$subarray_124[0],
"date"=>$subarray_124[1],
"open"=>$subarray_124[2],
"high"=>$subarray_124[3],
"low"=>$subarray_124[4],
"close"=>$subarray_124[5],
"volume"=>$subarray_124[6],
"adj_close"=>$subarray_124[7]
),
array(
"id"=>$subarray_125[0],
"date"=>$subarray_125[1],
"open"=>$subarray_125[2],
"high"=>$subarray_125[3],
"low"=>$subarray_125[4],
"close"=>$subarray_125[5],
"volume"=>$subarray_125[6],
"adj_close"=>$subarray_125[7]
),
array(
"id"=>$subarray_126[0],
"date"=>$subarray_126[1],
"open"=>$subarray_126[2],
"high"=>$subarray_126[3],
"low"=>$subarray_126[4],
"close"=>$subarray_126[5],
"volume"=>$subarray_126[6],
"adj_close"=>$subarray_126[7]
),
array(
"id"=>$subarray_127[0],
"date"=>$subarray_127[1],
"open"=>$subarray_127[2],
"high"=>$subarray_127[3],
"low"=>$subarray_17[4],
"close"=>$subarray_127[5],
"volume"=>$subarray_127[6],
"adj_close"=>$subarray_127[7]
),
array(
"id"=>$subarray_128[0],
```

```
                    "date"=>$subarray_128[1],
"open"=>$subarray_128[2],
                    "high"=>$subarray_128[3],
                    "low"=>$subarray_128[4],
                    "close"=>$subarray_128[5],
                    "volume"=>$subarray_128[6],
                    "adj_close"=>$subarray_128[7]
                    ),
                    array(
                "id"=>$subarray_129[0],
                    "date"=>$subarray_129[1],
"open"=>$subarray_129[2],
                    "high"=>$subarray_129[3],
                    "low"=>$subarray_129[4],
                    "close"=>$subarray_129[5],
                    "volume"=>$subarray_129[6],
                    "adj_close"=>$subarray_129[7]
                    ),
                      array(
                "id"=>$subarray_130[0],
                    "date"=>$subarray_130[1],
"open"=>$subarray_130[2],
                    "high"=>$subarray_130[3],
                    "low"=>$subarray_130[4],
                    "close"=>$subarray_130[5],
                    "volume"=>$subarray_130[6],
                    "adj_close"=>$subarray_130[7]
                    ),
                    array(
                "id"=>$subarray_131[0],
                    "date"=>$subarray_131[1],
"open"=>$subarray_131[2],
                    "high"=>$subarray_131[3],
                    "low"=>$subarray_131[4],
                    "close"=>$subarray_131[5],
                    "volume"=>$subarray_131[6],
                    "adj_close"=>$subarray_131[7]
                    ),
                      array(
                "id"=>$subarray_132[0],
                    "date"=>$subarray_132[1],
"open"=>$subarray_132[2],
```

```
                                        "high"=>$subarray_132[3],
                                        "low"=>$subarray_132[4],
                                        "close"=>$subarray_132[5],
                                        "volume"=>$subarray_132[6],
                                        "adj_close"=>$subarray_132[7]
                                        ),
                                        array(
                                  "id"=>$subarray_133[0],
                                        "date"=>$subarray_133[1],
"open"=>$subarray_133[2],
                                        "high"=>$subarray_133[3],
                                        "low"=>$subarray_133[4],
                                        "close"=>$subarray_133[5],
                                        "volume"=>$subarray_133[6],
                                        "adj_close"=>$subarray_133[7]
                                        ),
                                           array(
                                  "id"=>$subarray_134[0],
                                        "date"=>$subarray_134[1],
"open"=>$subarray_134[2],
                                        "high"=>$subarray_134[3],
                                        "low"=>$subarray_134[4],
                                        "close"=>$subarray_134[5],
                                        "volume"=>$subarray_134[6],
                                        "adj_close"=>$subarray_134[7]
                                        ),
                                        array(
                                  "id"=>$subarray_135[0],
                                        "date"=>$subarray_135[1],
"open"=>$subarray_135[2],
                                        "high"=>$subarray_135[3],
                                        "low"=>$subarray_135[4],
                                        "close"=>$subarray_135[5],
                                        "volume"=>$subarray_135[6],
                                        "adj_close"=>$subarray_135[7]
                                        ),
                                            array(
                                  "id"=>$subarray_136[0],
                                        "date"=>$subarray_136[1],
"open"=>$subarray_136[2],
                                        "high"=>$subarray_136[3],
                                        "low"=>$subarray_136[4],
```

```
                                        "close"=>$subarray_136[5],
                                        "volume"=>$subarray_136[6],
                                        "adj_close"=>$subarray_136[7]
                                        ),
                                        array(
                                "id"=>$subarray_137[0],
                                        "date"=>$subarray_137[1],
        "open"=>$subarray_137[2],
                                        "high"=>$subarray_137[3],
                                        "low"=>$subarray_137[4],
                                        "close"=>$subarray_137[5],
                                        "volume"=>$subarray_137[6],
                                        "adj_close"=>$subarray_137[7]
                                        ),
                                            array(
                                "id"=>$subarray_138[0],
                                        "date"=>$subarray_138[1],
        "open"=>$subarray_138[2],
                                        "high"=>$subarray_138[3],
                                        "low"=>$subarray_138[4],
                                        "close"=>$subarray_138[5],
                                        "volume"=>$subarray_138[6],
                                        "adj_close"=>$subarray_138[7]
                                        )

                                        );

//echo "<br/>"."The following is a summary of the Big_array:"."<br/>";
//foreach($Big_array as $c){
//while(list($k,$v)=each($c)){
//echo "$k ... $v <br/>";
//}
//}
header('content-type: text/xml');
print '<?xml version="1.0"?>' . "\n";
print "<Big_array>\n";
foreach ($Big_array as $subarray){
    print "    <subarray>\n";
    foreach($subarray as $tag => $data) {
        print "      <$tag>" . htmlspecialchars($data) . "</$tag>\n";
    }
    print "      </subarray>\n";
```

```
}
print " </Big_array>\n";

?>
```

In the above Php program, all the “echo” statements before the “header” statement have to be “commented-out”. Also, in the “fread” statement, sufficient amount of bytes has to be specified. 12000 is specified above. The Php program files and the final result “GE.xml” are in computer_files_9.1 folder.

9.2 Creating XML from an associate array.

In general, we can create an XML file from an associate array (which is also called “dictionary”, “hash”) as shown below:

```
<?php
//—http://localhost/new_sci2/array_to_xml_1.php
$material_property= array(
            array(
                "name" => "Aluminum",
                "density" => "169",
                "coefficient_of_thermal_expansion" => "13.7e-6",
                "specific_heat" => "0.237",
                "thermal_conductivity" => "128",
                "Youngs_modulus" => "8.5e6",
                "Poissons_ratio" => "0.33",
                "tensile_strength" => "3500"
            ),

            array(
                "name" => "Berylium",
                "density" => "115",
                "coefficient_of_thermal_expansion" => "10.0e-6",
                "specific_heat" => "0.570",
                "thermal_conductivity" => "68",
                "Youngs_modulus" => "39e6",
                "Poissons_ratio" => "0.024",
                "tensile_strength" => "41000"
            ),
            array(
                "name" => "Stainless_Steel",
```

```
                    "density" => "498",
                    "coefficient_of_thermal_expansion" => "10.0e-6",
                    "specific_heat" => "0.12",
                    "thermal_conductivity" => "12.6",
                    "Youngs_modulus" => "28e6",
                    "Poissons_ratio" => "0.29",
                    "tensile_strength" => "74500"
                ),
                array(
                    "name" => "Zirconium",
                    "density" => "406",
                    "coefficient_of_thermal_expansion" => "3.42e-6",
                    "specific_heat" => "0.0739",
                    "thermal_conductivity" => "11.4",
                    "Youngs_modulus" => "10.5e6",
                    "Poissons_ratio" => "0.32",
                    "tensile_strength" => "21000"
                )
                );
header('content-type: text/xml');
print '<?xml version="1.0"?>' . "\n";
print "<material_property>\n";
foreach ($material_property as $subarray){
   print "    <subarray>\n";
   foreach($subarray as $tag => $data) {
      print "      <$tag>" . htmlspecialchars($data) . "</$tag>\n";
   }
   print "      </subarray>\n";
}
print " </material_property>\n";
?>
```

The output of this program (called material_property_1.xml) is shown below:

```
&lt;?xml version="1.0" ?&gt;
 &lt;material_property&gt;
 &lt;subarray&gt;
 &lt;name&gt;Aluminum&lt;/name&gt;
 &lt;density&gt;169&lt;/density&gt;
 &lt;coefficient_of_thermal_expansion&gt;13.7e-6&lt;/coefficient_of_thermal_expansion&gt;
 &lt;specific_heat&gt;0.237&lt;/specific_heat&gt;
```

```
<thermal_conductivity>128</thermal_conductivity>
<Youngs_modulus>8.5e6</Youngs_modulus>
<Poissons_ratio>0.33</Poissons_ratio>
<tensile_strength>3500</tensile_strength>
</subarray>
<subarray>
<name>Berylium</name>
<density>115</density>
<coefficient_of_thermal_expansion>10.0e-6</coefficient_of_thermal_expansion>
<specific_heat>0.570</specific_heat>
<thermal_conductivity>68</thermal_conductivity>
<Youngs_modulus>39e6</Youngs_modulus>
<Poissons_ratio>0.024</Poissons_ratio>
<tensile_strength>41000</tensile_strength>
</subarray>
<subarray>

<name>Stainless_Steel</name>
<density>498</density>
<coefficient_of_thermal_expansion>10.0e-6</coefficient_of_thermal_expansion>
<specific_heat>0.12</specific_heat>
<thermal_conductivity>12.6</thermal_conductivity>
<Youngs_modulus>28e6</Youngs_modulus>
<Poissons_ratio>0.29</Poissons_ratio>
<tensile_strength>74500</tensile_strength>
</subarray>
<subarray>
<name>Zirconium</name>
<density>406</density>
<coefficient_of_thermal_expansion>3.42e-6</coefficient_of_thermal_expansion>
<specific_heat>0.0739</specific_heat>
<thermal_conductivity>11.4</thermal_conductivity>
<Youngs_modulus>10.5e6</Youngs_modulus>
<Poissons_ratio>0.32</Poissons_ratio>
<tensile_strength>21000</tensile_strength>
</subarray>
</material_property>
```

The computer files are included in computer_files_9.2.

9.3 Creating XML using DOM.

In this section, we shall create "steamTable.xml" as shown in Appendix 9.3, using the Document Object Model (DOM). Briefly it is a collection of processes of creating element tag followed by appending the child node with the text value. The steam table contains six items: temperature t, pressure p, specific volumes vf, vg for fluid and gas phases, specific internal energies uf, ug for fluid and gas phases. The data are taken from "Steam Tables (English Units) by Joseph H. Keenan et al".

The Php program is:

```
<?php
//...http://localhost/new_sci2/steamtable3rev.php
//
header('Content-Type: text/xml');
$dom = new DOMDocument();
$Steam_table = $dom->createElement('Steam_table');
$dom->appendChild($Steam_table);

input_data('450','422.1','0.019433','1.1011','428.6','1119.5');
input_data('475','539.3','0.019901','0.8594','456.6','1119.2');
input_data('500','680.0','0.02043','0.6761','485.1','1117.4');
input_data('525','847.1','0.02104','0.5350','514.5','1113.9');
input_data('550','1044.0','0.02175','0.4249','544.9','1108.6');
input_data('575','1274.0','0.02259','0.3378','576.5','1100.8');
input_data('600','1541.0','0.02363','0.2677','609.9','1090.0');
input_data('625','1849.7','0.02494','0.2103','645.7','1075.1');
input_data('650','2205.0','0.02673','0.16206','685.0','1053.7');
input_data('675','2616.0','0.02951','0.11952','731.0','1020.3');
input_data('700','3090.0','0.03666','0.07438','801.7','947.7');

// build the XML structure in a string variable
$xmlString = $dom->saveXML();
// output the XML string
echo $xmlString;

function input_data($tData,$pData,$vfData,$vgData,$ufData,$ugData){
global $dom,$temperature,$Steam_table;

// create the 't' element for the 'temperature'
$t = $dom->createElement('t');
```

```
$tText = $dom->createTextNode($tData);
$t->appendChild($tText);

// create the 'p' element for the 'temperature'
$p = $dom->createElement('p');
$pText = $dom->createTextNode($pData);
$p->appendChild($pText);

// create the 'vf' element for the 'temperature'
$vf = $dom->createElement('vf');
$vfText = $dom->createTextNode($vfData);
$vf->appendChild($vfText);

// create the 'vg' element for the 'temperature'
$vg = $dom->createElement('vg');
$vgText = $dom->createTextNode($vgData);
$vg->appendChild($vgText);

 // create the 'uf' element for the 'temperature'
$uf = $dom->createElement('uf');
$ufText = $dom->createTextNode($ufData);
$uf->appendChild($ufText);

// create the 'ug' element for the 'temperature'
$ug = $dom->createElement('ug');
$ugText = $dom->createTextNode($ugData);
$ug->appendChild($ugText);

// create the <temperature> element
$temperature = $dom->createElement('temperature');
$temperature->appendChild($t);
$temperature->appendChild($p);
$temperature->appendChild($vf);
$temperature->appendChild($vg);
$temperature->appendChild($uf);
$temperature->appendChild($ug);

// append <temperature> as a child of <Steam_table>
$Steam_table->appendChild($temperature);
}
?>
```

The computer file is in computer_files_9.3.

9.4 Parsing of the XML file, using SimpleXML.

Using SimpleXML, the user does not need to know the detailed structure of the XML file. The Php script is simple to use. The output is an associate array (also called a dictionary or a hash).

The following is an illustration for “steamTable.xml”. The Php script name is “steamTable_xml_dump.php”.

```
<?php
// ...http://localhost/new_sci2/steamTable_xml_dump.php
$theData = simplexml_load_file("steamTable.xml");
echo "<pre>";
print_r($theData);
echo "</pre>";
?>
```

The output associate array is:

```
SimpleXMLElement Object
(
   [temperature] => Array
      (
         [0] => SimpleXMLElement Object
            (
               [t] => 450
               [p] => 422.1
               [vf] => 0.019433
               [vg] => 1.1011
               [uf] => 428.6
               [ug] => 1119.5
            )

         [1] => SimpleXMLElement Object
            (
               [t] => 475
               [p] => 539.3
               [vf] => 0.019901
               [vg] => 0.8594
               [uf] => 456.6
               [ug] => 1119.2
            )
```

```
[2] => SimpleXMLElement Object
    (
        [t] => 500
        [p] => 680.0
        [vf] => 0.02043
        [vg] => 0.6761
        [uf] => 485.1
        [ug] => 1117.4
    )

[3] => SimpleXMLElement Object
    (
        [t] => 525
        [p] => 847.1
        [vf] => 0.02104
        [vg] => 0.5350
        [uf] => 514.5
        [ug] => 1113.9
    )

[4] => SimpleXMLElement Object
    (
        [t] => 550
        [p] => 1044.0
        [vf] => 0.02175
        [vg] => 0.4249
        [uf] => 544.9
        [ug] => 1108.6
    )

[5] => SimpleXMLElement Object
    (
        [t] => 575
        [p] => 1274.0
        [vf] => 0.02259
        [vg] => 0.3378
        [uf] => 576.5
        [ug] => 1100.8
    )
```

```
[6] => SimpleXMLElement Object
    (
        [t] => 600
        [p] => 1541.0
        [vf] => 0.02363
        [vg] => 0.2677
        [uf] => 609.9
        [ug] => 1090.0
    )

[7] => SimpleXMLElement Object
    (
        [t] => 625
        [p] => 1849.7
        [vf] => 0.02494
        [vg] => 0.2103
        [uf] => 645.7
        [ug] => 1075.1
    )

[8] => SimpleXMLElement Object
    (
        [t] => 650
        [p] => 2205.0
        [vf] => 0.02673
        [vg] => 0.16206
        [uf] => 685.0
        [ug] => 1053.7
    )

[9] => SimpleXMLElement Object
    (
        [t] => 675
        [p] => 2616.0
        [vf] => 0.02951
        [vg] => 0.11952
        [uf] => 731.0
        [ug] => 1020.3
    )
```

```
            [10] => SimpleXMLElement Object
                (
                    [t] => 700
                    [p] => 3090.0
                    [vf] => 0.03666
                    [vg] => 0.07438
                    [uf] => 801.7
                    [ug] => 947.7
                )

        )

)
```

We can also use another Php script (named “steamTable_xml_dump1.php”) to print out the data in text format:

```
<?php
// ...http://localhost/new_sci2/steamTable_xml_dump1.php

$theData = simplexml_load_file("steamTable.xml");

foreach($theData->Steam_table->temperature as $theTemperature){
//foreach($theData->temperature as $theTemperature){
$t=$theTemperature->t;
$p=$theTemperature->p;
$vf=$theTemperature->vf;
$vg=$theTemperature->vg;
$uf=$theTemperature->uf;
$ug=$theTemperature->ug;

$string=$t."\n";
$string.=$p."\n";
$string.=$vf."\n";
$string.=$vg."\n";
$string.=$uf."\n";
$string.=$ug."\n";

echo nl2br($string);
echo "<br />";
```

```
unset($t);
unset($p);
unset($vf);
unset($vg);
unset($uf);
unset($ug);

}
?>
```

The output is:

```
450
422.1
0.019433
1.1011
428.6
1119.5

475
539.3
0.019901
0.8594
456.6
1119.2

500
680.0
0.02043
0.6761
485.1
1117.4

525
847.1
0.02104
0.5350
514.5
1113.9
```

550
1044.0
0.02175
0.4249
544.9
1108.6

575
1274.0
0.02259
0.3378
576.5
1100.8

600
1541.0
0.02363
0.2677
609.9
1090.0

625
1849.7
0.02494
0.2103
645.7
1075.1

650
2205.0
0.02673
0.16206
685.0
1053.7

675
2616.0
0.02951
0.11952
731.0
1020.3

700
3090.0
0.03666
0.07438
801.7
947.7

A modified version of the above Php program is used to extract data from steamTable.xml to input to Matlab and Python. (See Chapter14.4.) The computer files are in computer_files_9.4.

9.5 Parsing of the XML file, using DOM.

In DOM, the document object model, the details of the XML tree structure must be known exacrly. The "steamTable.xml" created in Section 9.3 is now called "steamTable_1.xml" in computer_files_9.5. A similar version labeled as "steamTable.xml" generated elsewhere (during development) is also shown in computer_files_9.5. The difference between the two is that there is an extra level <response> </response> in the "steamTable.xml" whereas it is not in "steamTable_1.xml". The existence of this extra level really does not do anything except to make the model unnecessarily a little complicated. For all practical purpose, all the parsing programs work the same for either case, so it has not been very careful to label them differently. They have been just labeled as "steamTable.xml". But when working with DOM: An extra level will need an extra "foreach" loop so that DOM tree can be looped through properly, even though that extra level does not do anything useful. Here are the two different version of Php programs for the two different versions of XML files:

Version 1

```
<?php
//—http://localhost/new_sci2/to_use_DOM_steam.php
$dom = new DomDocument;
$dom->load("steamTable_1.xml");

foreach ($dom->documentElement->childNodes as $xml){
 if(($xml->nodeType==1)&&($xml->nodeName=="temperature")){

  foreach ($xml->childNodes as $theValue){
```

```
  if(($theValue->nodeType==1)&&($theValue->nodeName=="t")){
   $theValuet=$theValue->textContent;
   echo "t= ".$theValuet."</br />";
   unset($theValuet);
  }

  if(($theValue->nodeType==1)&&($theValue->nodeName=="p")){
   $theValuep=$theValue->textContent;
   echo "p= ".$theValuep."</br />";
   unset($theValuep);
  }

  if(($theValue->nodeType==1)&&($theValue->nodeName=="vf")){
   $theValuevf=$theValue->textContent;
   echo "vf= ".$theValuevf."</br />";
   unset($theValuevf);
  }

  if(($theValue->nodeType==1)&&($theValue->nodeName=="vg")){
   $theValuevg=$theValue->textContent;
   echo "vg= ".$theValuevg."</br />";
   unset($theValuevg);
  }

  if(($theValue->nodeType==1)&&($theValue->nodeName=="uf")){
   $theValueuf=$theValue->textContent;
   echo "uf= ".$theValueuf."</br />";
   unset($theValueuf);
  }
  if(($theValue->nodeType==1)&&($theValue->nodeName=="ug")){
   $theValueug=$theValue->textContent;
   echo "ug= ".$theValueug."</br />"."<br />";
   unset($theValueug);
  }
  }
 }
}
?>
```

Version 2

```
<?php
//—http://localhost/new_sci2/to_use_DOM_steam_mod.php
$dom = new DomDocument;
$dom->load("steamTable.xml");
foreach ($dom->documentElement->childNodes as $xml1){
if(($xml1->nodeType==1)&&($xml1->nodeName=="Steam_table")){
foreach ($xml1->childNodes as $xml){
 if(($xml->nodeType==1)&&($xml->nodeName=="temperature")){



   foreach ($xml->childNodes as $theValue){

    if(($theValue->nodeType==1)&&($theValue->nodeName=="t")){
     $theValuet=$theValue->textContent;
     echo "t= ".$theValuet."</br />";
     unset($theValuet);
    }

    if(($theValue->nodeType==1)&&($theValue->nodeName=="p")){
     $theValuep=$theValue->textContent;
     echo "p= ".$theValuep."</br />";
     unset($theValuep);
    }

    if(($theValue->nodeType==1)&&($theValue->nodeName=="vf")){
     $theValuevf=$theValue->textContent;
     echo "vf= ".$theValuevf."</br />";
     unset($theValuevf);
    }

    if(($theValue->nodeType==1)&&($theValue->nodeName=="vg")){
     $theValuevg=$theValue->textContent;
     echo "vg= ".$theValuevg."</br />";
     unset($theValuevg);
    }

    if(($theValue->nodeType==1)&&($theValue->nodeName=="uf")){
     $theValueuf=$theValue->textContent;
     echo "uf= ".$theValueuf."</br />";
```

```
    unset($theValueuf);
   }
   if(($theValue->nodeType==1)&&($theValue->nodeName=="ug")){
    $theValueug=$theValue->textContent;
    echo "ug= ".$theValueug."</br />"."<br />";
    unset($theValueug);
   }
   }
  }
 }
 }
 }
?>
```

The Php programs in this section are included in computer_files_9.5.

Chapter 10

PYTHON AND XML

10.1 CREATING XML USING PYTHON.

Two examples are described: In Example1, selected properties of some 49 chemical elements as listed (in printed form) in Appendix 10.1. The task is to type in the property data into a Python program to create an XML file. In Example 2, the electrical resistivity data in ohm meter at 20 deg C (in text format) is known as shown in Appendix 10.1, the task is to read this text file into a Python program to create an XML file. In both cases, (and in all cases with Python to create XML files), we need to use the statements:

```
from xml.dom.minidom import Document
doc = Document()
```

followed by repeating use of "createElement" and "appendChild" methods. The Python programs are given below. The resulting XML files are shown in Appendix 10.1.

Example 1

```
from xml.dom.minidom import Document
doc = Document()
Big_array = doc.createElement("Big_array")
doc.appendChild(Big_array)
def input_data(ix,itext,el,eltext,z,ztext,sy,sytext,w,wtext,a,atext,s;stext):

    global subarray,id,idtext,element,elementtext,atomic_number,atomic_numbertext
    global symbol,symboltext,atomic_weight,atomic_weighttext
    global absorption,absorptiontext,scattering,scatteringtext
```

```
    subarray = doc.createElement("subarray")

    id = doc.createElement(ix)
    subarray.appendChild(id)
    idtext = doc.createTextNode(itext)
    id.appendChild(idtext)

    element = doc.createElement(el)
    subarray.appendChild(element)
    elementtext = doc.createTextNode(eltext)
    element.appendChild(elementtext)

    atomic_number = doc.createElement(z)
    subarray.appendChild(atomic_number)
    atomic_numbertext = doc.createTextNode(ztext)
    atomic_number.appendChild(atomic_numbertext)

    symbol = doc.createElement(sy)
    subarray.appendChild(symbol)
    symboltext = doc.createTextNode(sytext)
    symbol.appendChild(symboltext)

    atomic_weight = doc.createElement(w)
    subarray.appendChild(atomic_weight)
    atomic_weighttext = doc.createTextNode(wtext)
    atomic_weight.appendChild(atomic_weighttext)

    absorption = doc.createElement(a)
    subarray.appendChild(absorption)
    absorptiontext = doc.createTextNode(atext)
    absorption.appendChild(absorptiontext)

    scattering = doc.createElement(s)
    subarray.appendChild(scattering)
    scatteringtext = doc.createTextNode(stext)
    scattering.appendChild(scatteringtext)

input_data('id','1','element','Hydrogen','atomic_number','1',\
        'symbol','H','atomic_weight','1.008','absorption','0.33','scattering','80')
Big_array.appendChild(subarray)
```

```
input_data('id','2','element','Deuterium','atomic_number','1',\
        'symbol','D','atomic_weight','2.015','absorption','0.00046','scattering','5.4')
Big_array.appendChild(subarray)

input_data('id','3','element','Helium','atomic_number','2',\
        'symbol','He','atomic_weight','4.003','absorption','0.0','scattering','0.8')
Big_array.appendChild(subarray)

input_data('id','4','element','Lithium','atomic_number','3',\
        'symbol','Li','atomic_weight','6.94','absorption','70','scattering','1.4')
Big_array.appendChild(subarray)

input_data('id','5','element','Berylium','atomic_number','4',\
        'symbol','Be','atomic_weight','9.01','absorption','0.009','scattering','7')
Big_array.appendChild(subarray)

input_data('id','6','element','Boron','atomic_number','5',\
        'symbol','B','atomic_weight','10.82','absorption','750','scattering','4')
Big_array.appendChild(subarray)

input_data('id','7','element','Carbon','atomic_number','6',\
        'symbol','C','atomic_weight','12.01','absorption','0.0045','scattering','4.8')
Big_array.appendChild(subarray)

input_data('id','8','element','Nitrogen','atomic_number','7',\
        'symbol','N','atomic_weight','14.008','absorption','1.8','scattering','10')
Big_array.appendChild(subarray)

input_data('id','9','element','Oxygen','atomic_number','8',\
        'symbol','O','atomic_weight','16','absorption','0.0002','scattering','4.2')
Big_array.appendChild(subarray)

input_data('id','10','element','Fluorine','atomic_number','9',\
        'symbol','F','atomic_weight','19','absorption','0.009','scattering','4.1')
Big_array.appendChild(subarray)

input_data('id','11','element','Neon','atomic_number','10',\
        'symbol','Ne','atomic_weight','20.18','absorption','2.8','scattering','2.4')
Big_array.appendChild(subarray)
```

```
input_data('id','12','element','Sodium','atomic_number','11',\
        'symbol','Na','atomic_weight','22.997','absorption','0.5','scattering','4')
Big_array.appendChild(subarray)

input_data('id','13','element','Magnesium','atomic_number','12',\
        'symbol','Mg','atomic_weight','24.32','absorption','0.06','scattering','3.6')
Big_array.appendChild(subarray)

input_data('id','14','element','Aluminum','atomic_number','13',\
        'symbol','Al','atomic_weight','26.98','absorption','0.21','scattering','1.4')
Big_array.appendChild(subarray)

input_data('id','15','element','Silicon','atomic_number','14',\
        'symbol','Si','atomic_weight','28.09','absorption','0.13','scattering','1.7')
Big_array.appendChild(subarray)

input_data('id','16','element','Phosphorus','atomic_number','15',\
        'symbol','P','atomic_weight','30.98','absorption','0.2','scattering','5')
Big_array.appendChild(subarray)

input_data('id','17','element','Sulfur','atomic_number','16',\
        'symbol','S','atomic_weight','32.07','absorption','0.49','scattering','1.1')
Big_array.appendChild(subarray)

input_data('id','18','element','Chlorine','atomic_number','17',\
        'symbol','Cl','atomic_weight','35.457','absorption','31.6','scattering','0')
Big_array.appendChild(subarray)

input_data('id','19','element','Argon','atomic_number','18',\
        'symbol','Ar','atomic_weight','39.94','absorption','0.62','scattering','1.5')
Big_array.appendChild(subarray)

input_data('id','20','element','Potassium','atomic_number','19',\
        'symbol','K','atomic_weight','39.1','absorption','2','scattering','1.5')
Big_array.appendChild(subarray)

input_data('id','21','element','Scandium','atomic_number','21',\
        'symbol','Sc','atomic_weight','45.1','absorption','23','scattering','0')
Big_array.appendChild(subarray)
```

```
input_data('id','22','element','Titanium','atomic_number','22',\
        'symbol','Ti','atomic_weight','47.9','absorption','5.6','scattering','4')
Big_array.appendChild(subarray)

input_data('id','23','element','Vanadium','atomic_number','23',\
        'symbol','V','atomic_weight','50.95','absorption','5.1','scattering','5')
Big_array.appendChild(subarray)

input_data('id','24','element','Chromium','atomic_number','24',\
        'symbol','Cr','atomic_weight','52.01','absorption','2.9','scattering','3')
Big_array.appendChild(subarray)

input_data('id','25','element','Calcium','atomic_number','20',\
        'symbol','Ca','atomic_weight','40.08','absorption','0.43','scattering','9')
Big_array.appendChild(subarray)

input_data('id','26','element','Manganese','atomic_number','25',\
        'symbol','Mn','atomic_weight','54.93','absorption','13','scattering','2.3')
Big_array.appendChild(subarray)

input_data('id','27','element','Iron','atomic_number','26',\
        'symbol','Fe','atomic_weight','55.85','absorption','2.4','scattering','11')
Big_array.appendChild(subarray)

input_data('id','28','element','Cobalt','atomic_number','27',\
        'symbol','Co','atomic_weight','58.94','absorption','37','scattering','5')
Big_array.appendChild(subarray)

input_data('id','29','element','Nickel','atomic_number','28',\
        'symbol','Ni','atomic_weight','58.69','absorption','4.5','scattering','17.5')
Big_array.appendChild(subarray)

input_data('id','30','element','Copper','atomic_number','29',\
        'symbol','Cu','atomic_weight','63.54','absorption','3.6','scattering','7.2')
Big_array.appendChild(subarray)

input_data('id','31','element','Zinc','atomic_number','30',\
        'symbol','Zn','atomic_weight','65.38','absorption','1.1','scattering','3.6')
Big_array.appendChild(subarray)
```

```
input_data('id','32','element','Lanthanum','atomic_number','57',\
        'symbol','La','atomic_weight','138.92','absorption','8.9','scattering','18')
Big_array.appendChild(subarray)

input_data('id','33','element','Yttrium','atomic_number','39',\
        'symbol','Y','atomic_weight','88.92','absorption','1.4','scattering','3')
Big_array.appendChild(subarray)

input_data('id','34','element','Neodymium','atomic_number','60',\
        'symbol','Nd','atomic_weight','144.27','absorption','44','scattering','25')
Big_array.appendChild(subarray)

input_data('id','35','element','Cerium','atomic_number','58',\
        'symbol','Ce','atomic_weight','140.13','absorption','0.7','scattering','9')
Big_array.appendChild(subarray)

input_data('id','36','element','Praseodymium','atomic_number','59',\
        'symbol','Pr','atomic_weight','140.92','absorption','11','scattering','0')
Big_array.appendChild(subarray)

input_data('id','37','element','Gadolinium','atomic_number','64',\
        'symbol','Gd','atomic_weight','156.9','absorption','44000','scattering','0')
Big_array.appendChild(subarray)

input_data('id','38','element','Dysprosium','atomic_number','66',\
        'symbol','Dy','atomic_weight','162.46','absorption','1100','scattering','0')
Big_array.appendChild(subarray)

input_data('id','39','element','Erbium','atomic_number','68',\
        'symbol','Er','atomic_weight','167.2','absorption','166','scattering','0')
Big_array.appendChild(subarray)

input_data('id','40','element','Samarium','atomic_number','62',\
        'symbol','Sm','atomic_weight','150.43','absorption','6500','scattering','0')
Big_array.appendChild(subarray)

input_data('id','41','element','Ytterbium','atomic_number','70',\
        'symbol','Yb','atomic_weight','173','absorption','36','scattering','12')
Big_array.appendChild(subarray)
```

```
input_data('id','42','element','Holmium','atomic_number','67',\
        'symbol','Ho','atomic_weight','164.94','absorption','64','scattering','0')
Big_array.appendChild(subarray)

input_data('id','43','element','Terbium','atomic_number','65',\
        'symbol','Tb','atomic_weight','159.2','absorption','44','scattering','0')
Big_array.appendChild(subarray)

input_data('id','44','element','Europium','atomic_number','63',\
        'symbol','Eu','atomic_weight','152','absorption','4500','scattering','0')
Big_array.appendChild(subarray)

input_data('id','45','element','Thulium','atomic_number','69',\
        'symbol','Tm','atomic_weight','169.4','absorption','118','scattering','0')
Big_array.appendChild(subarray)

input_data('id','46','element','Lutetium','atomic_number','71',\
        'symbol','Lu','atomic_weight','174.99','absorption','108','scattering','0')
Big_array.appendChild(subarray)

input_data('id','47','element','Promethium','atomic_number','61',\
        'symbol','Pm','atomic_weight','145','absorption','0','scattering','0')
Big_array.appendChild(subarray)

input_data('id','48','element','Uranium','atomic_number','92',\
        'symbol','U','atomic_weight','238.07','absorption','7.42','scattering','8.2')
Big_array.appendChild(subarray)

input_data('id','50','element','Thorium','atomic_number','90',\
        'symbol','Th','atomic_weight','232.12','absorption','7','scattering','13')
Big_array.appendChild(subarray)


print doc.toprettyxml(indent="  ")
```

Example 2

```
def read_resistivities(filename):
   infile = open(filename, 'r')
   resistivities = {}
   for line in infile:
```

```
        words = line.split()
        resistivity = float(words[-1])

        if len(words[:-1]) == 2:
            substance = words[0] + '_' + words[1]
        else:
            substance = words[0]

        resistivities[substance] = resistivity
    infile.close()
    return resistivities
#
resistivities = read_resistivities('resistivities.txt')
#
tags=resistivities.keys()
vals=resistivities.values()
print tags
print vals

from xml.dom.minidom import Document

doc = Document()

Big_array = doc.createElement("Big_array")
doc.appendChild(Big_array)

table = doc.createElement("table")
Big_array.appendChild(table)

index=0
while index < len(tags):
    tag=tags[index]
    val=str(vals[index])

    tag = doc.createElement(tag)
    table.appendChild(tag)
    val = doc.createTextNode(val)
    tag.appendChild(val)
    index += 1

print doc.toprettyxml(indent="  ")
```

10.2 Parsing XML files with Python.

To parse XML files from Python, we use "from xml.dom.minidom import parse". Two examples are shown below. Example 1 is to parse the XML file "basicdata1_py.xml" created in Section 10.1. Example 2 is to parse the XML file "steamTable.xml" and then directly plot the data. The plots shown in Appendix 10.2 are the same as those shown in Appendix 14.4B which is from data extracted from XML file using Php program.

Example 1

```
from xml.dom.minidom import parse
def getdata(nodes):
   rc = ''
   for node in nodes:
            if node.nodeType == node.TEXT_NODE:
                  rc = rc + node.data
   return rc

subarray = parse('C:/python-scripts/basicdata1_py.xml')
i=0
while i<49:
   element = subarray.getElementsByTagName("element")[i]
   print getdata(element.childNodes)
   atomic_number = subarray.getElementsByTagName("atomic_number")[i]
   print getdata(atomic_number.childNodes)
   symbol = subarray.getElementsByTagName("symbol")[i]
   print getdata(symbol.childNodes)
   atomic_weight = subarray.getElementsByTagName("atomic_weight")[i]
   print getdata(atomic_weight.childNodes)
   absorption = subarray.getElementsByTagName("absorption")[i]
   print getdata(absorption.childNodes)
   scattering = subarray.getElementsByTagName("scattering")[i]
   print getdata(scattering.childNodes)
   i=i+1
print ''
```

Example 2

```
from xml.dom.minidom import parse
from scitools.std import *
def getdata(nodes):
   rc = ''
   for node in nodes:
            if node.nodeType == node.TEXT_NODE:
                  rc = rc + node.data
   return rc
temperature = parse('C:/xampp/htdocs/new_sci2/steamTable.xml')
i=0
tt=[]
pp=[]
vvf=[]
vvg=[]
uuf=[]
uug=[]
while i<11:
   t = temperature.getElementsByTagName("t")[i]
   t1= getdata(t.childNodes)
   t1=float(t1)

   p = temperature.getElementsByTagName("p")[i]
   p1= getdata(p.childNodes)
   p1=float(p1)

   vf = temperature.getElementsByTagName("vf")[i]
   vf1= getdata(vf.childNodes)
   vf1=float(vf1)

   vg = temperature.getElementsByTagName("vg")[i]
   vg1= getdata(vg.childNodes)
   vg1=float(vg1)

   uf = temperature.getElementsByTagName("uf")[i]
   uf1= getdata(uf.childNodes)
   uf1=float(uf1)

   ug = temperature.getElementsByTagName("ug")[i]
   ug1= getdata(ug.childNodes)
   ug1=float(ug1)
```

```
    i=i+1
    print '%7.1f %7.1f %10.6f %8.4f %7.1f %8.1f' %(t1,p1,vf1,vg1,uf1,ug1)

    tt.append(float(t1))
    pp.append(float(p1))
    vvf.append(float(vf1))
    vvg.append(float(vg1))
    uuf.append(float(uf1))
    uug.append(float(ug1))

plot(tt,pp,'r-')
title('Saturation Pressure vs. Temperature')
xlabel('Temperature(degree F)')
ylabel('Pressure(psia)')
grid()
hardcopy('steam_table_plot1x.png')

semilogy(tt,vvf,'b-',tt,vvg,'g-')
title('Specific Volume vs. Temperature')
xlabel('Temperature(degree F)')
ylabel('Spec Vol (Ft3/lb) Blue-fluid Green=vapor')
grid()
hardcopy('steam_table_plot2x.png')

plot(tt,uuf,'b-',tt,uug,'g-')
title('Specific Internal Energy vs. Temperature')
xlabel('Temperature(degree F)')
ylabel('Spec Int Energy (Btu/lb) Blue-fluid Green=vapor')
grid()
hardcopy('steam_table_plot3x.png')
```

The computer files are in computer_files_10.2.

Chapter 11

Perl and XML

11.1 Creating an XML file using Perl.

The following Perl script is to create an XML file called “RLC.xml”. The Perl script is named “xmlDOM_write_RLC.pl”.

```
#!"C:\xampp\perl\bin\perl.exe"

print "Content-type: text/html\n\n";

# http://localhost/cgi-bin/xampp_perl/xmlDOM_write_RLC.pl

use strict;
use XML::DOM;
use CGI::Carp qw(fatalsToBrowser);
my $doc = XML::DOM::Document->new;
my $xml_pi = $doc->createXMLDecl ('1.0');
my $root = $doc->createElement('RLC');
my $data = $doc->createElement('data');
$root->appendChild($data);
my $link=$doc->createElement('Resistance');
my $text=$doc->createTextNode("20");
$link->appendChild($text);
$data->appendChild($link);
my $link=$doc->createElement('Inductance');
my $text=$doc->createTextNode("10");
$link->appendChild($text);
$data->appendChild($link);
```

```
my $link=$doc->createElement('Capacitance');
my $text=$doc->createTextNode("2.5e-4");
$link->appendChild($text);
$data->appendChild($link);
my $link=$doc->createElement('Voltage');
my $text=$doc->createTextNode("10");
$link->appendChild($text);
$data->appendChild($link);
my $link=$doc->createElement('Frequency');
my $text=$doc->createTextNode("1.5915");
$link->appendChild($text);
$data->appendChild($link);
#print $xml_pi->toString;
#print $root->toString;
#$doc->saveXML(); Perl doesnot have saveXML.
$root->printToFile("RLC.xml");
print 'Task completed';
```

The output XML file is:

```
<RLC>
<data>
<Resistance>20</Resistance>
<Inductance>10</Inductance>
<Capacitance>2.5e-4</Capacitance>
<Voltage>10</Voltage>
<Frequency>1.5915</Frequency>
</data>
</RLC>
```

The above Perl script and the output XML files are included in computer_files_11.2.

11.2 Parsing XML files using Perl.

Three examples are given below. Example 1 is to parse “RLV.xml” created in Section 11.1; Example 2 is to parse “steamTable.xml” created in Section 9.3; Example 3 is to parse “resistivities_py.xml” created in Section 10.1.

Example 1

```
#!"C:\xampp\perl\bin\perl.exe"

print "Content-type: text/html\n\n";

# http://localhost/cgi-bin/xampp_perl/xmlDOM_read_RLC.pl


use XML::DOM;
use CGI::Carp qw(fatalsToBrowser);
my $parser = new XML::DOM::Parser;
my $doc = $parser->parsefile('RLC.xml');
foreach $data1 ($doc->getElementsByTagName('data')){
 print $data1->getElementsByTagName('Resistance')->item(0)
          ->getFirstChild->getNodeValue;
 print "<br />";
 print $data1->getElementsByTagName('Inductance')->item(0)
          ->getFirstChild->getNodeValue;
 print "<br />";
 print $data1->getElementsByTagName('Capacitance')->item(0)
          ->getFirstChild->getNodeValue;
 print "<br />";
 print $data1->getElementsByTagName('Voltage')->item(0)
          ->getFirstChild->getNodeValue;
 print "<br />";
 print $data1->getElementsByTagName('Frequency')->item(0)
          ->getFirstChild->getNodeValue;
 print "<br />";
 print "<br />";
 }
```

Example 2

```
#!"C:\xampp\perl\bin\perl.exe"

print "Content-type: text/html\n\n";

# http://localhost/cgi-bin/xampp_perl/xmlDOM_read_ST.pl
```

```
use XML::DOM;
use CGI::Carp qw(fatalsToBrowser);
my $parser = new XML::DOM::Parser;
my $doc = $parser->parsefile('steamTable.xml');
foreach $data ($doc->getElementsByTagName('temperature')){
  print $data->getElementsByTagName('t')->item(0)
          ->getFirstChild->getNodeValue;
  print "<br />";
  print $data->getElementsByTagName('p')->item(0)
          ->getFirstChild->getNodeValue;
  print "<br />";
  print $data->getElementsByTagName('vf')->item(0)
          ->getFirstChild->getNodeValue;
  print "<br />";
  print $data->getElementsByTagName('vg')->item(0)
          ->getFirstChild->getNodeValue;
  print "<br />";
  print $data->getElementsByTagName('uf')->item(0)
          ->getFirstChild->getNodeValue;
  print "<br />";
  print $data->getElementsByTagName('ug')->item(0)
          ->getFirstChild->getNodeValue;
  print "<br />";
  print "<br />";
}
```

Example 3

```
#!"C:\xampp\perl\bin\perl.exe"

print "Content-type: text/html\n\n";

# http://localhost/cgi-bin/xampp_perl/xmlDOM_read_res.pl


use XML::DOM;
use CGI::Carp qw(fatalsToBrowser);
my $parser = new XML::DOM::Parser;
my $doc = $parser->parsefile('resistivities_py.xml');
foreach $table ($doc->getElementsByTagName('table')){
  print $table->getElementsByTagName('copper')->item(0)
```

```
        ->getFirstChild->getNodeValue;
print "<br />";
print $table->getElementsByTagName('constantan')->item(0)
        ->getFirstChild->getNodeValue;
print "<br />";
print $table->getElementsByTagName('gold')->item(0)
        ->getFirstChild->getNodeValue;
print "<br />";
print $table->getElementsByTagName('germanium')->item(0)
        ->getFirstChild->getNodeValue;
print "<br />";
print $table->getElementsByTagName('titanium')->item(0)
        ->getFirstChild->getNodeValue;
print "<br />";
print $table->getElementsByTagName('zinc')->item(0)
        ->getFirstChild->getNodeValue;
print "<br />";
print $table->getElementsByTagName('mercury')->item(0)
        ->getFirstChild->getNodeValue;
print "<br />";
print $table->getElementsByTagName('lead')->item(0)
        ->getFirstChild->getNodeValue;
print "<br />";
print $table->getElementsByTagName('amorphous_carbon')->item(0)
        ->getFirstChild->getNodeValue;
print "<br />";
print $table->getElementsByTagName('platium')->item(0)
        ->getFirstChild->getNodeValue;
print "<br />";
print $table->getElementsByTagName('tin')->item(0)
        ->getFirstChild->getNodeValue;
print "<br />";
print $table->getElementsByTagName('annealed_copper')->item(0)
        ->getFirstChild->getNodeValue;
print "<br />";
print $table->getElementsByTagName('lithium')->item(0)
        ->getFirstChild->getNodeValue;
print "<br />";
print $table->getElementsByTagName('nichrome')->item(0)
        ->getFirstChild->getNodeValue;
print "<br />";
print $table->getElementsByTagName('teflon')->item(0)
```

```
        ->getFirstChild->getNodeValue;
  print "<br />";
  print $table->getElementsByTagName('nickel')->item(0)
        ->getFirstChild->getNodeValue;
  print "<br />";
  print $table->getElementsByTagName('fused_quartz')->item(0)
        ->getFirstChild->getNodeValue;
  print "<br />";
  print $table->getElementsByTagName('tungsten')->item(0)
        ->getFirstChild->getNodeValue;
  print "<br />";
  print $table->getElementsByTagName('silver')->item(0)
        ->getFirstChild->getNodeValue;
  print "<br />";
  print $table->getElementsByTagName('aluminum')->item(0)
        ->getFirstChild->getNodeValue;
  print "<br />";
  print $table->getElementsByTagName('stainless_steel')->item(0)
        ->getFirstChild->getNodeValue;
  print "<br />";
  print $table->getElementsByTagName('manganese')->item(0)
        ->getFirstChild->getNodeValue;
  print "<br />";
  print $table->getElementsByTagName('silicon')->item(0)
        ->getFirstChild->getNodeValue;
  print "<br />";
  print $table->getElementsByTagName('calcium')->item(0)
        ->getFirstChild->getNodeValue;
  print "<br />";
   print $table->getElementsByTagName('iron')->item(0)
        ->getFirstChild->getNodeValue;
  print "<br />";
  print "<br />";
}
```

These computer files are included in computer_files_11.2.

Chapter 12

MATLAB AND XML

12.1 CREATING XML USING MATLAB

Matlab has built-in "xmlread" and "xmlwrite" commands, but they are not yet useful for creating and parsing XML documents. (These two commands alone will allow users to read and print the entire XML documents, but not to extract data from it.)

The following is in accordance with the "xmltree" software in http://www.artefact.tk/software/matlab/xml/. The software package is shown in the folder "xmltree" in the computer_files_12.1. It is recommended to copy all the files in this folder directly into the MATLAB root folder, in addition to the other files described in this section and the next section. This way will definitely make sure all the files needed are in the Matlab path for execution.

The Matlab path for creating basicdata1_ml.xml is:

```
% xmldemo1x
%
%  This script demonstrates the use of the xmltree class to
%  create an XML tree from scratch and save it in a file.
%
clear; help xmldemo1x;
tree = xmltree;
tree = set(tree,root(tree),'name','Big_array');
tree = add(tree,root(tree),'comment','This is to create an xml file
basicdata1_ml.xml');
%
```

```
[tree, subarray_uid] = add(tree,root(tree),'element','subarray');
subarray = struct('id','1',...
            'element','Hydrogen',...
                        'atomic_number','1',...
            'symbol','H',...
            'atomic_weight','1.008',...
            'absorption','0.33',...
            'scattering','80');

[tree, uid] = add(tree,subarray_uid,'element','id');
tree = add(tree,uid,'chardata',subarray.id);
[tree, uid] = add(tree,subarray_uid,'element','element');
tree = add(tree,uid,'chardata',subarray.element);
[tree, uid] = add(tree,subarray_uid,'element','atomic_number');
tree = add(tree,uid,'chardata',subarray.atomic_number);
[tree, uid] = add(tree,subarray_uid,'element','symbol');
tree = add(tree,uid,'chardata',subarray.symbol);
[tree, uid] = add(tree,subarray_uid,'element','atomic_weight');
tree = add(tree,uid,'chardata',subarray.atomic_weight);
[tree, uid] = add(tree,subarray_uid,'element','absorption');
tree = add(tree,uid,'chardata',subarray.absorption);
[tree, uid] = add(tree,subarray_uid,'element','scattering');
tree = add(tree,uid,'chardata',subarray.scattering);
%
[tree, subarray_uid] = add(tree,root(tree),'element','subarray');
subarray = struct('id','2',...
            'element','Deuterium',...
                        'atomic_number','1',...
            'symbol','D',...
            'atomic_weight','2.015',...
            'absorption','0.00046',...
            'scattering','5.4');

[tree, uid] = add(tree,subarray_uid,'element','id');
tree = add(tree,uid,'chardata',subarray.id);
[tree, uid] = add(tree,subarray_uid,'element','element');
tree = add(tree,uid,'chardata',subarray.element);
[tree, uid] = add(tree,subarray_uid,'element','atomic_number');
tree = add(tree,uid,'chardata',subarray.atomic_number);
[tree, uid] = add(tree,subarray_uid,'element','symbol');
```

```
tree = add(tree,uid,'chardata',subarray.symbol);
[tree, uid] = add(tree,subarray_uid,'element','atomic_weight');
tree = add(tree,uid,'chardata',subarray.atomic_weight);
[tree, uid] = add(tree,subarray_uid,'element','absorption');
tree = add(tree,uid,'chardata',subarray.absorption);
[tree, uid] = add(tree,subarray_uid,'element','scattering');
tree = add(tree,uid,'chardata',subarray.scattering);
%
[tree, subarray_uid] = add(tree,root(tree),'element','subarray');
subarray = struct('id','3',...
            'element','Helium',...
                        'atomic_number','2',...
            'symbol','He',...
            'atomic_weight','4.003',...
            'absorption','0.0',...
            'scattering','0.8');

[tree, uid] = add(tree,subarray_uid,'element','id');
tree = add(tree,uid,'chardata',subarray.id);
[tree, uid] = add(tree,subarray_uid,'element','element');
tree = add(tree,uid,'chardata',subarray.element);
[tree, uid] = add(tree,subarray_uid,'element','atomic_number');
tree = add(tree,uid,'chardata',subarray.atomic_number);
[tree, uid] = add(tree,subarray_uid,'element','symbol');
tree = add(tree,uid,'chardata',subarray.symbol);
[tree, uid] = add(tree,subarray_uid,'element','atomic_weight');
tree = add(tree,uid,'chardata',subarray.atomic_weight);
[tree, uid] = add(tree,subarray_uid,'element','absorption');
tree = add(tree,uid,'chardata',subarray.absorption);
[tree, uid] = add(tree,subarray_uid,'element','scattering');
tree = add(tree,uid,'chardata',subarray.scattering);
%
[tree, subarray_uid] = add(tree,root(tree),'element','subarray');
subarray = struct('id','4',...
            'element','Lithium',...
                        'atomic_number','3',...
            'symbol','Li',...
            'atomic_weight','6.94',...
            'absorption','70.0',...
            'scattering','1.4');

[tree, uid] = add(tree,subarray_uid,'element','id');
```

```
tree = add(tree,uid,'chardata',subarray.id);
[tree, uid] = add(tree,subarray_uid,'element','element');
tree = add(tree,uid,'chardata',subarray.element);
[tree, uid] = add(tree,subarray_uid,'element','atomic_number');
tree = add(tree,uid,'chardata',subarray.atomic_number);
[tree, uid] = add(tree,subarray_uid,'element','symbol');
tree = add(tree,uid,'chardata',subarray.symbol);
[tree, uid] = add(tree,subarray_uid,'element','atomic_weight');
tree = add(tree,uid,'chardata',subarray.atomic_weight);
[tree, uid] = add(tree,subarray_uid,'element','absorption');
tree = add(tree,uid,'chardata',subarray.absorption);
[tree, uid] = add(tree,subarray_uid,'element','scattering');
tree = add(tree,uid,'chardata',subarray.scattering);
%
[tree, subarray_uid] = add(tree,root(tree),'element','subarray');
subarray = struct('id','5',...
            'element','Berylium',...
                        'atomic_number','4',...
            'symbol','Be',...
            'atomic_weight','9.01',...
            'absorption','0.009',...
            'scattering','7');

[tree, uid] = add(tree,subarray_uid,'element','id');
tree = add(tree,uid,'chardata',subarray.id);
[tree, uid] = add(tree,subarray_uid,'element','element');
tree = add(tree,uid,'chardata',subarray.element);
[tree, uid] = add(tree,subarray_uid,'element','atomic_number');
tree = add(tree,uid,'chardata',subarray.atomic_number);
[tree, uid] = add(tree,subarray_uid,'element','symbol');
tree = add(tree,uid,'chardata',subarray.symbol);
[tree, uid] = add(tree,subarray_uid,'element','atomic_weight');
tree = add(tree,uid,'chardata',subarray.atomic_weight);
[tree, uid] = add(tree,subarray_uid,'element','absorption');
tree = add(tree,uid,'chardata',subarray.absorption);
[tree, uid] = add(tree,subarray_uid,'element','scattering');
tree = add(tree,uid,'chardata',subarray.scattering);
%
[tree, subarray_uid] = add(tree,root(tree),'element','subarray');
subarray = struct('id','6',...
            'element','Boron',...
                        'atomic_number','5',...
```

```
            'symbol','B',...
            'atomic_weight','10.82',...
            'absorption','750',...
            'scattering','4');

[tree, uid] = add(tree,subarray_uid,'element','id');
tree = add(tree,uid,'chardata',subarray.id);
[tree, uid] = add(tree,subarray_uid,'element','element');
tree = add(tree,uid,'chardata',subarray.element);
[tree, uid] = add(tree,subarray_uid,'element','atomic_number');
tree = add(tree,uid,'chardata',subarray.atomic_number);
[tree, uid] = add(tree,subarray_uid,'element','symbol');
tree = add(tree,uid,'chardata',subarray.symbol);
[tree, uid] = add(tree,subarray_uid,'element','atomic_weight');
tree = add(tree,uid,'chardata',subarray.atomic_weight);
[tree, uid] = add(tree,subarray_uid,'element','absorption');
tree = add(tree,uid,'chardata',subarray.absorption);
[tree, uid] = add(tree,subarray_uid,'element','scattering');
tree = add(tree,uid,'chardata',subarray.scattering);
%
[tree, subarray_uid] = add(tree,root(tree),'element','subarray');
subarray = struct('id','7',...
            'element','Carbon',...
                        'atomic_number','6',...
            'symbol','C',...
            'atomic_weight','12.01',...
            'absorption','0.0045',...
            'scattering','4.8');

[tree, uid] = add(tree,subarray_uid,'element','id');
tree = add(tree,uid,'chardata',subarray.id);
[tree, uid] = add(tree,subarray_uid,'element','element');
tree = add(tree,uid,'chardata',subarray.element);
[tree, uid] = add(tree,subarray_uid,'element','atomic_number');
tree = add(tree,uid,'chardata',subarray.atomic_number);
[tree, uid] = add(tree,subarray_uid,'element','symbol');
tree = add(tree,uid,'chardata',subarray.symbol);
[tree, uid] = add(tree,subarray_uid,'element','atomic_weight');
tree = add(tree,uid,'chardata',subarray.atomic_weight);
[tree, uid] = add(tree,subarray_uid,'element','absorption');
tree = add(tree,uid,'chardata',subarray.absorption);
[tree, uid] = add(tree,subarray_uid,'element','scattering');
```

```
tree = add(tree,uid,'chardata',subarray.scattering);
%
[tree, subarray_uid] = add(tree,root(tree),'element','subarray');
subarray = struct('id','8',...
            'element','Nitrogen',...
                        'atomic_number','7',...
            'symbol','N',...
            'atomic_weight','14.008',...
            'absorption','1.8',...
            'scattering','10');

[tree, uid] = add(tree,subarray_uid,'element','id');
tree = add(tree,uid,'chardata',subarray.id);
[tree, uid] = add(tree,subarray_uid,'element','element');
tree = add(tree,uid,'chardata',subarray.element);
[tree, uid] = add(tree,subarray_uid,'element','atomic_number');
tree = add(tree,uid,'chardata',subarray.atomic_number);
[tree, uid] = add(tree,subarray_uid,'element','symbol');
tree = add(tree,uid,'chardata',subarray.symbol);
[tree, uid] = add(tree,subarray_uid,'element','atomic_weight');
tree = add(tree,uid,'chardata',subarray.atomic_weight);
[tree, uid] = add(tree,subarray_uid,'element','absorption');
tree = add(tree,uid,'chardata',subarray.absorption);
[tree, uid] = add(tree,subarray_uid,'element','scattering');
tree = add(tree,uid,'chardata',subarray.scattering);
%
[tree, subarray_uid] = add(tree,root(tree),'element','subarray');
subarray = struct('id','9',...
            'element','Oxygen',...
                        'atomic_number','8',...
            'symbol','O',...
            'atomic_weight','16',...
            'absorption','0.0002',...
            'scattering','4.2');

[tree, uid] = add(tree,subarray_uid,'element','id');
tree = add(tree,uid,'chardata',subarray.id);
[tree, uid] = add(tree,subarray_uid,'element','element');
tree = add(tree,uid,'chardata',subarray.element);
[tree, uid] = add(tree,subarray_uid,'element','atomic_number');
tree = add(tree,uid,'chardata',subarray.atomic_number);
[tree, uid] = add(tree,subarray_uid,'element','symbol');
```

```
tree = add(tree,uid,'chardata',subarray.symbol);
[tree, uid] = add(tree,subarray_uid,'element','atomic_weight');
tree = add(tree,uid,'chardata',subarray.atomic_weight);
[tree, uid] = add(tree,subarray_uid,'element','absorption');
tree = add(tree,uid,'chardata',subarray.absorption);
[tree, uid] = add(tree,subarray_uid,'element','scattering');
tree = add(tree,uid,'chardata',subarray.scattering);
%
[tree, subarray_uid] = add(tree,root(tree),'element','subarray');
subarray = struct('id','10',...
        'element','Fluorine',...
                'atomic_number','9',...
        'symbol','F',...
        'atomic_weight','19',...
        'absorption','0.009',...
        'scattering','4.1');

[tree, uid] = add(tree,subarray_uid,'element','id');
tree = add(tree,uid,'chardata',subarray.id);
[tree, uid] = add(tree,subarray_uid,'element','element');
tree = add(tree,uid,'chardata',subarray.element);
[tree, uid] = add(tree,subarray_uid,'element','atomic_number');
tree = add(tree,uid,'chardata',subarray.atomic_number);
[tree, uid] = add(tree,subarray_uid,'element','symbol');
tree = add(tree,uid,'chardata',subarray.symbol);
[tree, uid] = add(tree,subarray_uid,'element','atomic_weight');
tree = add(tree,uid,'chardata',subarray.atomic_weight);
[tree, uid] = add(tree,subarray_uid,'element','absorption');
tree = add(tree,uid,'chardata',subarray.absorption);
[tree, uid] = add(tree,subarray_uid,'element','scattering');
tree = add(tree,uid,'chardata',subarray.scattering);
%
[tree, subarray_uid] = add(tree,root(tree),'element','subarray');
subarray = struct('id','11',...
        'element','Neon',...
                'atomic_number','10',...
        'symbol','Ne',...
        'atomic_weight','20.18',...
        'absorption','2.8',...
        'scattering','2.4');

[tree, uid] = add(tree,subarray_uid,'element','id');
```

```
tree = add(tree,uid,'chardata',subarray.id);
[tree, uid] = add(tree,subarray_uid,'element','element');
tree = add(tree,uid,'chardata',subarray.element);
[tree, uid] = add(tree,subarray_uid,'element','atomic_number');
tree = add(tree,uid,'chardata',subarray.atomic_number);
[tree, uid] = add(tree,subarray_uid,'element','symbol');
tree = add(tree,uid,'chardata',subarray.symbol);
[tree, uid] = add(tree,subarray_uid,'element','atomic_weight');
tree = add(tree,uid,'chardata',subarray.atomic_weight);
[tree, uid] = add(tree,subarray_uid,'element','absorption');
tree = add(tree,uid,'chardata',subarray.absorption);
[tree, uid] = add(tree,subarray_uid,'element','scattering');
tree = add(tree,uid,'chardata',subarray.scattering);
%
[tree, subarray_uid] = add(tree,root(tree),'element','subarray');
subarray = struct('id','12',...
            'element','Sodium',...
                    'atomic_number','11',...
            'symbol','Na',...
            'atomic_weight','22.997',...
            'absorption','0.5',...
            'scattering','4');

[tree, uid] = add(tree,subarray_uid,'element','id');
tree = add(tree,uid,'chardata',subarray.id);
[tree, uid] = add(tree,subarray_uid,'element','element');
tree = add(tree,uid,'chardata',subarray.element);
[tree, uid] = add(tree,subarray_uid,'element','atomic_number');
tree = add(tree,uid,'chardata',subarray.atomic_number);
[tree, uid] = add(tree,subarray_uid,'element','symbol');
tree = add(tree,uid,'chardata',subarray.symbol);
[tree, uid] = add(tree,subarray_uid,'element','atomic_weight');
tree = add(tree,uid,'chardata',subarray.atomic_weight);
[tree, uid] = add(tree,subarray_uid,'element','absorption');
tree = add(tree,uid,'chardata',subarray.absorption);
[tree, uid] = add(tree,subarray_uid,'element','scattering');
tree = add(tree,uid,'chardata',subarray.scattering);
%
[tree, subarray_uid] = add(tree,root(tree),'element','subarray');
subarray = struct('id','13',...
            'element','Magnesium',...
                    'atomic_number','12',...
```

```
            'symbol','Mg',...
            'atomic_weight','24.32',...
            'absorption','0.06',...
            'scattering','3.6');

[tree, uid] = add(tree,subarray_uid,'element','id');
tree = add(tree,uid,'chardata',subarray.id);
[tree, uid] = add(tree,subarray_uid,'element','element');
tree = add(tree,uid,'chardata',subarray.element);
[tree, uid] = add(tree,subarray_uid,'element','atomic_number');
tree = add(tree,uid,'chardata',subarray.atomic_number);
[tree, uid] = add(tree,subarray_uid,'element','symbol');
tree = add(tree,uid,'chardata',subarray.symbol);
[tree, uid] = add(tree,subarray_uid,'element','atomic_weight');
tree = add(tree,uid,'chardata',subarray.atomic_weight);
[tree, uid] = add(tree,subarray_uid,'element','absorption');
tree = add(tree,uid,'chardata',subarray.absorption);
[tree, uid] = add(tree,subarray_uid,'element','scattering');
tree = add(tree,uid,'chardata',subarray.scattering);
%
[tree, subarray_uid] = add(tree,root(tree),'element','subarray');
subarray = struct('id','14',...
            'element','Aluminum',...
                        'atomic_number','13',...
            'symbol','Al',...
            'atomic_weight','26.98',...
            'absorption','0.21',...
            'scattering','1.4');

[tree, uid] = add(tree,subarray_uid,'element','id');
tree = add(tree,uid,'chardata',subarray.id);
[tree, uid] = add(tree,subarray_uid,'element','element');
tree = add(tree,uid,'chardata',subarray.element);
[tree, uid] = add(tree,subarray_uid,'element','atomic_number');
tree = add(tree,uid,'chardata',subarray.atomic_number);
[tree, uid] = add(tree,subarray_uid,'element','symbol');
tree = add(tree,uid,'chardata',subarray.symbol);
[tree, uid] = add(tree,subarray_uid,'element','atomic_weight');
tree = add(tree,uid,'chardata',subarray.atomic_weight);
[tree, uid] = add(tree,subarray_uid,'element','absorption');
tree = add(tree,uid,'chardata',subarray.absorption);
[tree, uid] = add(tree,subarray_uid,'element','scattering');
```

```
tree = add(tree,uid,'chardata',subarray.scattering);
%
[tree, subarray_uid] = add(tree,root(tree),'element','subarray');
subarray = struct('id','15',...
            'element','Silicon',...
                        'atomic_number','14',...
            'symbol','Si',...
            'atomic_weight','28.09',...
            'absorption','0.13',...
            'scattering','1.7');

[tree, uid] = add(tree,subarray_uid,'element','id');
tree = add(tree,uid,'chardata',subarray.id);
[tree, uid] = add(tree,subarray_uid,'element','element');
tree = add(tree,uid,'chardata',subarray.element);
[tree, uid] = add(tree,subarray_uid,'element','atomic_number');
tree = add(tree,uid,'chardata',subarray.atomic_number);
[tree, uid] = add(tree,subarray_uid,'element','symbol');
tree = add(tree,uid,'chardata',subarray.symbol);
[tree, uid] = add(tree,subarray_uid,'element','atomic_weight');
tree = add(tree,uid,'chardata',subarray.atomic_weight);
[tree, uid] = add(tree,subarray_uid,'element','absorption');
tree = add(tree,uid,'chardata',subarray.absorption);
[tree, uid] = add(tree,subarray_uid,'element','scattering');
tree = add(tree,uid,'chardata',subarray.scattering);
%
[tree, subarray_uid] = add(tree,root(tree),'element','subarray');
subarray = struct('id','16',...
            'element','Phosphorus',...
                        'atomic_number','15',...
            'symbol','P',...
            'atomic_weight','30.98',...
            'absorption','0.2',...
            'scattering','5');

[tree, uid] = add(tree,subarray_uid,'element','id');
tree = add(tree,uid,'chardata',subarray.id);
[tree, uid] = add(tree,subarray_uid,'element','element');
tree = add(tree,uid,'chardata',subarray.element);
[tree, uid] = add(tree,subarray_uid,'element','atomic_number');
tree = add(tree,uid,'chardata',subarray.atomic_number);
[tree, uid] = add(tree,subarray_uid,'element','symbol');
```

```
tree = add(tree,uid,'chardata',subarray.symbol);
[tree, uid] = add(tree,subarray_uid,'element','atomic_weight');
tree = add(tree,uid,'chardata',subarray.atomic_weight);
[tree, uid] = add(tree,subarray_uid,'element','absorption');
tree = add(tree,uid,'chardata',subarray.absorption);
[tree, uid] = add(tree,subarray_uid,'element','scattering');
tree = add(tree,uid,'chardata',subarray.scattering);
%
[tree, subarray_uid] = add(tree,root(tree),'element','subarray');
subarray = struct('id','17',...
            'element','Sulfur',...
                        'atomic_number','16',...
            'symbol','S',...
            'atomic_weight','32.07',...
            'absorption','0.49',...
            'scattering','1.1');

[tree, uid] = add(tree,subarray_uid,'element','id');
tree = add(tree,uid,'chardata',subarray.id);
[tree, uid] = add(tree,subarray_uid,'element','element');
tree = add(tree,uid,'chardata',subarray.element);
[tree, uid] = add(tree,subarray_uid,'element','atomic_number');
tree = add(tree,uid,'chardata',subarray.atomic_number);
[tree, uid] = add(tree,subarray_uid,'element','symbol');
tree = add(tree,uid,'chardata',subarray.symbol);
[tree, uid] = add(tree,subarray_uid,'element','atomic_weight');
tree = add(tree,uid,'chardata',subarray.atomic_weight);
[tree, uid] = add(tree,subarray_uid,'element','absorption');
tree = add(tree,uid,'chardata',subarray.absorption);
[tree, uid] = add(tree,subarray_uid,'element','scattering');
tree = add(tree,uid,'chardata',subarray.scattering);
%
[tree, subarray_uid] = add(tree,root(tree),'element','subarray');
subarray = struct('id','18',...
            'element','Chlorine',...
                        'atomic_number','17',...
            'symbol','Cl',...
            'atomic_weight','35.457',...
            'absorption','31.6',...
            'scattering','0');

[tree, uid] = add(tree,subarray_uid,'element','id');
```

```
tree = add(tree,uid,'chardata',subarray.id);
[tree, uid] = add(tree,subarray_uid,'element','element');
tree = add(tree,uid,'chardata',subarray.element);
[tree, uid] = add(tree,subarray_uid,'element','atomic_number');
tree = add(tree,uid,'chardata',subarray.atomic_number);
[tree, uid] = add(tree,subarray_uid,'element','symbol');
tree = add(tree,uid,'chardata',subarray.symbol);
[tree, uid] = add(tree,subarray_uid,'element','atomic_weight');
tree = add(tree,uid,'chardata',subarray.atomic_weight);
[tree, uid] = add(tree,subarray_uid,'element','absorption');
tree = add(tree,uid,'chardata',subarray.absorption);
[tree, uid] = add(tree,subarray_uid,'element','scattering');
tree = add(tree,uid,'chardata',subarray.scattering);
%
[tree, subarray_uid] = add(tree,root(tree),'element','subarray');
subarray = struct('id','19',...
        'element','Argon',...
                'atomic_number','18',...
        'symbol','Ar',...
        'atomic_weight','39.94',...
        'absorption','0.62',...
        'scattering','1.5');

[tree, uid] = add(tree,subarray_uid,'element','id');
tree = add(tree,uid,'chardata',subarray.id);
[tree, uid] = add(tree,subarray_uid,'element','element');
tree = add(tree,uid,'chardata',subarray.element);
[tree, uid] = add(tree,subarray_uid,'element','atomic_number');
tree = add(tree,uid,'chardata',subarray.atomic_number);
[tree, uid] = add(tree,subarray_uid,'element','symbol');
tree = add(tree,uid,'chardata',subarray.symbol);
[tree, uid] = add(tree,subarray_uid,'element','atomic_weight');
tree = add(tree,uid,'chardata',subarray.atomic_weight);
[tree, uid] = add(tree,subarray_uid,'element','absorption');
tree = add(tree,uid,'chardata',subarray.absorption);
[tree, uid] = add(tree,subarray_uid,'element','scattering');
tree = add(tree,uid,'chardata',subarray.scattering);
%
[tree, subarray_uid] = add(tree,root(tree),'element','subarray');
subarray = struct('id','20',...
        'element','Potassium',...
                'atomic_number','19',...
```

```
            'symbol','K',...
            'atomic_weight','39.1',...
            'absorption','2',...
            'scattering','1.5');

[tree, uid] = add(tree,subarray_uid,'element','id');
tree = add(tree,uid,'chardata',subarray.id);
[tree, uid] = add(tree,subarray_uid,'element','element');
tree = add(tree,uid,'chardata',subarray.element);
[tree, uid] = add(tree,subarray_uid,'element','atomic_number');
tree = add(tree,uid,'chardata',subarray.atomic_number);
[tree, uid] = add(tree,subarray_uid,'element','symbol');
tree = add(tree,uid,'chardata',subarray.symbol);
[tree, uid] = add(tree,subarray_uid,'element','atomic_weight');
tree = add(tree,uid,'chardata',subarray.atomic_weight);
[tree, uid] = add(tree,subarray_uid,'element','absorption');
tree = add(tree,uid,'chardata',subarray.absorption);
[tree, uid] = add(tree,subarray_uid,'element','scattering');
tree = add(tree,uid,'chardata',subarray.scattering);
%
[tree, subarray_uid] = add(tree,root(tree),'element','subarray');
subarray = struct('id','21',...
            'element','Scandium',...
                        'atomic_number','21',...
            'symbol','Sc',...
            'atomic_weight','45.1',...
            'absorption','23',...
            'scattering','0');

[tree, uid] = add(tree,subarray_uid,'element','id');
tree = add(tree,uid,'chardata',subarray.id);
[tree, uid] = add(tree,subarray_uid,'element','element');
tree = add(tree,uid,'chardata',subarray.element);
[tree, uid] = add(tree,subarray_uid,'element','atomic_number');
tree = add(tree,uid,'chardata',subarray.atomic_number);
[tree, uid] = add(tree,subarray_uid,'element','symbol');
tree = add(tree,uid,'chardata',subarray.symbol);
[tree, uid] = add(tree,subarray_uid,'element','atomic_weight');
tree = add(tree,uid,'chardata',subarray.atomic_weight);
[tree, uid] = add(tree,subarray_uid,'element','absorption');
tree = add(tree,uid,'chardata',subarray.absorption);
[tree, uid] = add(tree,subarray_uid,'element','scattering');
```

```
tree = add(tree,uid,'chardata',subarray.scattering);
%
[tree, subarray_uid] = add(tree,root(tree),'element','subarray');
subarray = struct('id','22',...
            'element','Titanium',...
                        'atomic_number','22',...
            'symbol','Ti',...
            'atomic_weight','47.9',...
            'absorption','5.6',...
            'scattering','4');

[tree, uid] = add(tree,subarray_uid,'element','id');
tree = add(tree,uid,'chardata',subarray.id);
[tree, uid] = add(tree,subarray_uid,'element','element');
tree = add(tree,uid,'chardata',subarray.element);
[tree, uid] = add(tree,subarray_uid,'element','atomic_number');
tree = add(tree,uid,'chardata',subarray.atomic_number);
[tree, uid] = add(tree,subarray_uid,'element','symbol');
tree = add(tree,uid,'chardata',subarray.symbol);
[tree, uid] = add(tree,subarray_uid,'element','atomic_weight');
tree = add(tree,uid,'chardata',subarray.atomic_weight);
[tree, uid] = add(tree,subarray_uid,'element','absorption');
tree = add(tree,uid,'chardata',subarray.absorption);
[tree, uid] = add(tree,subarray_uid,'element','scattering');
tree = add(tree,uid,'chardata',subarray.scattering);
%
[tree, subarray_uid] = add(tree,root(tree),'element','subarray');
subarray = struct('id','23',...
            'element','Vanadium',...
                        'atomic_number','23',...
            'symbol','V',...
            'atomic_weight','50.95',...
            'absorption','5.1',...
            'scattering','5');

[tree, uid] = add(tree,subarray_uid,'element','id');
tree = add(tree,uid,'chardata',subarray.id);
[tree, uid] = add(tree,subarray_uid,'element','element');
tree = add(tree,uid,'chardata',subarray.element);
[tree, uid] = add(tree,subarray_uid,'element','atomic_number');
tree = add(tree,uid,'chardata',subarray.atomic_number);
[tree, uid] = add(tree,subarray_uid,'element','symbol');
```

```
tree = add(tree,uid,'chardata',subarray.symbol);
[tree, uid] = add(tree,subarray_uid,'element','atomic_weight');
tree = add(tree,uid,'chardata',subarray.atomic_weight);
[tree, uid] = add(tree,subarray_uid,'element','absorption');
tree = add(tree,uid,'chardata',subarray.absorption);
[tree, uid] = add(tree,subarray_uid,'element','scattering');
tree = add(tree,uid,'chardata',subarray.scattering);
%
[tree, subarray_uid] = add(tree,root(tree),'element','subarray');
subarray = struct('id','24',...
            'element','Chromium',...
                        'atomic_number','24',...
            'symbol','Cr',...
            'atomic_weight','52.01',...
            'absorption','2.9',...
            'scattering','3');

[tree, uid] = add(tree,subarray_uid,'element','id');
tree = add(tree,uid,'chardata',subarray.id);
[tree, uid] = add(tree,subarray_uid,'element','element');
tree = add(tree,uid,'chardata',subarray.element);
[tree, uid] = add(tree,subarray_uid,'element','atomic_number');
tree = add(tree,uid,'chardata',subarray.atomic_number);
[tree, uid] = add(tree,subarray_uid,'element','symbol');
tree = add(tree,uid,'chardata',subarray.symbol);
[tree, uid] = add(tree,subarray_uid,'element','atomic_weight');
tree = add(tree,uid,'chardata',subarray.atomic_weight);
[tree, uid] = add(tree,subarray_uid,'element','absorption');
tree = add(tree,uid,'chardata',subarray.absorption);
[tree, uid] = add(tree,subarray_uid,'element','scattering');
tree = add(tree,uid,'chardata',subarray.scattering);
%
[tree, subarray_uid] = add(tree,root(tree),'element','subarray');
subarray = struct('id','25',...
            'element','Calcium',...
                        'atomic_number','20',...
            'symbol','Ca',...
            'atomic_weight','40.08',...
            'absorption','0.43',...
            'scattering','9');

[tree, uid] = add(tree,subarray_uid,'element','id');
```

```
tree = add(tree,uid,'chardata',subarray.id);
[tree, uid] = add(tree,subarray_uid,'element','element');
tree = add(tree,uid,'chardata',subarray.element);
[tree, uid] = add(tree,subarray_uid,'element','atomic_number');
tree = add(tree,uid,'chardata',subarray.atomic_number);
[tree, uid] = add(tree,subarray_uid,'element','symbol');
tree = add(tree,uid,'chardata',subarray.symbol);
[tree, uid] = add(tree,subarray_uid,'element','atomic_weight');
tree = add(tree,uid,'chardata',subarray.atomic_weight);
[tree, uid] = add(tree,subarray_uid,'element','absorption');
tree = add(tree,uid,'chardata',subarray.absorption);
[tree, uid] = add(tree,subarray_uid,'element','scattering');
tree = add(tree,uid,'chardata',subarray.scattering);
%
[tree, subarray_uid] = add(tree,root(tree),'element','subarray');
subarray = struct('id','26',...
            'element','Manganese',...
                        'atomic_number','25',...
            'symbol','Mn',...
            'atomic_weight','54.93',...
            'absorption','13',...
            'scattering','2.3');

[tree, uid] = add(tree,subarray_uid,'element','id');
tree = add(tree,uid,'chardata',subarray.id);
[tree, uid] = add(tree,subarray_uid,'element','element');
tree = add(tree,uid,'chardata',subarray.element);
[tree, uid] = add(tree,subarray_uid,'element','atomic_number');
tree = add(tree,uid,'chardata',subarray.atomic_number);
[tree, uid] = add(tree,subarray_uid,'element','symbol');
tree = add(tree,uid,'chardata',subarray.symbol);
[tree, uid] = add(tree,subarray_uid,'element','atomic_weight');
tree = add(tree,uid,'chardata',subarray.atomic_weight);
[tree, uid] = add(tree,subarray_uid,'element','absorption');
tree = add(tree,uid,'chardata',subarray.absorption);
[tree, uid] = add(tree,subarray_uid,'element','scattering');
tree = add(tree,uid,'chardata',subarray.scattering);
%
[tree, subarray_uid] = add(tree,root(tree),'element','subarray');
subarray = struct('id','27',...
            'element','Iron',...
                        'atomic_number','26',...
```

```
            'symbol','Fe',...
            'atomic_weight','55.85',...
            'absorption','2.4',...
            'scattering','11');

[tree, uid] = add(tree,subarray_uid,'element','id');
tree = add(tree,uid,'chardata',subarray.id);
[tree, uid] = add(tree,subarray_uid,'element','element');
tree = add(tree,uid,'chardata',subarray.element);
[tree, uid] = add(tree,subarray_uid,'element','atomic_number');
tree = add(tree,uid,'chardata',subarray.atomic_number);
[tree, uid] = add(tree,subarray_uid,'element','symbol');
tree = add(tree,uid,'chardata',subarray.symbol);
[tree, uid] = add(tree,subarray_uid,'element','atomic_weight');
tree = add(tree,uid,'chardata',subarray.atomic_weight);
[tree, uid] = add(tree,subarray_uid,'element','absorption');
tree = add(tree,uid,'chardata',subarray.absorption);
[tree, uid] = add(tree,subarray_uid,'element','scattering');
tree = add(tree,uid,'chardata',subarray.scattering);
%
[tree, subarray_uid] = add(tree,root(tree),'element','subarray');
subarray = struct('id','28',...
            'element','Cobalt',...
                        'atomic_number','27',...
            'symbol','Co',...
            'atomic_weight','58.94',...
            'absorption','37',...
            'scattering','5');

[tree, uid] = add(tree,subarray_uid,'element','id');
tree = add(tree,uid,'chardata',subarray.id);
[tree, uid] = add(tree,subarray_uid,'element','element');
tree = add(tree,uid,'chardata',subarray.element);
[tree, uid] = add(tree,subarray_uid,'element','atomic_number');
tree = add(tree,uid,'chardata',subarray.atomic_number);
[tree, uid] = add(tree,subarray_uid,'element','symbol');
tree = add(tree,uid,'chardata',subarray.symbol);
[tree, uid] = add(tree,subarray_uid,'element','atomic_weight');
tree = add(tree,uid,'chardata',subarray.atomic_weight);
[tree, uid] = add(tree,subarray_uid,'element','absorption');
tree = add(tree,uid,'chardata',subarray.absorption);
[tree, uid] = add(tree,subarray_uid,'element','scattering');
```

```
tree = add(tree,uid,'chardata',subarray.scattering);
%
[tree, subarray_uid] = add(tree,root(tree),'element','subarray');
subarray = struct('id','29',...
            'element','Nickel',...
                        'atomic_number','28',...
            'symbol','Ni',...
            'atomic_weight','58.69',...
            'absorption','4.5',...
            'scattering','17.5');

[tree, uid] = add(tree,subarray_uid,'element','id');
tree = add(tree,uid,'chardata',subarray.id);
[tree, uid] = add(tree,subarray_uid,'element','element');
tree = add(tree,uid,'chardata',subarray.element);
[tree, uid] = add(tree,subarray_uid,'element','atomic_number');
tree = add(tree,uid,'chardata',subarray.atomic_number);
[tree, uid] = add(tree,subarray_uid,'element','symbol');
tree = add(tree,uid,'chardata',subarray.symbol);
[tree, uid] = add(tree,subarray_uid,'element','atomic_weight');
tree = add(tree,uid,'chardata',subarray.atomic_weight);
[tree, uid] = add(tree,subarray_uid,'element','absorption');
tree = add(tree,uid,'chardata',subarray.absorption);
[tree, uid] = add(tree,subarray_uid,'element','scattering');
tree = add(tree,uid,'chardata',subarray.scattering);
%
[tree, subarray_uid] = add(tree,root(tree),'element','subarray');
subarray = struct('id','30',...
            'element','Copper',...
                        'atomic_number','29',...
            'symbol','Cu',...
            'atomic_weight','63.54',...
            'absorption','3.6',...
            'scattering','7.2');

[tree, uid] = add(tree,subarray_uid,'element','id');
tree = add(tree,uid,'chardata',subarray.id);
[tree, uid] = add(tree,subarray_uid,'element','element');
tree = add(tree,uid,'chardata',subarray.element);
[tree, uid] = add(tree,subarray_uid,'element','atomic_number');
tree = add(tree,uid,'chardata',subarray.atomic_number);
[tree, uid] = add(tree,subarray_uid,'element','symbol');
```

```
tree = add(tree,uid,'chardata',subarray.symbol);
[tree, uid] = add(tree,subarray_uid,'element','atomic_weight');
tree = add(tree,uid,'chardata',subarray.atomic_weight);
[tree, uid] = add(tree,subarray_uid,'element','absorption');
tree = add(tree,uid,'chardata',subarray.absorption);
[tree, uid] = add(tree,subarray_uid,'element','scattering');
tree = add(tree,uid,'chardata',subarray.scattering);
%
[tree, subarray_uid] = add(tree,root(tree),'element','subarray');
subarray = struct('id','31',...
        'element','Zinc',...
                'atomic_number','30',...
        'symbol','Zn',...
        'atomic_weight','65.38',...
        'absorption','1.1',...
        'scattering','3.6');

[tree, uid] = add(tree,subarray_uid,'element','id');
tree = add(tree,uid,'chardata',subarray.id);
[tree, uid] = add(tree,subarray_uid,'element','element');
tree = add(tree,uid,'chardata',subarray.element);
[tree, uid] = add(tree,subarray_uid,'element','atomic_number');
tree = add(tree,uid,'chardata',subarray.atomic_number);
[tree, uid] = add(tree,subarray_uid,'element','symbol');
tree = add(tree,uid,'chardata',subarray.symbol);
[tree, uid] = add(tree,subarray_uid,'element','atomic_weight');
tree = add(tree,uid,'chardata',subarray.atomic_weight);
[tree, uid] = add(tree,subarray_uid,'element','absorption');
tree = add(tree,uid,'chardata',subarray.absorption);
[tree, uid] = add(tree,subarray_uid,'element','scattering');
tree = add(tree,uid,'chardata',subarray.scattering);
%
[tree, subarray_uid] = add(tree,root(tree),'element','subarray');
subarray = struct('id','32',...
        'element','Lanthanum',...
                'atomic_number','57',...
        'symbol','La',...
        'atomic_weight','138.92',...
        'absorption','8.9',...
        'scattering','18');

[tree, uid] = add(tree,subarray_uid,'element','id');
```

```
tree = add(tree,uid,'chardata',subarray.id);
[tree, uid] = add(tree,subarray_uid,'element','element');
tree = add(tree,uid,'chardata',subarray.element);
[tree, uid] = add(tree,subarray_uid,'element','atomic_number');
tree = add(tree,uid,'chardata',subarray.atomic_number);
[tree, uid] = add(tree,subarray_uid,'element','symbol');
tree = add(tree,uid,'chardata',subarray.symbol);
[tree, uid] = add(tree,subarray_uid,'element','atomic_weight');
tree = add(tree,uid,'chardata',subarray.atomic_weight);
[tree, uid] = add(tree,subarray_uid,'element','absorption');
tree = add(tree,uid,'chardata',subarray.absorption);
[tree, uid] = add(tree,subarray_uid,'element','scattering');
tree = add(tree,uid,'chardata',subarray.scattering);
%
[tree, subarray_uid] = add(tree,root(tree),'element','subarray');
subarray = struct('id','33',...
        'element','Yttrium',...
                'atomic_number','39',...
        'symbol','Y',...
        'atomic_weight','88.92',...
        'absorption','1.4',...
        'scattering','3');

[tree, uid] = add(tree,subarray_uid,'element','id');
tree = add(tree,uid,'chardata',subarray.id);
[tree, uid] = add(tree,subarray_uid,'element','element');
tree = add(tree,uid,'chardata',subarray.element);
[tree, uid] = add(tree,subarray_uid,'element','atomic_number');
tree = add(tree,uid,'chardata',subarray.atomic_number);
[tree, uid] = add(tree,subarray_uid,'element','symbol');
tree = add(tree,uid,'chardata',subarray.symbol);
[tree, uid] = add(tree,subarray_uid,'element','atomic_weight');
tree = add(tree,uid,'chardata',subarray.atomic_weight);
[tree, uid] = add(tree,subarray_uid,'element','absorption');
tree = add(tree,uid,'chardata',subarray.absorption);
[tree, uid] = add(tree,subarray_uid,'element','scattering');
tree = add(tree,uid,'chardata',subarray.scattering);
%
[tree, subarray_uid] = add(tree,root(tree),'element','subarray');
subarray = struct('id','34',...
        'element','Neodymium',...
                'atomic_number','60',...
```

```
            'symbol','Nd',...
            'atomic_weight','144.27',...
            'absorption','44',...
            'scattering','25');

[tree, uid] = add(tree,subarray_uid,'element','id');
tree = add(tree,uid,'chardata',subarray.id);
[tree, uid] = add(tree,subarray_uid,'element','element');
tree = add(tree,uid,'chardata',subarray.element);
[tree, uid] = add(tree,subarray_uid,'element','atomic_number');
tree = add(tree,uid,'chardata',subarray.atomic_number);
[tree, uid] = add(tree,subarray_uid,'element','symbol');
tree = add(tree,uid,'chardata',subarray.symbol);
[tree, uid] = add(tree,subarray_uid,'element','atomic_weight');
tree = add(tree,uid,'chardata',subarray.atomic_weight);
[tree, uid] = add(tree,subarray_uid,'element','absorption');
tree = add(tree,uid,'chardata',subarray.absorption);
[tree, uid] = add(tree,subarray_uid,'element','scattering');
tree = add(tree,uid,'chardata',subarray.scattering);
%
[tree, subarray_uid] = add(tree,root(tree),'element','subarray');
subarray = struct('id','35',...
            'element','Cerium',...
                        'atomic_number','58',...
            'symbol','Ce',...
            'atomic_weight','140.13',...
            'absorption','0.7',...
            'scattering','9');

[tree, uid] = add(tree,subarray_uid,'element','id');
tree = add(tree,uid,'chardata',subarray.id);
[tree, uid] = add(tree,subarray_uid,'element','element');
tree = add(tree,uid,'chardata',subarray.element);
[tree, uid] = add(tree,subarray_uid,'element','atomic_number');
tree = add(tree,uid,'chardata',subarray.atomic_number);
[tree, uid] = add(tree,subarray_uid,'element','symbol');
tree = add(tree,uid,'chardata',subarray.symbol);
[tree, uid] = add(tree,subarray_uid,'element','atomic_weight');
tree = add(tree,uid,'chardata',subarray.atomic_weight);
[tree, uid] = add(tree,subarray_uid,'element','absorption');
tree = add(tree,uid,'chardata',subarray.absorption);
[tree, uid] = add(tree,subarray_uid,'element','scattering');
```

```
tree = add(tree,uid,'chardata',subarray.scattering);
%
[tree, subarray_uid] = add(tree,root(tree),'element','subarray');
subarray = struct('id','36',...
            'element','Praseodymium',...
                        'atomic_number','59',...
            'symbol','Pr',...
            'atomic_weight','140.92',...
            'absorption','11',...
            'scattering','0');

[tree, uid] = add(tree,subarray_uid,'element','id');
tree = add(tree,uid,'chardata',subarray.id);
[tree, uid] = add(tree,subarray_uid,'element','element');
tree = add(tree,uid,'chardata',subarray.element);
[tree, uid] = add(tree,subarray_uid,'element','atomic_number');
tree = add(tree,uid,'chardata',subarray.atomic_number);
[tree, uid] = add(tree,subarray_uid,'element','symbol');
tree = add(tree,uid,'chardata',subarray.symbol);
[tree, uid] = add(tree,subarray_uid,'element','atomic_weight');
tree = add(tree,uid,'chardata',subarray.atomic_weight);
[tree, uid] = add(tree,subarray_uid,'element','absorption');
tree = add(tree,uid,'chardata',subarray.absorption);
[tree, uid] = add(tree,subarray_uid,'element','scattering');
tree = add(tree,uid,'chardata',subarray.scattering);
%
[tree, subarray_uid] = add(tree,root(tree),'element','subarray');
subarray = struct('id','37',...
            'element','Gadolinium',...
                        'atomic_number','64',...
            'symbol','Gd',...
            'atomic_weight','156.9',...
            'absorption','44000',...
            'scattering','0');

[tree, uid] = add(tree,subarray_uid,'element','id');
tree = add(tree,uid,'chardata',subarray.id);
[tree, uid] = add(tree,subarray_uid,'element','element');
tree = add(tree,uid,'chardata',subarray.element);
[tree, uid] = add(tree,subarray_uid,'element','atomic_number');
tree = add(tree,uid,'chardata',subarray.atomic_number);
[tree, uid] = add(tree,subarray_uid,'element','symbol');
```

```
tree = add(tree,uid,'chardata',subarray.symbol);
[tree, uid] = add(tree,subarray_uid,'element','atomic_weight');
tree = add(tree,uid,'chardata',subarray.atomic_weight);
[tree, uid] = add(tree,subarray_uid,'element','absorption');
tree = add(tree,uid,'chardata',subarray.absorption);
[tree, uid] = add(tree,subarray_uid,'element','scattering');
tree = add(tree,uid,'chardata',subarray.scattering);
%
[tree, subarray_uid] = add(tree,root(tree),'element','subarray');
subarray = struct('id','38',...
        'element','Dysprosium',...
                'atomic_number','66',...
        'symbol','Dy',...
        'atomic_weight','162.46',...
        'absorption','1100',...
        'scattering','0');

[tree, uid] = add(tree,subarray_uid,'element','id');
tree = add(tree,uid,'chardata',subarray.id);
[tree, uid] = add(tree,subarray_uid,'element','element');
tree = add(tree,uid,'chardata',subarray.element);
[tree, uid] = add(tree,subarray_uid,'element','atomic_number');
tree = add(tree,uid,'chardata',subarray.atomic_number);
[tree, uid] = add(tree,subarray_uid,'element','symbol');
tree = add(tree,uid,'chardata',subarray.symbol);
[tree, uid] = add(tree,subarray_uid,'element','atomic_weight');
tree = add(tree,uid,'chardata',subarray.atomic_weight);
[tree, uid] = add(tree,subarray_uid,'element','absorption');
tree = add(tree,uid,'chardata',subarray.absorption);
[tree, uid] = add(tree,subarray_uid,'element','scattering');
tree = add(tree,uid,'chardata',subarray.scattering);
%
[tree, subarray_uid] = add(tree,root(tree),'element','subarray');
subarray = struct('id','39',...
        'element','Erbium',...
                'atomic_number','68',...
        'symbol','Er',...
        'atomic_weight','167.2',...
        'absorption','166',...
        'scattering','0');

[tree, uid] = add(tree,subarray_uid,'element','id');
```

```
tree = add(tree,uid,'chardata',subarray.id);
[tree, uid] = add(tree,subarray_uid,'element','element');
tree = add(tree,uid,'chardata',subarray.element);
[tree, uid] = add(tree,subarray_uid,'element','atomic_number');
tree = add(tree,uid,'chardata',subarray.atomic_number);
[tree, uid] = add(tree,subarray_uid,'element','symbol');
tree = add(tree,uid,'chardata',subarray.symbol);
[tree, uid] = add(tree,subarray_uid,'element','atomic_weight');
tree = add(tree,uid,'chardata',subarray.atomic_weight);
[tree, uid] = add(tree,subarray_uid,'element','absorption');
tree = add(tree,uid,'chardata',subarray.absorption);
[tree, uid] = add(tree,subarray_uid,'element','scattering');
tree = add(tree,uid,'chardata',subarray.scattering);
%
[tree, subarray_uid] = add(tree,root(tree),'element','subarray');
subarray = struct('id','40',...
            'element','Samarium',...
                    'atomic_number','62',...
            'symbol','Sm',...
            'atomic_weight','150.43',...
            'absorption','6500',...
            'scattering','0');

[tree, uid] = add(tree,subarray_uid,'element','id');
tree = add(tree,uid,'chardata',subarray.id);
[tree, uid] = add(tree,subarray_uid,'element','element');
tree = add(tree,uid,'chardata',subarray.element);
[tree, uid] = add(tree,subarray_uid,'element','atomic_number');
tree = add(tree,uid,'chardata',subarray.atomic_number);
[tree, uid] = add(tree,subarray_uid,'element','symbol');
tree = add(tree,uid,'chardata',subarray.symbol);
[tree, uid] = add(tree,subarray_uid,'element','atomic_weight');
tree = add(tree,uid,'chardata',subarray.atomic_weight);
[tree, uid] = add(tree,subarray_uid,'element','absorption');
tree = add(tree,uid,'chardata',subarray.absorption);
[tree, uid] = add(tree,subarray_uid,'element','scattering');
tree = add(tree,uid,'chardata',subarray.scattering);
%
[tree, subarray_uid] = add(tree,root(tree),'element','subarray');
subarray = struct('id','41',...
            'element','Ytterbium',...
                    'atomic_number','70',...
```

```
            'symbol','Yb',...
            'atomic_weight','173',...
            'absorption','36',...
            'scattering','12');

[tree, uid] = add(tree,subarray_uid,'element','id');
tree = add(tree,uid,'chardata',subarray.id);
[tree, uid] = add(tree,subarray_uid,'element','element');
tree = add(tree,uid,'chardata',subarray.element);
[tree, uid] = add(tree,subarray_uid,'element','atomic_number');
tree = add(tree,uid,'chardata',subarray.atomic_number);
[tree, uid] = add(tree,subarray_uid,'element','symbol');
tree = add(tree,uid,'chardata',subarray.symbol);
[tree, uid] = add(tree,subarray_uid,'element','atomic_weight');
tree = add(tree,uid,'chardata',subarray.atomic_weight);
[tree, uid] = add(tree,subarray_uid,'element','absorption');
tree = add(tree,uid,'chardata',subarray.absorption);
[tree, uid] = add(tree,subarray_uid,'element','scattering');
tree = add(tree,uid,'chardata',subarray.scattering);
%
[tree, subarray_uid] = add(tree,root(tree),'element','subarray');
subarray = struct('id','42',...
            'element','Holmium',...
                        'atomic_number','67',...
            'symbol','Ho',...
            'atomic_weight','164.94',...
            'absorption','64',...
            'scattering','0');

[tree, uid] = add(tree,subarray_uid,'element','id');
tree = add(tree,uid,'chardata',subarray.id);
[tree, uid] = add(tree,subarray_uid,'element','element');
tree = add(tree,uid,'chardata',subarray.element);
[tree, uid] = add(tree,subarray_uid,'element','atomic_number');
tree = add(tree,uid,'chardata',subarray.atomic_number);
[tree, uid] = add(tree,subarray_uid,'element','symbol');
tree = add(tree,uid,'chardata',subarray.symbol);
[tree, uid] = add(tree,subarray_uid,'element','atomic_weight');
tree = add(tree,uid,'chardata',subarray.atomic_weight);
[tree, uid] = add(tree,subarray_uid,'element','absorption');
tree = add(tree,uid,'chardata',subarray.absorption);
[tree, uid] = add(tree,subarray_uid,'element','scattering');
```

```
tree = add(tree,uid,'chardata',subarray.scattering);
%
[tree, subarray_uid] = add(tree,root(tree),'element','subarray');
subarray = struct('id','43',...
              'element','Terbium',...
                           'atomic_number','65',...
              'symbol','Tb',...
              'atomic_weight','159.2',...
              'absorption','44',...
              'scattering','0');

[tree, uid] = add(tree,subarray_uid,'element','id');
tree = add(tree,uid,'chardata',subarray.id);
[tree, uid] = add(tree,subarray_uid,'element','element');
tree = add(tree,uid,'chardata',subarray.element);
[tree, uid] = add(tree,subarray_uid,'element','atomic_number');
tree = add(tree,uid,'chardata',subarray.atomic_number);
[tree, uid] = add(tree,subarray_uid,'element','symbol');
tree = add(tree,uid,'chardata',subarray.symbol);
[tree, uid] = add(tree,subarray_uid,'element','atomic_weight');
tree = add(tree,uid,'chardata',subarray.atomic_weight);
[tree, uid] = add(tree,subarray_uid,'element','absorption');
tree = add(tree,uid,'chardata',subarray.absorption);
[tree, uid] = add(tree,subarray_uid,'element','scattering');
tree = add(tree,uid,'chardata',subarray.scattering);
%
[tree, subarray_uid] = add(tree,root(tree),'element','subarray');
subarray = struct('id','44',...
              'element','Europium',...
                           'atomic_number','63',...
              'symbol','Eu',...
              'atomic_weight','152',...
              'absorption','4500',...
              'scattering','0');

[tree, uid] = add(tree,subarray_uid,'element','id');
tree = add(tree,uid,'chardata',subarray.id);
[tree, uid] = add(tree,subarray_uid,'element','element');
tree = add(tree,uid,'chardata',subarray.element);
[tree, uid] = add(tree,subarray_uid,'element','atomic_number');
tree = add(tree,uid,'chardata',subarray.atomic_number);
[tree, uid] = add(tree,subarray_uid,'element','symbol');
```

```
tree = add(tree,uid,'chardata',subarray.symbol);
[tree, uid] = add(tree,subarray_uid,'element','atomic_weight');
tree = add(tree,uid,'chardata',subarray.atomic_weight);
[tree, uid] = add(tree,subarray_uid,'element','absorption');
tree = add(tree,uid,'chardata',subarray.absorption);
[tree, uid] = add(tree,subarray_uid,'element','scattering');
tree = add(tree,uid,'chardata',subarray.scattering);
%
[tree, subarray_uid] = add(tree,root(tree),'element','subarray');
subarray = struct('id','45',...
            'element','Thulium',...
                    'atomic_number','69',...
            'symbol','Tm',...
            'atomic_weight','169.4',...
            'absorption','118',...
            'scattering','0');

[tree, uid] = add(tree,subarray_uid,'element','id');
tree = add(tree,uid,'chardata',subarray.id);
[tree, uid] = add(tree,subarray_uid,'element','element');
tree = add(tree,uid,'chardata',subarray.element);
[tree, uid] = add(tree,subarray_uid,'element','atomic_number');
tree = add(tree,uid,'chardata',subarray.atomic_number);
[tree, uid] = add(tree,subarray_uid,'element','symbol');
tree = add(tree,uid,'chardata',subarray.symbol);
[tree, uid] = add(tree,subarray_uid,'element','atomic_weight');
tree = add(tree,uid,'chardata',subarray.atomic_weight);
[tree, uid] = add(tree,subarray_uid,'element','absorption');
tree = add(tree,uid,'chardata',subarray.absorption);
[tree, uid] = add(tree,subarray_uid,'element','scattering');
tree = add(tree,uid,'chardata',subarray.scattering);
%
[tree, subarray_uid] = add(tree,root(tree),'element','subarray');
subarray = struct('id','46',...
            'element','Lutetium',...
                    'atomic_number','71',...
            'symbol','Lu',...
            'atomic_weight','174.99',...
            'absorption','108',...
            'scattering','0');

[tree, uid] = add(tree,subarray_uid,'element','id');
```

```
tree = add(tree,uid,'chardata',subarray.id);
[tree, uid] = add(tree,subarray_uid,'element','element');
tree = add(tree,uid,'chardata',subarray.element);
[tree, uid] = add(tree,subarray_uid,'element','atomic_number');
tree = add(tree,uid,'chardata',subarray.atomic_number);
[tree, uid] = add(tree,subarray_uid,'element','symbol');
tree = add(tree,uid,'chardata',subarray.symbol);
[tree, uid] = add(tree,subarray_uid,'element','atomic_weight');
tree = add(tree,uid,'chardata',subarray.atomic_weight);
[tree, uid] = add(tree,subarray_uid,'element','absorption');
tree = add(tree,uid,'chardata',subarray.absorption);
[tree, uid] = add(tree,subarray_uid,'element','scattering');
tree = add(tree,uid,'chardata',subarray.scattering);
%
[tree, subarray_uid] = add(tree,root(tree),'element','subarray');
subarray = struct('id','47',...
          'element','Promethium',...
                    'atomic_number','61',...
          'symbol','Pm',...
          'atomic_weight','145',...
          'absorption','0',...
          'scattering','0');

[tree, uid] = add(tree,subarray_uid,'element','id');
tree = add(tree,uid,'chardata',subarray.id);
[tree, uid] = add(tree,subarray_uid,'element','element');
tree = add(tree,uid,'chardata',subarray.element);
[tree, uid] = add(tree,subarray_uid,'element','atomic_number');
tree = add(tree,uid,'chardata',subarray.atomic_number);
[tree, uid] = add(tree,subarray_uid,'element','symbol');
tree = add(tree,uid,'chardata',subarray.symbol);
[tree, uid] = add(tree,subarray_uid,'element','atomic_weight');
tree = add(tree,uid,'chardata',subarray.atomic_weight);
[tree, uid] = add(tree,subarray_uid,'element','absorption');
tree = add(tree,uid,'chardata',subarray.absorption);
[tree, uid] = add(tree,subarray_uid,'element','scattering');
tree = add(tree,uid,'chardata',subarray.scattering);
%
[tree, subarray_uid] = add(tree,root(tree),'element','subarray');
subarray = struct('id','48',...
          'element','Uranium',...
                    'atomic_number','92',...
```

```
            'symbol','U',...
            'atomic_weight','238.07',...
            'absorption','7.42',...
            'scattering','8.2');

[tree, uid] = add(tree,subarray_uid,'element','id');
tree = add(tree,uid,'chardata',subarray.id);
[tree, uid] = add(tree,subarray_uid,'element','element');
tree = add(tree,uid,'chardata',subarray.element);
[tree, uid] = add(tree,subarray_uid,'element','atomic_number');
tree = add(tree,uid,'chardata',subarray.atomic_number);
[tree, uid] = add(tree,subarray_uid,'element','symbol');
tree = add(tree,uid,'chardata',subarray.symbol);
[tree, uid] = add(tree,subarray_uid,'element','atomic_weight');
tree = add(tree,uid,'chardata',subarray.atomic_weight);
[tree, uid] = add(tree,subarray_uid,'element','absorption');
tree = add(tree,uid,'chardata',subarray.absorption);
[tree, uid] = add(tree,subarray_uid,'element','scattering');
tree = add(tree,uid,'chardata',subarray.scattering);
%
[tree, subarray_uid] = add(tree,root(tree),'element','subarray');
subarray = struct('id','50',...
            'element','Thorium',...
                        'atomic_number','90',...
            'symbol','Th',...
            'atomic_weight','232.12',...
            'absorption','7',...
            'scattering','13');

[tree, uid] = add(tree,subarray_uid,'element','id');
tree = add(tree,uid,'chardata',subarray.id);
[tree, uid] = add(tree,subarray_uid,'element','element');
tree = add(tree,uid,'chardata',subarray.element);
[tree, uid] = add(tree,subarray_uid,'element','atomic_number');
tree = add(tree,uid,'chardata',subarray.atomic_number);
[tree, uid] = add(tree,subarray_uid,'element','symbol');
tree = add(tree,uid,'chardata',subarray.symbol);
[tree, uid] = add(tree,subarray_uid,'element','atomic_weight');
tree = add(tree,uid,'chardata',subarray.atomic_weight);
[tree, uid] = add(tree,subarray_uid,'element','absorption');
tree = add(tree,uid,'chardata',subarray.absorption);
```

```
[tree, uid] = add(tree,subarray_uid,'element','scattering');
tree = add(tree,uid,'chardata',subarray.scattering);

%
view(tree);
save(tree,'basicdata1_ml.xml');
```

The computer file of this Matlab script and the output XML file is in computer_files_12.1.

12.2 Parsing XML files with Matlab

The following examples are to retrieve data from an XML file using the "xmltree" package described in Section 12.1:

Example 1

The program "xmldemo2x.m" is to modify one value in "basicdata1_ml.xml" from absorption =0.0 to absorption =0.0001, and to save the revised xml file as "basicdata1_mlmod.xml". Note that Matlab counts from 1, not from 0. So subarray[3] is that for Helium.

```
% xmldemo2x
%
%  This script demonstrates the use of the xmltree class to
%  open an XML file, access data stored in it, modify a value
%  and save the new XML file.
%
clear; help xmldemo2x;
t = xmltree('basicdata1_ml.xml');
methods xmltree;
absorption_tag = find(t,'/Big_array/subarray[3]/absorption');
absorption = children(t,absorption_tag);
get(t,absorption,'value');

t = set(t,absorption,'value','0.0001');

save(t,'basicdata1_mlmod.xml');
```

Example 2

"xmldemo2xA.m" is an extension of "xmldemo2x.m", to print out the information of the XML file ("basicdata1_ml.xml") in the format of Matlab construct. Hence it is a Matlab program for parsing an XML file.

```
% xmldemo2xA
%
%   This script demonstrates the use of the xmltree class to
%   open an XML file, access data stored in it.
%
%
clear; help xmldemo2x;
t = xmltree('basicdata1_ml.xml');
methods xmltree;


element_tag = find(t,'/Big_array/subarray[1]/element');
element = children(t,element_tag);
element_ = get(t,element,'value')

atomic_number_tag = find(t,'/Big_array/subarray[1]/atomic_number');
atomic_number = children(t,atomic_number_tag);
atomic_number_ = get(t,atomic_number,'value')

symbol_tag = find(t,'/Big_array/subarray[1]/symbol');
symbol = children(t,symbol_tag);
symbol_ = get(t,symbol,'value')

atomic_weight_tag = find(t,'/Big_array/subarray[1]/atomic_weight');
atomic_weight = children(t,atomic_weight_tag);
atomic_weight_ = get(t,atomic_weight,'value')

absorption_tag = find(t,'/Big_array/subarray[1]/absorption');
absorption = children(t,absorption_tag);
absorption_=get(t,absorption,'value')

scattering_tag = find(t,'/Big_array/subarray[1]/scattering');
scattering = children(t,scattering_tag);
scattering_=get(t,scattering,'value')
```

```
%

element_tag = find(t,'/Big_array/subarray[2]/element');
element = children(t,element_tag);
element_ = get(t,element,'value')

atomic_number_tag = find(t,'/Big_array/subarray[2]/atomic_number');
atomic_number = children(t,atomic_number_tag);
atomic_number_ = get(t,atomic_number,'value')

symbol_tag = find(t,'/Big_array/subarray[2]/symbol');
symbol = children(t,symbol_tag);
symbol_ = get(t,symbol,'value')

atomic_weight_tag = find(t,'/Big_array/subarray[2]/atomic_weight');
atomic_weight = children(t,atomic_weight_tag);
atomic_weight_ = get(t,atomic_weight,'value')

absorption_tag = find(t,'/Big_array/subarray[2]/absorption');
absorption = children(t,absorption_tag);
absorption_=get(t,absorption,'value')

scattering_tag = find(t,'/Big_array/subarray[2]/scattering');
scattering = children(t,scattering_tag);
scattering_=get(t,scattering,'value')

%

element_tag = find(t,'/Big_array/subarray[3]/element');
element = children(t,element_tag);
element_ = get(t,element,'value')

atomic_number_tag = find(t,'/Big_array/subarray[3]/atomic_number');
atomic_number = children(t,atomic_number_tag);
atomic_number_ = get(t,atomic_number,'value')

symbol_tag = find(t,'/Big_array/subarray[3]/symbol');
symbol = children(t,symbol_tag);
symbol_ = get(t,symbol,'value')
```

```
atomic_weight_tag = find(t,'/Big_array/subarray[3]/atomic_weight');
atomic_weight = children(t,atomic_weight_tag);
atomic_weight_ = get(t,atomic_weight,'value')

absorption_tag = find(t,'/Big_array/subarray[3]/absorption');
absorption = children(t,absorption_tag);
absorption_=get(t,absorption,'value')

scattering_tag = find(t,'/Big_array/subarray[3]/scattering');
scattering = children(t,scattering_tag);
scattering_=get(t,scattering,'value')

% etc. etc.
```

The computer files are in computer_files_12.2.

Chapter 13

Interface of Matlab with other programs

13.1 From Matlab to execute Perl

We can execute Perl from Matlab command window.

Example 1

We shall consider the following simple Perl program:

```
#!"C:\xampp\perl\bin\perl.exe"

print "Content-type: text/plain \n\n"; #HTTP HEADER

# http://localhost/cgi-bin/xampp_perl/hello.pl

$input = $ARGV[0];
print "Hello $input.";
```

The following shows the commands and the responses on the Matlab command window:

```
>> perl('C:/xampp/cgi-bin/xampp_perl/hello.pl','World')
```

```
ans =

Content-type: text/plain

Hello World.

>>
```

Note that: To pass arguments from Matlab to Perl, we use perl('file.pl','....') on the Matlab command window as shown above.

Example 2

We shall consider the following Perl program "table_of_squares.pl":

```
#!"C:\xampp\perl\bin\perl.exe"

print "Content-type: text/html \n\n"; #HTTP HEADER

# http://localhost/cgi-bin/xampp_perl/table_of_squares.pl

$title = "Table of Squares";
$rows=10;

print "Content-Type: text/html\n\n";

print header();
print body();

sub header() {

   return qq{<HTML>\n<HEAD>\n<title>$title</title></head>};

}

sub body() {

   $body = qq{
<BODY>
<div align="center">
```

```
<H4>$title</H4>
<P>
<table border="1">
};

   for $i (1 .. $rows) {
      $body .= qq{<tr><td>Row $i</td>};
      $body .= qq{<td width="50" align="center">};
      $body .= $i*$i;
      $body .= qq{</td></tr>\n};
   }

   $body .= qq{
</table>
</div>
</BODY>
</HTML>};

   return $body;
}
```

The following shows the commands and responses on the Matlab command window:

```
>> perl('C:/xampp/cgi-bin/xampp_perl/table_of_squares.pl')

ans =

Content-type: text/html

Content-Type: text/html

<HTML>
<HEAD>
<title>Table of Squares</title></head>
<BODY>
<div align="center">
<H4>Table of Squares</H4>
<P>
<table border="1">
<tr><td>Row 1</td><td width="50" align="center">1</td></tr>
<tr><td>Row 2</td><td width="50" align="center">4</td></tr>
```

```
<tr><td>Row 3</td><td width="50" align="center">9</td></tr>
<tr><td>Row 4</td><td width="50" align="center">16</td></tr>
<tr><td>Row 5</td><td width="50" align="center">25</td></tr>
<tr><td>Row 6</td><td width="50" align="center">36</td></tr>
<tr><td>Row 7</td><td width="50" align="center">49</td></tr>
<tr><td>Row 8</td><td width="50" align="center">64</td></tr>
<tr><td>Row 9</td><td width="50" align="center">81</td></tr>
<tr><td>Row 10</td><td width="50" align="center">100</td></tr>

</table>
</div>
</BODY>
</HTML>
```

This html file, when executed, will produce the same “table of squares” as the original perl script executed directly. That is http://localhost/cgi-bin/xampp_perl/table_of_squares.pl

Note that Matlab cannot interpret html without an html toolbox. So the HTML file is output as a text.

The computer files are included in computer_files_13.1.

13.2 From Matlab to execute Python

The original Matlab program from Mathsoft does not directly interface with Python. It can be made so by making use of the analogy with Perl. The method is based on http://Stackoverflow.com/questions/1707780/call-python-function-from-matlab

First, make a copy of the M-file in “\toolbox\matlab\general\perl.m”.

Then, in that copy of the file, change all “perl” to “python”, also change perlCmd from ‘sys\perl\win32\bin’ to ‘C:\Python27\’.

Then put this new python.m file in “\MATLAB” folder and run python files from Matlab command window, as for the case of Perl. This “python.m” is included in the computer_files_13.2. The following shows how to execute Python programs from Matlab command window:

Example 1

We shall consider the following Python script “Fibonacci.py”:

```
def fib(n):    # write Fibonacci series up to n
    """Print a Fibonacci series up to n."""
    a, b = 0, 1
    while a < n:
        print a,
        a, b = b, a+b

# Now call the function we just defined:

fib(2000)
```

The following shows the commands and responses on the Matlab command window:

```
>> python('C:/python-scripts/Fibonacci.py')

ans =

0 1 1 2 3 5 8 13 21 34 55 89 144 233 377 610 987 1597
```

Example 2

We shall consider the following Python script “sqd_1.py”:

```
import sys

def squared(x):
    y = x * x
    return y

if __name__ == '__main__':
    x = float(sys.argv[1])
    sys.stdout.write(str(squared(x)))
```

The following shows the commands and responses on Matlab command window:

```
>> python('C:/python-scripts/sqd_1.py','4.5')

ans =

20.25

>>
```

13.3 From Php to execute Matlab.

It is possible to execute a Matlab program in batch mode from Php. In the following example, the Matlab script “eigen_A.m” is:

```
% eigen_A
clear; help eigen_A;
% To read matrix A from file.
fid1=fopen('phpToFile.txt','r');
a=fscanf(fid1,'%g',[1 inf]);
a=a';
fclose(fid1);

A=zeros(2,2);
A(1,1)=a(1);
A(1,2)=a(2);
A(2,1)=a(3);
A(2,2)=a(4);

[V,D]=eig(A);
[m,n]=size(A);
fid=fopen('eigen_values_vectors_A.txt','w');
fprintf(fid,'Matrix A is\r\n');
fprintf(fid,'_____________\r\n');
fprintf(fid,'%6.4f %6.4f\r\n',A(1,1),A(1,2));
fprintf(fid,'%6.4f %6.4f\r\n',A(2,1),A(2,2));
fprintf(fid,'_____________\r\n');
fprintf(fid,'The eigenvalues are \r\n');
fprintf(fid,'_____________\r\n');
```

```
fprintf(fid,'%6.4f %6.4f\r\n',D(1,1),D(2,2));
fprintf(fid,'_____________\r\n');
fprintf(fid,'The corresponding eigenvectors are the columns of the following matrix
\r\n');
fprintf(fid,'_____________\r\n');
fprintf(fid,'%6.4f %6.4f\r\n',V(1,1),V(1,2));
fprintf(fid,'%6.4f %6.4f\r\n',V(2,1),V(2,2));
fprintf(fid,'_____________\r\n');
fclose(fid);
quit;
```

The Php script “testphpmatlab_eigen_A.php” is:

```
<?php
// http://localhost/new_sci3/testphpmatlab_eigen_A.php

$A[0][0]="5";
$A[0][1]="6";
$A[1][0]="7";
$A[1][1]="8";
$filename="phpToFile.txt";
$fp=fopen($filename,"w") or die("Could not open $filename");
fwrite($fp,$A[0][0]."\n");
fwrite($fp,$A[0][1]."\n");
fwrite($fp,$A[1][0]."\n");
fwrite($fp,$A[1][1]."\n");
fclose($fp);
usleep(1000000); // Sleep for 1 sec.
echo "Finish sleeping, and start the matlab command"."\n";
if(file_exists($filename)) {

$command="matlab -sd C:\\xampp\\htdocs\\new_sci3\\ -r eigen_A -logfile C:\\tmp\\
logfile";

 echo $command;
 exec($command);
}
usleep(10000000); // Sleep for 10 sec.
echo "Finish sleeping, and start reading results from file"."\n";
$filename2="eigen_values_vectors_A.txt";
```

```
$fp2=fopen($filename2,"r") or die ("Could not open $filename2");
while(!feof($fp2)){
$line=fgets($fp2,1024);
echo $line."<br />";
}
fclose($fp2);

?>
```

In this example, the Php script creates a 2x2 matrix A and writes the values to a file named “phpToFile.txt”. Then sleeps for 1 second. Then execute the command to run “eigen_A.m” in batch mode:

```
$command=”matlab -sd C:\\xampp\\htdocs\\new_sci3\\ -r eigen_A -logfile C:\\tmp\\
logfile”;
```

The Matlab script reads the file “phpToFile.txt” and performs the analysis. It writes the output to another file named “eigen_values_vectors_A.txt”. The Php script sleeps for 10 seconds and reads this “eigen_values_vectors_A.txt” file and writes out the result. (Note the double \\ ‘s are needed because Php consider “\” as to delete the letter immediately after it. Use \\ to get the actual \ in the address of URL.)

The output of the Php is:

Finish sleeping, and start the matlab command matlab -sd C:\xampp\htdocs\xampp_sci\ -r eigen_A -logfile C:\tmp\logfileFinish sleeping, and start reading results from file Matrix A is

____

5.0000 6.0000
7.0000 8.0000

____

The eigenvalues are

____

-0.1521 13.1521

____

The corresponding eigenvectors are the columns of the following matrix

____

-0.7587 -0.5928
0.6515 -0.8054

____

13.4 From Perl and Python to execute Matlab

From Perl

Using Microsoft's Component Object Model (COM), it is possible to pass the data from Perl to Matlab. The listings of the following Perl programs are included in computer_files_13.4. They are:

Matlab_from_Perl.pl - to execute 'magicArray = magic(4)'
Matlab_from_Perl_A.pl - to execute 'magicArray = magic(3)'
Matlab_from_Perl_B.pl - to execute '[V,D]=eig([1 2;3 4])'
Matlab_from_Perl_C.pl - to execute 'A=[1 2;3 4];[V,D]=eig(A)'
Matlab_from_Perl_D.pl - to execute '[V,D]=eig(A)'
Matlab_from_Perl_E.pl - to execute 'p=[1 6 72 -27];r=roots(p)'
Matlab_from_Perl_F.pl - to execute 'A=[3 2;1 -1];B=[19;-2];X=A\B;'
Matlab_from_Perl_G.pl - to execute 'answer=quad('sin',0,pi)'

From Python

The following is a demonstration of calling Matlab from Python in interactive mode:

```
Python 2.7.1 |EPD 7.0-2 (32-bit)| (r271:86832, Dec 2 2010, 10:35:02) [MSC v.1500
32 bit (Intel)] on win32
Type "copyright", "credits" or "license()" for more information.
>>> import win32com.client
>>> ml=win32com.client.Dispatch("Matlab.Application")
>>> from numpy import *

>>> ml.Execute('H2MT1=[1. 2. 3.; 4. 5. 6.;7. 8. 9.];[V,D]=eig(H2MT1)')
u'\nV =\n\n   -0.2320   -0.7858    0.4082\n   -0.5253   -0.0868   -0.8165\n   -0.8187
0.6123    0.4082\n\n\nD =\n\n   16.1168         0         0\n         0   -1.1168         0\n
0         0   -0.0000\n\n'
>>>
>>> ml.Visible
1
>>>
>>> H2MT1=[1. 2. 3.; 4. 5. 6.;7. 8. 9.];[V,D]=eig(H2MT1)
```

```
V =
  -0.2320  -0.7858   0.4082
  -0.5253  -0.0868  -0.8165
  -0.8187   0.6123   0.4082
D =
  16.1168        0         0
       0   -1.1168         0
       0         0   -0.0000
```

Chapter 14

Comparison of Matlab and Python

14.1 Solution of a system of ordinary differential equations.

In this section, we shall illustrate the solution of the following set of ordinary differential equations:

$$\frac{dI}{dt} = -\lambda_I I$$

$$\frac{dX}{dt} = -\lambda_X X + \lambda_I I$$

where $\lambda_I = 2.8737 \times 10^{-5}\ \sec^{-1}$ and $\lambda_X = 2.1 \times 10^{0}\ \sec^{-1}$

The initial conditions are: X0=1.6739e15 per cm^3; I0=3.98615e16 per cm^3.

We are not interested in the details of the physics involved here. Briefly the set of equations describes the build-up of xenon-135 (denoted by X) from the decay of Iodine-135 (denoted by I); (lam_X) and (lam_I) are their respective decay constants having the unit of inverse time; and t is time after reactor shutdown. Before the shutdown, the reactor had been operated at constant power, having a neutron flux of 2.0e14 n/cm^2 sec. The initial values of X (denoted by X0) and of I(denoted by I0) are typical values for a commercial power reactor. The reason for analyzing the xenon build-up after reactor shutdown is that even in the absence of fission reactions, the xenon-135 continues to build up at the expense of Iodine-135. Xenon-135 has high neutron absorption cross section. If the reactor is designed without enough excess reactivity to over ride the Xenon-135 build-up, it cannot be restarted some 11 hours after shutdown when the Xenon-135 reaches its peak.

In the Matlab script, we shall use y(1)=I; y(2)=X; ydot(1)=dI/dt; ydot(2)=dX/dt. In Python, we shall use y[0]=I and y[1] =X.

The set of equations is simple enough to be solved analytically, but we shall use Matlab and Python functions based on Runge-Kutta formulas.

The Matlab scripts are "xenon_ode_2.m" and "Xe_2.m":

```
% xenon_ode_2
clear; help xenon_ode_2;
global lam_I lam_X;
t0=0;
tf=50*3600;
tspan=t0:(tf-t0)/600:tf;

lam_I=2.8737e-5;
lam_X=2.1e-5;
I0=3.98615e16;
X0=1.6739e15;
y0=[I0 X0]';
[t,s]=ode23('Xe_2',tspan,y0);
I=s(:,1);
X=s(:,2);
n=size(t);
for i=1:n
t(i)=t(i)/3600;
end;
plot(t,X,'b-');
xlabel('Time in hrs after reactor shutdown');
ylabel('Xenon concentration number/cc');
title('Xenon Build-up after shutdown at 2.0e14 n/cm^2 sec');
grid on;
print xenon_matlab.png -dpng;

function ydot=Xe_2(t,y)
global lam_I lam_X;
ydot(1)=-lam_I*y(1);
ydot(2)=lam_I*y(1)-lam_X*y(2);
ydot=ydot(:);
```

The Python script is xenon_ode_2.py:

```
from numpy import linspace
from scipy.integrate import odeint
from scitools.std import *

# Define the initial conditions
inic = array([3.98615e16,1.6739e15])

# Times to evaluate the ODEs. 600 times from 0 to 50 hr (inclusive).
t = linspace(0.0,50.0,600)

# The derivative function.
def f(y,time):
    """ Compute the derivate of 'y' at time 'time'.
        'y' is a list of two elements.
    """
    lam_I=0.1034532;
    lam_X=0.0756;
    return array([-lam_I*y[0], lam_I*y[0]-lam_X*y[1] ])

# Compute the ODE
res = odeint(f, inic, t)

# Plot the results
plot(t,res[:,1],'b-')
title('Xenon Build-up after shutdown at 2.0e14 n/cm2 sec')

xlabel('Time in hrs after reactor shutdown')
ylabel('Xenon concentration number/cc')
show()
hardcopy('xenon_python.png')
```

The results of the analysis together with the Matlab's Simulink model "xenon.mdl" are shown in Appendix 14.1. The Matlab and Python scripts are included in the computer_file_14.1.

14.2 RLC Circuit

In this section, we shall consider using Matlab and Python to solve the second order ordinary equation of the RLC series circuit:

$$L\frac{di}{dt}+Ri+\frac{1}{C}\int idt=V_0\sin\omega t$$

Or

$$L\frac{d^2i}{dt^2}+R\frac{di}{dt}+\frac{i}{C}=\omega V_0\cos\omega t$$

for L=10 henry, R=20 ohm, C=1/4000=2.5e-4 farad, V0=10 volt, w=10 rad/s (f=1.5915 hertz), i(0)=0.01 amp, i'(0)=0.

The second order differential equation is first converted to a set of coupled first order ordinary differential equations and then solved with Matlab or Python's ODE solver based on Runge Kutta algorithm. That is,

Let X(1)=i; X(2)=di/dt=dX(1)/dt.
We have a set of coupled ODE:
dX(1)/dt = X(2)
dX(2)/dt= -R X(2)/L - X(1)/L C + w V0 cos(w t)/L

The Matlab scrips "RLC_Matlab_test.m"and "rlc.m" are:

```
% RLC_Matlab_test
clear; help RLC_Matlab_test;
global R L C w V0;

V0=10;
R=20;
L=10;
C=2.5e-4;
w=10;
```

```
t0=0;
tf=3;
tspan=t0:(tf-t0)/100:tf;
x0=[0.01 0]';
[t,s]=ode23('rlc',tspan,x0);
x1=s(:,1);
x2=s(:,2);

plot(t,x1,'r-',t,x2,'b-');
xlabel('Time (s)');
ylabel('x1(red) or x2(blue)');
title('Solution of RLC in Series');
text(0.5,-0.5,'L d^2i/dt^2+R di/dt+i/C=w V0 cos(w t)');
text(0.5,-0.6,'L=10 h,R=20 ohm,C=2.5e-4 f,V0=10 v,w=10 rad/s');
text(0.5,-0.7,'x1=i (red),x2=di/dt (blue),x1(0)=0.01 amp,x2(0)=0');
grid on;
print RLC_series.png -dpng;

function xdot=rlc(t,x)
global R L C w V0;
xdot=[x(2);(-R*x(2)-x(1)/C+w*V0*cos(w*t))/L];
```

The corresponding Python script “RLC_Python_test.py” is:

```
from numpy import linspace
from scipy.integrate import odeint
from scitools.std import *

# Define the initial conditions
inic = array([0.01,0.0])

# Times to evaluate the ODEs. 100 times from 0 to 3 sec (inclusive).
t = linspace(0.0,3.0,100)

V0=10
R=20
L=10
C=2.5e-4
w=10
```

```
# The derivative function.
def f(y,time):
   """ Compute the derivate of 'y' at time 'time'.
      'y' is a list of two elements.
   """

   return array([y[1],(-R*y[1]-y[0]/C+w*V0*cos(w*time))/L ])
# Compute the ODE
res = odeint(f, inic, t)

# Plot the results
plot(t,res[:,0],'r-',t,res[:,1],'b-')
xlabel('Time (s)')
ylabel('i(red) or di/dt(blue)')
title('Solution of RLC in Series')
hardcopy('RLC_series.png')
```

The results are shown in Appendix 14.2. The computer files are included in computer_files_14-2.

14.3 Plotting curves.

In this section, we shall compare the plotting routines of Matlab with Matplotlib in Python, and the independent version of Gnuplot. The input data are helium densities as a function of temperature and pressure taken from a textbook "Nuclear Power Engineering by El-Wakil". The printed table was converted to a MySQL table "helium" as shown in Appendix 14.3A. A Php program was used to extract the data of helium densities and to write them to a few simple text files for use by Matlab and Python to plot the graphs. The following shows the steps:

Step 1. The following MySQL commands was to create and populate the MySQL table "helium". Note that P stands for pressure in psia. A,B,C,D,E,F stand for, respectively, 100,200,300,400,500,600 degree Fahrenheit.

```
CREATE TABLE stocks.helium(
id INT NOT NULL PRIMARY KEY AUTO_INCREMENT,
P FLOAT NOT NULL,
A FLOAT NOT NULL,
```

```
B FLOAT NOT NULL,
C FLOAT NOT NULL,
D FLOAT NOT NULL,
E FLOAT NOT NULL,
F FLOAT NOT NULL);

INSERT INTO stocks.helium
(P,A,B,C,D,E,F)VALUES
('14.696', '0.0097820', '0.0082997', '0.0072076', '0.0063694', '0.0057059', '0.0051676'),
('50.0',   '0.033239',  '0.028208',  '0.024500',  '0.021653',  '0.019399',  '0.017570'),
('150.0',  '0.099372',  '0.084372',  '0.073310',  '0.064812',  '0.058078',  '0.052610'),
('400.0',  '0.26273',   '0.22334',   '0.194225',  '0.171831',  '0.154072',  '0.139633'),
('600.0',  '0.39146',   '0.33308',   '0.28986',   '0.25658',   '0.23016',   '0.20867'),
('900.0',  '0.58139',   '0.49537',   '0.43154',   '0.38230',   '0.34317',   '0.31129'),
('1500.0', '0.95064',   '0.81207',   '0.70880',   '0.62897',   '0.56528',   '0.51328'),
('2500.0', '1.53741',   '1.31845',   '1.15427',   '1.02659',   '0.92442',   '0.84071'),
('4000.0', '2.3598',    '2.0341',    '1.78789',   '1.59503',   '1.44000',   '1.31248');

SELECT * FROM stocks.helium;
```

Step 2. Use Php program to extract data from the MySQL table "helium", and to write text files:

```
<?php
//—http://localhost/new_sci2/to_retrieve_helium.php
//*******
// To log in
$db_hostname = 'localhost';
$db_database = 'stocks';
$db_username = 'root1';
$db_password = 'xxxxxxxx';
// To connect to MySQL
$db_server = mysql_connect($db_hostname, $db_username, $db_password);
if (!$db_server) die("Unable to connect to MySQL: " . mysql_error());
// To select a database
mysql_select_db($db_database,$db_server)
        or die("Unable to select database: " . mysql_error());
// To query a database
$query = "SELECT * FROM helium";
$result = mysql_query($query,$db_server);
```

```
if (!$result) die ("Database access failed: " . mysql_error());
$rows=mysql_num_rows($result);
$fpP=fopen("file_helium_P.txt","w");
$fpA=fopen("file_helium_A.txt","w");
$fpB=fopen("file_helium_B.txt","w");
$fpC=fopen("file_helium_C.txt","w");
$fpD=fopen("file_helium_D.txt","w");
$fpE=fopen("file_helium_E.txt","w");
$fpF=fopen("file_helium_F.txt","w");
// To fetch results one row at a time
for ($j = 0 ; $j < $rows ; ++$j)
{
        $row = mysql_fetch_row($result);
        echo 'id: ' .       $row[0] . '<br />';
        echo 'P: ' .        $row[1] . '<br />';
        fwrite($fpP,$row[1]);
        fwrite($fpP,"\n");
        echo 'A: ' .        $row[2] . '<br />';
        fwrite($fpA,$row[2]);
        fwrite($fpA,"\n");
        echo 'B: ' .                $row[3] . '<br />';
        fwrite($fpB,$row[3]);
        fwrite($fpB,"\n");
        echo 'C: ' .                $row[4] . '<br />';
        fwrite($fpC,$row[4]);
        fwrite($fpC,"\n");
        echo 'D: ' .                $row[5] . '<br />';
        fwrite($fpD,$row[5]);
        fwrite($fpD,"\n");
        echo 'E: ' .                $row[6] . '<br />';
        fwrite($fpE,$row[6]);
        fwrite($fpE,"\n");
        echo 'F: ' .                $row[7] . '<br /><br />';
        fwrite($fpF,$row[7]);
        fwrite($fpF,"\n");
}
// To close the database connection
mysql_close($db_server);
?>
```

Step 3: Use Matlab and Python to plot the graphs:

Matlab program

```
% curve_plot_helium
clear; help curve_plot_helium;
%
fidP=fopen('file_helium_P.txt','r');
P=fscanf(fidP,'%g',[1 inf]);
P=P';
np=size(P)
fclose(fidP);

fidA=fopen('file_helium_A.txt','r');
a=fscanf(fidA,'%g',[1 inf]);
a=a';
fclose(fidA);

fidB=fopen('file_helium_B.txt','r');
b=fscanf(fidB,'%g',[1 inf]);
b=b';
fclose(fidB);

fidC=fopen('file_helium_C.txt','r');
c=fscanf(fidC,'%g',[1 inf]);
c=c';
fclose(fidC);

fidD=fopen('file_helium_D.txt','r');
d=fscanf(fidD,'%g',[1 inf]);
d=d';
fclose(fidD);

fidE=fopen('file_helium_E.txt','r');
e=fscanf(fidE,'%g',[1 inf]);
e=e';
fclose(fidE);

fidF=fopen('file_helium_F.txt','r');
f=fscanf(fidF,'%g',[1 inf]);
f=f';
fclose(fidF);
```

```
T=100:100:600;
T=T';

DA=[a(1) b(1) c(1) d(1) e(1) f(1)]';
DB=[a(2) b(2) c(2) d(2) e(2) f(2)]';
DC=[a(3) b(3) c(3) d(3) e(3) f(3)]';
DD=[a(4) b(4) c(4) d(4) e(4) f(4)]';
DE=[a(5) b(5) c(5) d(5) e(5) f(5)]';
DF=[a(6) b(6) c(6) d(6) e(6) f(6)]';
DG=[a(7) b(7) c(7) d(7) e(7) f(7)]';
DH=[a(8) b(8) c(8) d(8) e(8) f(8)]';
DI=[a(9) b(9) c(9) d(9) e(9) f(9)]';

plot(P,a,'m-',P,b,'c-',P,c,'r-',P,d,'g-',P,e,'b-',P,f,'k-');
title('Helium Densities vs. Pressures at Various Temperatures');
xlabel('Pressure(psia)');
ylabel('Density(lb/ft^3)');
text(1000,0.7,'100^oF');
text(1500,0.85,'200^oF');
text(2200,1.1,'300^oF');
text(2700,1.2,'400^oF');
text(3300,1.3,'500^oF');
text(3600,1.1,'600^oF');
grid on;
pause;
plot(T,DA,'m-',T,DB,'c-',T,DC,'r-',T,DD,'g-',T,DE,'b-',T,DF,'k-',T,DG,'m--',T,DH,'c--',T,DI,'r--');
title('Helium Densities vs. Temperatures at Various Pressures');
xlabel('Temperature(^oF)');
ylabel('Density(lb/ft^3)');
text(200,2,'4000 psi');
text(200,1.3,'2500 psi');
text(200,0.7,'1500 psi');
text(300,0.4,'900 psi');
text(400,0.25,'600 psi');
text(200,0.25,'400 psi');
text(300,0.1,'150 psi');
grid on;
```

The results are displayed in Appendix 14.3B.

The Python program:

```
from scitools.std import * # for curve plotting
from numpy import *

infile=open('file_helium_P.txt','r')
P=[]
for line in infile:
   P.append(float(line))
infile.close()

infile=open('file_helium_A.txt','r')
a=[]
for line in infile:
   a.append(float(line))
infile.close()

infile=open('file_helium_B.txt','r')
b=[]
for line in infile:
   b.append(float(line))
infile.close()

infile=open('file_helium_C.txt','r')
c=[]
for line in infile:
   c.append(float(line))
infile.close()

infile=open('file_helium_D.txt','r')
d=[]
for line in infile:
   d.append(float(line))
infile.close()

infile=open('file_helium_E.txt','r')
e=[]
for line in infile:
   e.append(float(line))
infile.close()
```

```
infile=open('file_helium_F.txt','r')
f=[]
for line in infile:
   f.append(float(line))
infile.close()

T=linspace(100,600,6)

DA=[a[0], b[0], c[0], d[0], e[0], f[0]]
DB=[a[1], b[1], c[1], d[1], e[1], f[1]]
DC=[a[2], b[2], c[2], d[2], e[2], f[2]]
DD=[a[3], b[3], c[3], d[3], e[3], f[3]]
DE=[a[4], b[4], c[4], d[4], e[4], f[4]]
DF=[a[5], b[5], c[5], d[5], e[5], f[5]]
DG=[a[6], b[6], c[6], d[6], e[6], f[6]]
DH=[a[7], b[7], c[7], d[7], e[7], f[7]]
DI=[a[8], b[8], c[8], d[8], e[8], f[8]]

plot(P,a,'m-',P,b,'c-',P,c,'r-',P,d,'g-',P,e,'b-',P,f,'k-')
title('Helium Densities vs. Pressures at Various Temperatures')
xlabel('Pressure(psia)')
ylabel('Density(lb/ft**3)')
#legend('magenta=100F,cyan=200F,red=300F,green=400F,blue=500F,black=600F')
hardcopy('density_vs_pressure.png')
show()
figure() #new figure
plot(T,DA,'m-',T,DB,'c-',T,DC,'r-',T,DD,'g-',T,DE,'b-',T,DF,'k-',T,DG,'m--',T,DH,'c--',T,DI,'r--')
title('Helium Densities vs. Temperatures at Various Pressures')
xlabel('Temperature(F)')
ylabel('Density(lb/ft**3)')
#legend('red dash=4000psi,cyan dash=2500psi,magenta dash=1500psi,
#solid black=900psi,solid blue=600psi,solid green=400psi,solid red=150psi')
hardcopy('density_vs_temperature.png')
show()
```

The results are shown in Appendix 14.3C.

Appendix 14.3D shows the details of Gnuplot input and output.

14.4 Steam Table Plots

In this section, we shall extract data from an XML file, "steamTable.xml", created with Php program in Section 9.3, as input to Matlab and Python to plot functional relationships between temperature, pressure, specific volume, specific internal energy of saturated steam. The original data were based on a reference book, "Steam Tables by Joseph H. Keenan et al". Certainly there is no need to use XML to run scientific programs, because the input data can be simply extract directly from the reference book. But XML represents a portable, convenient way to transmit digital data through the internet. XML is popular in commercial programming. However, it has not been widely used in scientific programming. We shall think of XML as an additional tool for scientific programming as well.

The XML file is shown in Appendix 9.3. For convenience, it is also given below:


```
<response>

<Steam_table>

<temperature>
<t>450</t>
<p>422.1</p>
<vf>0.019433</vf>
<vg>1.1011</vg>
<uf>428.6</uf>
<ug>1119.5</ug>
</temperature>

<temperature>
<t>475</t>
<p>539.3</p>
<vf>0.019901</vf>
<vg>0.8594</vg>
<uf>456.6</uf>
<ug>1119.2</ug>
</temperature>
```

<temperature>
<t>500</t>
<p>680.0</p>
<vf>0.02043</vf>
<vg>0.6761</vg>
<uf>485.1</uf>
<ug>1117.4</ug>
</temperature>

<temperature>
<t>525</t>
<p>847.1</p>
<vf>0.02104</vf>
<vg>0.5350</vg>
<uf>514.5</uf>
<ug>1113.9</ug>
</temperature>

<temperature>
<t>550</t>
<p>1044.0</p>
<vf>0.02175</vf>
<vg>0.4249</vg>
<uf>544.9</uf>
<ug>1108.6</ug>
</temperature>

<temperature>
<t>575</t>
<p>1274.0</p>
<vf>0.02259</vf>
<vg>0.3378</vg>
<uf>576.5</uf>
<ug>1100.8</ug>
</temperature>

<temperature>
<t>600</t>
<p>1541.0</p>
<vf>0.02363</vf>
<vg>0.2677</vg>

```
<uf>609.9</uf>
<ug>1090.0</ug>
</temperature>

<temperature>
<t>625</t>
<p>1849.7</p>
<vf>0.02494</vf>
<vg>0.2103</vg>
<uf>645.7</uf>
<ug>1075.1</ug>
</temperature>

<temperature>
<t>650</t>
<p>2205.0</p>
<vf>0.02673</vf>
<vg>0.16206</vg>
<uf>685.0</uf>
<ug>1053.7</ug>
</temperature>

<temperature>
<t>675</t>
<p>2616.0</p>
<vf>0.02951</vf>
<vg>0.11952</vg>
<uf>731.0</uf>
<ug>1020.3</ug>
</temperature>

<temperature>
<t>700</t>
<p>3090.0</p>
<vf>0.03666</vf>
<vg>0.07438</vg>
<uf>801.7</uf>
<ug>947.7</ug>
</temperature>
</Steam_table>
</response>
```

The Php program to extract data from the XML file is:

```
<?php
// ...http://localhost/new_sci2/steamTable_xml_dump2.php
$theData = simplexml_load_file("steamTable.xml");

$fp1=fopen("file_t.txt","w");
$fp2=fopen("file_p.txt","w");
$fp3=fopen("file_vf.txt","w");
$fp4=fopen("file_vg.txt","w");
$fp5=fopen("file_uf.txt","w");
$fp6=fopen("file_ug.txt","w");

foreach($theData->Steam_table->temperature as $theTemperature){

$t=$theTemperature->t;
$p=$theTemperature->p;
$vf=$theTemperature->vf;
$vg=$theTemperature->vg;
$uf=$theTemperature->uf;
$ug=$theTemperature->ug;

fwrite($fp1,$t." ");
fwrite($fp2,$p." ");
fwrite($fp3,$vf." ");
fwrite($fp4,$vg." ");
fwrite($fp5,$uf." ");
fwrite($fp6,$ug." ");

}

fclose($fp1);
fclose($fp2);
fclose($fp3);
fclose($fp4);
fclose($fp5);
fclose($fp6);

echo "Task completed";

?>
```

The Php program writes six text files which are then used as input files to the Matlab and Python programs:

The Matlab program is:

```
% Steam_Table
clear; help Steam_Table;
fid1=fopen('file_t.txt','r');
fid2=fopen('file_p.txt','r');
fid3=fopen('file_vf.txt','r');
fid4=fopen('file_vg.txt','r');
fid5=fopen('file_uf.txt','r');
fid6=fopen('file_ug.txt','r');

t=fscanf(fid1,'%g',[1 inf]);
p=fscanf(fid2,'%g',[1 inf]);
vf=fscanf(fid3,'%g',[1 inf]);
vg=fscanf(fid4,'%g',[1 inf]);
uf=fscanf(fid5,'%g',[1 inf]);
ug=fscanf(fid6,'%g',[1 inf]);

t=t';
p=p';
vf=vf';
vg=vg';
uf=uf';
ug=ug';

% n=size(t)

fclose(fid1);
fclose(fid2);
fclose(fid3);
fclose(fid4);
fclose(fid5);
fclose(fid6);

plot(t,p,'r-');
title('Saturation Pressure vs. Temperature');
xlabel('Temperature(degree F)');
ylabel('Pressure(psia)');
```

```
grid on;
pause;

semilogy(t,vf,'b-',t,vg,'g-');
title('Specific Volume vs. Temperature');
xlabel('Temperature(degree F)');
ylabel('Spec Vol (Ft3/lb) Blue-fluid Green=vapor');
grid on;
pause;

plot(t,uf,'b-',t,ug,'g-');
title('Specific Internal Energy vs. Temperature');
xlabel('Temperature(degree F)');
ylabel('Spec Int Energy (Btu/lb) Blue-fluid Green=vapor');
grid on;
```

The corresponding Python program is:

```
from scitools.std import * # for curve plotting
from numpy import *

infile=open('file_p.txt','r')
line=infile.readline()
words=line.split()
p=[0,0,0,0,0,0,0,0,0,0,0]
for i in range(len(p)):
   p[i]=float(words[i])
infile.close()

infile=open('file_t.txt','r')
line=infile.readline()
words=line.split()
t=[0,0,0,0,0,0,0,0,0,0,0]
for i in range(len(t)):
   t[i]=float(words[i])
infile.close()

infile=open('file_vg.txt','r')
line=infile.readline()
words=line.split()
vg=[0,0,0,0,0,0,0,0,0,0,0]
```

```
for i in range(len(vg)):
   vg[i]=float(words[i])
infile.close()

infile=open('file_vf.txt','r')
line=infile.readline()
words=line.split()
vf=[0,0,0,0,0,0,0,0,0,0,0,0]
for i in range(len(vf)):
   vf[i]=float(words[i])
infile.close()

infile=open('file_ug.txt','r')
line=infile.readline()
words=line.split()
ug=[0,0,0,0,0,0,0,0,0,0,0,0]
for i in range(len(ug)):
   ug[i]=float(words[i])
infile.close()

infile=open('file_uf.txt','r')
line=infile.readline()
words=line.split()
uf=[0,0,0,0,0,0,0,0,0,0,0,0]
for i in range(len(uf)):
   uf[i]=float(words[i])
infile.close()

plot(t,p,'r-')
title('Saturation Pressure vs. Temperature')
xlabel('Temperature(degree F)')
ylabel('Pressure(psia)')
grid()
hardcopy('steam_table_plot1.png')

semilogy(t,vf,'b-',t,vg,'g-')
title('Specific Volume vs. Temperature')
xlabel('Temperature(degree F)')
ylabel('Spec Vol (Ft3/lb) Blue-fluid Green=vapor')
grid()
hardcopy('steam_table_plot2.png')
```

```
plot(t,uf,'b-',t,ug,'g-')
title('Specific Internal Energy vs. Temperature')
xlabel('Temperature(degree F)')
ylabel('Spec Int Energy (Btu/lb) Blue-fluid Green=vapor')
grid()
hardcopy('steam_table_plot3.png')
```

The Matlab plots are shown in Appendix 14.4A; the Python plots are in Appendix 14.4B. The computer files are in computer_files_14.4.

14.5 Heat conduction equation.

The following one dimensional heat conduction equation is solved with both Matlab and Python:

$$\frac{\partial T}{\partial t} = \alpha \frac{\partial^2 T}{\partial x^2}$$

We shall consider the case of a quartz slab, 2 cm thick, initially at uniform temperature of 400 K, suddenly immerged into an environment such that the slab surface temperature is kept at 293 K. To take advantage of the symmetry, only half of the slab thickness is modeled, with X=0 at the insulated center plane, where the temperature gradient is zero. The half slab of 0.01 meter thickness is divided into 9 equal thickness slices, so that there are 10 nodal points across the half thickness. For Matlab analysis, the node at the center plane is node #1; the node at the right surface is node #10 (N=10). Nodes #2,3,4,...,9 are internal nodes. The approach here is to use finite difference approximation to represent the second partial derivative with respect to spatial variable X, then to convert the partial differential equation into a set of coupled ordinary differential equations with "t" (time) as the only independent variable. The set of coupled ordinary differential equations can then be solved by Runge Kutta method. Matlab has built-in functions ODE23 and ODE45 for that. The set of coupled ordinary differential equations is:

```
dT1/dt = a*(T2 -2*T1 +T0) =2*a*(T2-T1)    because T0=T2 by symmetry
dT2/dt = a*(T3 -2*T2 +T1)
dT3/dt = a* (T4 -2*T3 +T2)
...etc.
dT9/dt= a*(T10-2*T9+T8)
```

T10/dt=a*(T11-2*T10+T9) = a*(Ts-2*T10+T9) because T11=Ts =293 K, the surface temperature.

In the above equations, a=(alpha)/(h**2), where h=L/(N-1); L=0.01 meter; N=10; alpha = thermal diffusivity of quartz =1.4e-6 M**2/sec.

Note that for Python, which uses 0 as the first number in counts, not 1, the above equations have to be adjusted accordingly. (Also, to use "range" in Python, for example, range(n) will count 1,2,3,...(n-1). The last one "n" is not included.)

The Matlab scripts named "heat_slab.m" and "heat.m" are as follows:

```
% heat_slab
clear; help heat_slab;
global a Ts N;
%
t0=0;
tf=120.0;  % time in seconds.
tspan=t0:(tf-t0)/120:tf;
%
L=0.01;  % slab thickness=0.01 meter.
N=10;   % consider 10 equidistant points.
h=L/(N-1);  % space mesh size.
alpha=1.4e-6; % diffusivity of quartz in m^2/sec.
a=alpha/(h^2);  % 'a' has a unit of sec^-1.
Ts=293.0;  % outer surface temperature, assumed constant.
%
% initial condition
%
y0=zeros(1,N);
Tin=400.0;
for j=1:N
y0(1,j)=Tin;
end
%
%T=zeros(N);
[t,s]=ode23('heat',tspan,y0);
nt=size(t);
T=zeros(N,nt);
```

```
for i=1:N
for j=1:nt
T(i,j)=s(j,i);  % Temperature of each spatial node, in deg K.
end
end
%
X=0:h:L;  % spatial nodes.
X=X';
%
for j=1:nt
fprintf('%7.2f %7.2f %7.2f %7.2f %7.2f\n',T(1,j),T(2,j),T(3,j),T(4,j),T(5,j));
end
disp('  ');
for j=1:nt
fprintf('%7.2f %7.2f %7.2f %7.2f %7.2f\n',T(6,j),T(7,j),T(8,j),T(9,j),T(10,j));
end
%
plot(X,T(:,6),'r-',X,T(:,31),'b-',X,T(:,61),'k-',X,T(:,91),'m-',X,T(:,121),'g-');
title('Heat Conduction Across a Quartz Slab');
xlabel('Distance from the center plane (m)');
ylabel('Temperature (^oK)');
text(0.0015,385,'Red=5 sec');
text(0.0015,380,'Blue=30 sec');
text(0.0015,375,'Black=60 sec');
text(0.0015,370,'Magenta=90 sec');
text(0.0015,365,'Green=120 sec');
grid on

function ydot=heat(t,y)
global a Ts N;
%
ydot(1)=2.0*a*(y(2)-y(1));
for i=2:(N-1)
ydot(i)=a*(y(i+1)-2*y(i)+y(i-1));
end
ydot(N)=a*(Ts-2*y(N)+y(N-1));
ydot=ydot(:);
```

The Python script "heat_slab_2.py" is:

```
from numpy import linspace
from scipy.integrate import odeint
from scitools.std import *

# Define the initial conditions
inic = array([400.0,400.0,400.0,400.0,400.0,400.0,400.0,400.0,400.0,400.0])

# Times to evaluate the ODEs. 121 times from 0 to 120 sec (inclusive).
t = linspace(0.0,120.0,121)

#
L=0.01  # slab thickness=0.01 meter.
N=10   # consider 10 equidistant points.
h=L/(N-1)  # space mesh size.
alpha=1.4e-6  # diffusivity of quartz in m**2/sec.
a=alpha/(h**2)  # 'a' has a unit of sec**-1.
Ts=293.0  # outer surface temperature, assumed constant.
#
ydot=[0.0,0.0,0.0,0.0,0.0,0.0,0.0,0.0,0.0,0.0]
# The derivative function.
def f(y,time):
   ydot[0]=2.0*a*(y[1]-y[0])
   for i in range(1,N-1):
      ydot[i]=a*(y[i+1]-2*y[i]+y[i-1])
   ydot[N-1]=a*(Ts-2*y[N-1]+y[N-2])
   return array([ydot[0],ydot[1],ydot[2],ydot[3],ydot[4],ydot[5],ydot[6],ydot[7],ydot[
8],ydot[9]])
#
# Compute the ODE
res = odeint(f, inic, t)
#
for i in range(121):
   print '%7.2f %7.2f %7.2f %7.2f %7.2f' %(res[i][0],res[i][1],res[i][2],res[i][3],res[i][4])
print ' '
for i in range(121):
   print '%7.2f %7.2f %7.2f %7.2f %7.2f' %(res[i][5],res[i][6],res[i][7],res[i][8],res[i][9])
```

```
X=[0.0,h,2.0*h,3.0*h,4.0*h,5.0*h,6.0*h,7.0*h,8.0*h,9.0*h]
plot(X,res[5,:],'r-',X,res[30,:],'b-',X,res[60,:],'k-',X,res[90,:],'m-',X,res[120,:],'g-')
title('Heat Conduction Across a Quartz Slab')
xlabel('Distance from the center plane (m)')
ylabel('Temperature (deg K)')
legend('red 5s','blue 30s','black 60s','magenta 90s','green 120s')
show()
hardcopy('heat_quartz_python.png')
```

The result is shown in Appendix 14.5. The Matlab and Python scripts are included in the computer _files_14.5.

14.6 Waves on a string.

We shall consider the one-dimensional wave equation:

$$\frac{\partial^2 u}{\partial t^2} = c^2 \frac{\partial^2 u}{\partial x^2} + f(x,t)$$

where c is the wave speed; u is lateral displacement; f(x,t) is the external acceleration term on the string.

To convert this second order partial differential equation to a set of coupled ordinary differential equations, we shall imagine to divide the string into N equal segments (N=20). We shall assume that each segment has a length h (h=0.6 meter) so the entire length of the string is 12 meters. There are N+1=21 spatial nodes. For Matlab, we shall label the nodes as 1,2,...,N+1; for Python, the labels are 0,1,2,...N. We shall use Matlab's label in the following discussion. We shall consider the case that node 1 is fixed throughout the transient; node N+1 is subjected to external acceleration f(x,t)=A sin wt, where A=0.05 m/sec^2, w is the frequency in radian/sec. In the simulation, we want to choose w so that we shall observe three complete cycles of oscillation.

With the string represented by spatial nodes, the partial derivatives become derivative with respect to t only. Let X(:,1)=u(:); X(:,2)=du(:)/dt, where (:) represents the spatial nodes. Then for i=2,3,4,...N,

dX(i,1)/dt=X(i,2)
dX(i,2)/dt=(c/h)^2 *{ X(i+1,1)-2 X(i,1) +X(i-1,1) }

For i=1,
dX(1,1)/dt=X(1,2)
dX(1,2)/dt=(c/h)^2 *{ X(2,1)-2 X(1,1) }
For i=N+1,
dX(N+1,1)/dt=X(N+1,2)
dX(N+1,2)/dt=(c/h)^2 *{ A sin wt-2 X(N+1,1) +X(N,1) }
Now let
y(1)=X(1,1); y(2)=X(2,1); y(3)=X(3,1); ..., y(N+1)=X(N+1,1);
y(N+2)=X(1,2); y(N+3)=X(2,2); y(N+4)=X(3,2); ..., y(2 N+2)=X(N+1,2)
And so,
dy(1)/dt = X(1,2); dy(2)/dt = X(2,2); dy(3)/dt = X(3,2); ..., dy(N+1)/dt = X(N+1,2);
dy(N+2)/dt = dX(1,2)/dt = (c/h)^2 *{ X(2,1)-2 X(1,1) };
dy(N+3)/dt = dX(2,2)/dt = (c/h)^2 *{ X(3,1)-2 X(2,1) +X(1,1) };
dy(N+4)/dt = dX(3,2)/dt = (c/h)^2 *{ X(4,1)-2 X(3,1) +X(2,1) };
....
dy(2N+2)/dt = dX(N+1,2)/dt = (c/h)^2 *{ A sin wt-2 X(N+1,1) +X(N,1) }

The following are the implementations of the above scheme in Matlab and in Python:

The Matlab script is:

```
% wave_string
clear; help wave_string;
global c h N w A;
t0=0.0;
tf=12.0;  %time in seconds
tspan=t0:(tf-t0)/120.0:tf;
%
w=6*pi/tf;  % rad/sec
A=0.05; % amplitude (m)
h=0.6;  %spatial mesh size in meter
N=20; % number of spatial meshes
L=N*h; % length of the string in meter
c=3.0*L/tf; % speed of sound on the string in m/sec.
% Left end of the string is fixed.
%
% Initial condition
%
y0=zeros(1,2*N+2);
%
[t,s]=ode23('wave',tspan,y0);
```

```
nt=size(t);
u=zeros(N+1,nt);  % lateral displacements in meter
for i=1:N+1
for j=1:nt
u(i,j)=s(j,i);
end
end
%
X=0:h:L;  % spatial nodes.
X=X';
%
for j=1:nt
fprintf('%12.4e %12.4e %12.4e %12.4e %12.4fe\n',u(1,j),u(2,j),u(3,j),u(4,j),u(5,j));
end
disp('  ');
for j=1:nt
fprintf('%12.4e %12.4e %12.4e %12.4e %12.4e\n',u(6,j),u(7,j),u(8,j),u(9,j),u(10,j));
end
disp('  ');
for j=1:nt
fprintf('%12.4e %12.4e %12.4e %12.4e %12.4e\n',u(11,j),u(12,j),u(13,j),u(14,j),u(15,j));
end
disp('  ');
for j=1:nt
fprintf('%12.4e %12.4e %12.4e %12.4e %12.4e\n',u(16,j),u(17,j),u(18,j),u(19,j),u(20,j));
end
disp('  ');
for j=1:nt
fprintf('%12.4e\n',u(21,j));
end
%
plot(X,u(:,6),'r-',X,u(:,31),'b-',X,u(:,61),'k-',X,u(:,91),'m-',X,u(:,121),'g-');
title('Waves on a string fixed at left, sine wave on right');
xlabel('Distance (m)');
ylabel('Lateral displacement(m)');
text(2,0.055,'Red=0.5 sec');
text(2,0.05,'Blue=3 sec');
text(2,0.045,'Black=6 sec');
text(2,0.04,'Magenta=9 sec');
text(2,0.035,'Green=12 sec');
grid on;
```

```
function ydot=wave(t,y)
global c h N w A;
%
for i=1:N+1
ydot(i)=y(N+1+i);
end
%
ydot(N+2)=(c/h)^2*(y(2)-2*y(1));
for i=(N+3):(2*N+1)
ydot(i)=(c/h)^2*(y(i+1)-2*y(i)+y(i-1));
end
ydot(2*N+2)=(c/h)^2*(-2*y(2*N+2)+y(2*N+1)+A*sin(w*t));
ydot=ydot(:);
```

The Python script is:

```
from numpy import linspace
from scipy.integrate import odeint
from scitools.std import *
from math import *
tf=12.0   # time in seconds
# Times to evaluate the ODEs. 121 times from 0 to 12 sec (inclusive).
t = linspace(0.0,tf,121)
#
w=6*pi/tf   # rad/sec
A=0.05  # amplitude (m)
h=0.6   #spatial mesh size in meter
N=20  # number of spatial meshes
L=N*h  # length of the string in meter
c=3.0*L/tf  # speed of sound on the string in m/sec.
# Left end of the string is fixed.
#
# Define the initial conditions
inic =array([0.,0.,0.,0.,0.,0.,0.,0.,0.,0.,0.,0.,0.,0.,0.,0.,0.,0.,0.,0.,0.,0.,0.,0.,0.,0.,0.,0
.,0.,0.,0.,0.,0.,0.,0.,0.,0.,0.,0.,0.,0.])
#
ydot=[0.,0.,0.,0.,0.,0.,0.,0.,0.,0.,0.,0.,0.,0.,0.,0.,0.,0.,0.,0.,0.,0.,0.,0.,0.,0.,0.,0.,0.,0.
,0.,0.,0.,0.,0.,0.,0.,0.,0.,0.,0.,0.]
#
# The derivative function.
```

```
def f(y,time):
   ydot[0]=y[N+1]
   for i in range(1,N+1):
      ydot[i]=y[N+1+i]
   ydot[N+1]=(c/h)**2*(y[1]-2*y[0])
   for i in range(N+2,2*N+1):
      ydot[i]=(c/h)**2*(y[i+1]-2*y[i]+y[i-1])
   ydot[2*N+1]=(c/h)**2*(-2*y[2*N+1]+y[2*N]+A*sin(w*time))
   return array([ydot[0],ydot[1],ydot[2],ydot[3],ydot[4],ydot[5],ydot[6],ydot[7],ydot[8
],ydot[9],ydot[10],
                  ydot[11],ydot[12],ydot[13],ydot[14],ydot[15],ydot[16],ydot[17],ydot[
18],ydot[19],ydot[20],
                        ydot[21],ydot[22],ydot[23],ydot[24],ydot[25],ydot[26],ydot[
27],ydot[28],ydot[29],ydot[30],
                          ydot[31],ydot[32],ydot[33],ydot[34],ydot[35],ydot[36],yd
ot[37],ydot[38],ydot[39],ydot[40],ydot[41]])
#
# Compute the ODE
res = odeint(f, inic, t)
#
for i in range(121):
   print '%12.4e %12.4e %12.4e %12.4e %12.4e' %(res[i][0],res[i][1],res[i]
[2],res[i][3],res[i][4])
print ' '
for i in range(121):
   print '%12.4e %12.4e %12.4e %12.4e %12.4e' %(res[i][5],res[i][6],res[i]
[7],res[i][8],res[i][9])
print ' '
for i in range(121):
   print '%12.4e %12.4e %12.4e %12.4e %12.4e' %(res[i][10],res[i][11],res[i]
[12],res[i][13],res[i][14])
print ' '
for i in range(121):
   print '%12.4e %12.4e %12.4e %12.4e %12.4e' %(res[i][15],res[i][16],res[i]
[17],res[i][18],res[i][19])
print ' '
for i in range(121):
   print '%12.4e' %(res[i][20])
#
X=[0.0,h,2.0*h,3.0*h,4.0*h,5.0*h,6.0*h,7.0*h,8.0*h,9.0*h,10.0*h,11.0*h,12.0*h,13.
0*h,14.0*h,15.0*h,16.0*h,17.0*h,18.0*h,19.0*h,20.0*h]
u=zeros((21,121))
```

```
for i in range(0,N+1):
    for j in range(0,121):
        u[i][j]=res[j][i]
plot(X,u[:,5],'r-',X,u[:,30],'b-',X,u[:,60],'k-',X,u[:,90],'m-',X,u[:,120],'g-')
title('Waves on a string, fixed on left end, sine wave on right')
xlabel('Distance (m)')
ylabel('Lateral diaplacement (m)')
legend('red 0.5s','blue 3s','black 6s','magenta 9s','green 12s')
show()
hardcopy('wave_on_string_python.png')
```

The results are shown in Appendix 14.6. The Matlab and Python scripts are included in the computer_files_14.6.

14.7 Electric field due to line source.

We want calculate the magnitude of electric field from a line charge λ =1 C/m at a perpendicular distance z meters from its mid-point. The line source has a length 2L, where L=1 meter. This is just an exercise of evaluating the definite integral

$$E = \frac{1}{4\pi\varepsilon_o}\int_{-L}^{L}\frac{\lambda z dx}{\left(x^2 + z^2\right)^{\frac{3}{2}}}$$

using the function "quad" of Matlab and Python. The Matlab script is very straight forward. The important point to pay attention is that in the script, the term x.^2 has to be used rather than x^2 because x is not a square matrix. Also the integrand becomes singular at z=0. The Matlab script is "electric_field_2.m" with function "integrand1.m". We shall use $k = \frac{1}{4\pi\varepsilon_o}$.

```
% electric_field_2
clear; help electric_field_2;
global zz;
k=8.99e9;% Newton meter^2/coulomb^2
lam=1.0; % coulomb/meter
L=1.0; % meter
z=1.0:0.1:5.0; % meter
z=z';
```

```
n=size(z);
E=zeros(n); % magnitude of electric field volt/m
for i=1:n
zz=z(i);
E(i)=lam*k*z(i)*quad('integrand1',-L,L);
end


fid=fopen('E_field_matlab.txt','w');
for i=1:n
fprintf(fid,'%g %g\r\n',z(i),E(i));
end
fclose(fid);
semilogy(z,E,'r-');
xlabel('Distance (meter) perpendicular to the line');
ylabel('Magnitude of electric field (volt/m)');
title('Demonstration of integration using quad');
text(2,6e10,'1 coulomb/m; 2 m long,');
text(2,4e10,'Distance measured from mid point of the line.')
grid on;
function fun=integrand1(x)
global zz;
fun=(x.^2+zz^2).^(-1.5);
```

Besides plotting out the graph of electric field, it also writes a text file of E vs. z. (E_field_matlab.txt).

The Python script is "test_integrate14.py":

```
from scipy.integrate import quad
from pylab import *
k=8.99e9 # Newton meter^2/coulomb^2
lam=1.0 # coulomb/meter
L=1.0 # meter
def intgrnd2(x,z):
return lam*k*(x**2+z**2)**(-1.5)
def intgrl2(m): # make the parameter a variable
return quad(intgrnd2, -L, L, args=(m))
vintgrl2=vectorize(intgrl2)
```

```
zlist=linspace(1.0,5.0,50) #50 points between 1.0 and 5.0
results, errs =vintgrl2(zlist)
outfile = open('E_field.txt','w')
for i in range(len(zlist)):
outfile.write('%15.4e %15.4e' % (zlist[i],results[i]*zlist[i]))
outfile.write('\n')
outfile.close()
```

In Python, it is necessary to include the parameter z to be an additional variable. Since z (or zlist) is a list, an intermediate step of vectorization is needed. Note that the vectorized function vintgrl2 has a different name from its original "intgrl2". Finally, it also writes an output text file "E_field.txt" using "outfile.write".

Finally, the following Matlab program "electric_field_comp.m" is to compare the results of Matlab, Python and the analytical solution of the problem.

```
% electric_field_comp
clear; help electric_field_comp;
fid=fopen('E_field.txt','r');
A=fscanf(fid,'%g %g',[2 inf]);
fclose(fid)
A=A';
[m,n]=size(A);
z=zeros(m);
E=zeros(m);
for i=1:m
z(i)=A(i,1);
E(i)=A(i,2);
end
fid=fopen('E_field_matlab.txt','r');
B=fscanf(fid,'%g %g',[2 inf]);
fclose(fid)
B=B';
[m,n]=size(B);
zm=zeros(m);
Em=zeros(m);
for i=1:m
zm(i)=B(i,1);
Em(i)=B(i,2);
end
```

```
k=8.99e9;% Newton meter^2/coulomb^2
lam=1.0; % coulomb/meter
L=1.0;  % meter

za=zeros(m);
Ea=zeros(m);
for i=1:m
za(i)=zm(i);
Ea(i)=(2.0*k*lam*L/za(i))/sqrt(L^2+za(i)^2);  %Analytical Solution
end
semilogy(z,E,'r-',zm,Em,'b-',za,Ea,'k-');
xlabel('Distance (meter) perpendicular to the line');
ylabel('Magnitude of electric field (volt/m)');
title('Demonstration of integration using quad');
text(1.5,6e10,'1 coulomb/m; 2 m long,');
text(1.5,4e10,'Distance measured from mid point of the line.');
text(1.5,2e10,'Red=Python,Blue=Matlab,Black=Analytical');
grid on;
```

The scripts of this section are included in the computer_files_14.7. The result is shown in Appendix 14.7.

14.8 Plot of stock market data

We shall perform the following tasks:

(1) Obtain stock market data from an open source database which is in text format.
(2) Convert the text database into a MySQL database table using Php.
(3) Selecting data from the MySQL database table and converting them into input data for Matlab and Python for plotting, using Php.
(4) Make the plots using Matlab and Python.

To obtain the stock market data, we can go to http://finance.yahoo.com/. We have chosen General Electric historical monthly stock prices from January 2, 2000 to July 17, 2011. After downloading the data to a spreadsheet, the result was saved as a comma-separated text file called "table_wordpad.txt" as shown below:

```
Date,Open,High,Low,Close,Volume,Adj Close
2011-07-01,18.86,19.45,18.29,18.41,52463100,18.41
```

2011-06-01,19.47,19.60,17.97,18.86,53953900,18.86
2011-05-02,20.70,20.71,18.97,19.64,45910500,19.48
2011-04-01,20.14,20.85,19.51,20.45,56260900,20.28
2011-03-01,21.12,21.17,18.60,20.05,63914200,19.89
2011-02-01,20.38,21.65,20.08,20.92,52895600,20.75
2011-01-03,18.49,20.74,18.12,20.14,76413100,19.84
2010-12-01,16.03,18.49,16.03,18.29,57131500,18.02
2010-11-01,16.09,16.86,15.63,15.83,55387200,15.47
2010-10-01,16.40,17.49,15.88,16.02,64676100,15.66
2010-09-01,14.73,16.70,14.60,16.25,60450700,15.88
2010-08-02,16.32,16.54,14.25,14.48,60617900,14.05
2010-07-01,14.33,16.57,13.75,16.12,75597900,15.64
2010-06-01,16.24,16.51,14.27,14.42,83717300,13.99
2010-05-03,18.97,19.34,15.15,16.35,106550400,15.76
2010-04-01,18.27,19.70,18.18,18.86,82505100,18.18
2010-03-01,16.10,18.94,15.83,18.20,93006300,17.55
2010-02-01,16.20,17.03,15.25,16.06,77313200,15.48
2010-01-04,15.22,16.92,15.15,16.08,88647000,15.41
2009-12-01,16.27,16.49,15.13,15.13,62454500,14.50
2009-11-02,14.30,16.25,14.15,16.02,80429200,15.25
2009-10-01,16.31,16.87,14.15,14.26,103007100,13.57
2009-09-01,13.74,17.52,13.03,16.42,132466400,15.63
2009-08-03,13.65,14.88,13.16,13.90,86516200,13.15
2009-07-01,11.76,13.45,10.50,13.40,100768400,12.68
2009-06-01,13.82,13.99,11.25,11.72,87259400,11.09
2009-05-01,12.74,14.55,12.22,13.48,104569000,12.65
2009-04-01,9.91,12.81,9.80,12.65,133547800,11.87
2009-03-02,8.29,11.35,5.87,10.11,277426300,9.49
2009-02-02,12.03,12.90,8.40,8.51,194928800,7.99
2009-01-02,16.51,17.24,11.87,12.13,117846700,11.06
2008-12-01,16.36,19.30,15.35,16.20,98683700,14.77
2008-11-03,19.78,21.04,12.58,17.17,134841700,15.36
2008-10-01,24.00,25.75,17.27,19.51,164650600,17.45
2008-09-02,28.54,29.28,22.16,25.50,105769100,22.81
2008-08-01,28.43,30.39,27.76,28.10,43604700,24.80
2008-07-01,26.42,29.89,25.60,28.29,69943000,24.97
2008-06-02,30.75,31.14,26.15,26.69,75216900,23.56
2008-05-01,32.80,33.62,30.21,30.72,52851400,26.82
2008-04-01,37.36,38.52,31.55,32.70,64485500,28.55
2008-03-03,33.34,37.74,31.65,37.01,59927700,32.31
2008-02-01,35.59,36.30,33.09,33.14,44926300,28.93
2008-01-02,37.10,37.45,32.92,35.36,55123800,30.59

2007-12-03,38.20,38.20,36.07,37.07,42936400,32.07
2007-11-01,40.89,40.98,36.52,38.29,45181800,32.84
2007-10-01,41.28,42.15,39.40,41.16,32919400,35.31
2007-09-04,38.84,42.07,38.45,41.40,37426500,35.51
2007-08-01,38.60,40.46,36.20,38.87,46947200,33.12
2007-07-02,38.42,40.98,37.73,38.76,43667100,33.02
2007-06-01,37.68,39.77,36.65,38.28,43860200,32.62
2007-05-01,36.82,37.81,36.45,37.58,31562900,31.79
2007-04-02,35.36,37.24,34.55,36.86,41666000,31.18
2007-03-01,34.61,36.00,33.90,35.36,37497700,29.91
2007-02-01,36.18,36.50,34.50,34.91,34598700,29.53
2007-01-03,37.41,38.28,35.76,36.05,34343900,30.26
2006-12-01,35.38,38.49,34.96,37.21,33604700,31.23
2006-11-01,35.20,36.28,34.62,35.28,23114100,29.39
2006-10-02,35.40,36.48,34.92,35.11,26500400,29.25
2006-09-01,34.18,35.65,33.76,35.30,24034200,29.41
2006-08-01,32.65,34.44,32.20,34.06,18494400,28.17
2006-07-03,33.10,33.62,32.06,32.69,24910500,27.04
2006-06-01,34.30,34.92,32.78,32.96,27849600,27.26
2006-05-01,34.64,35.24,33.70,34.26,24209600,28.13
2006-04-03,34.79,34.99,33.07,34.59,26428700,28.40
2006-03-01,32.97,35.00,32.58,34.78,26519300,28.56
2006-02-01,32.66,33.75,32.21,32.87,26951100,26.99
2006-01-03,35.10,35.63,32.63,32.75,34947000,26.69
2005-12-01,35.85,36.26,34.95,35.05,22568500,28.56
2005-11-01,33.97,36.34,33.51,35.72,22225800,28.90
2005-10-03,33.60,34.50,32.67,33.91,23636600,27.44
2005-09-01,33.43,34.58,33.00,33.67,22843400,27.25
2005-08-01,34.57,34.62,32.85,33.61,19156900,27.02
2005-07-01,34.85,35.78,33.93,34.50,22692600,27.73
2005-06-01,36.48,37.13,34.15,34.65,24312400,27.85
2005-05-02,36.08,37.34,35.56,36.48,17054700,29.15
2005-04-01,36.18,36.60,35.02,36.20,21540700,28.92
2005-03-01,35.27,36.48,35.06,36.06,18737000,28.81
2005-02-01,36.00,36.61,35.05,35.20,17348000,28.12
2005-01-03,36.71,36.89,34.95,36.13,19883000,28.69
2004-12-01,35.36,37.75,35.27,36.50,18800400,28.98
2004-11-01,34.10,36.86,33.81,35.36,18420700,27.91
2004-10-01,33.70,34.40,32.65,34.12,16090400,26.93
2004-09-01,32.79,34.53,32.62,33.58,18122500,26.50
2004-08-02,32.65,33.35,31.42,32.79,15559200,25.73
2004-07-01,32.40,33.62,31.50,33.25,22230200,26.09

```
2004-06-01,31.00,33.49,30.82,32.40,28805300,25.42
2004-05-03,30.12,31.47,29.55,31.12,20702700,24.27
2004-04-01,30.42,31.85,29.80,29.95,32068200,23.36
2004-03-01,32.69,33.48,28.88,30.52,40261200,23.80
2004-02-02,33.69,33.99,32.35,32.52,18725500,25.36
2004-01-02,31.00,34.57,30.92,33.63,23093800,26.07
2003-12-01,29.20,31.29,28.78,30.98,20243900,24.02
2003-11-03,29.05,29.95,27.37,28.67,22067400,22.08
2003-10-01,29.81,31.30,28.00,29.01,21493200,22.34
2003-09-02,29.75,32.42,29.31,29.81,21533800,22.96
2003-08-01,28.20,30.39,27.18,29.57,16648400,22.63
2003-07-01,28.48,29.50,26.90,28.44,22288900,21.77
2003-06-02,29.42,31.66,28.53,28.68,20550900,21.95
2003-05-01,29.45,29.45,27.35,28.70,19460600,21.82
2003-04-01,25.55,29.78,25.50,29.45,21207800,22.39
2003-03-03,24.20,28.00,23.16,25.50,26107100,19.39
2003-02-03,23.35,24.20,21.30,24.05,23505800,18.29
2003-01-02,24.65,26.26,22.45,23.14,23240300,17.46
2002-12-02,27.98,27.98,24.10,24.35,20521100,18.37
2002-11-01,25.28,27.40,23.20,27.12,28840700,20.31
2002-10-01,24.75,27.21,21.40,25.25,34091600,18.91
2002-09-03,29.50,29.70,23.51,24.65,31835500,18.46
2002-08-01,32.10,32.98,28.27,30.15,26539000,22.42
2002-07-01,29.06,32.20,23.02,32.20,39648900,23.94
2002-06-03,31.14,31.40,27.42,29.05,29971600,21.60
2002-05-01,31.75,33.45,30.40,31.14,23783100,23.01
2002-04-01,37.05,37.80,30.15,31.55,31131400,23.31
2002-03-01,39.10,41.84,36.83,37.40,25796800,27.63
2002-02-01,36.90,39.65,34.72,38.50,25112400,28.45
2002-01-02,40.30,41.34,34.49,37.15,24680100,27.32
2001-12-03,38.40,41.39,36.21,40.08,23080100,29.48
2001-11-01,36.25,41.78,36.05,38.50,16974400,28.19
2001-10-01,37.30,39.49,36.04,36.41,19544800,26.66
2001-09-04,40.90,42.17,28.50,37.20,42638800,27.24
2001-08-01,43.00,43.53,39.84,40.90,16831300,29.81
2001-07-02,48.92,50.20,42.99,43.50,20559200,31.71
2001-06-01,48.99,52.61,46.26,49.00,29526100,35.60
2001-05-01,48.05,53.55,47.51,49.00,16915500,35.60
2001-04-02,41.52,50.01,39.04,48.53,22337500,35.26
2001-03-01,45.50,46.60,36.42,41.86,30658800,30.41
2001-02-01,46.50,48.45,45.02,46.50,20455600,33.66
2001-01-02,46.75,48.75,42.63,45.98,24345500,33.29
```

2000-12-01,50.88,56.19,47.19,47.94,17054700,34.71
2000-11-01,54.75,55.25,47.94,49.56,14524300,35.76
2000-10-02,58.00,59.94,49.00,54.81,20282300,39.55
2000-09-01,59.25,60.06,55.00,57.81,12225400,41.71
2000-08-01,51.94,60.50,51.19,58.63,11558800,42.21
2000-07-03,52.50,54.75,49.50,51.69,13163300,37.21
2000-06-01,52.06,54.00,47.94,53.00,12857500,38.05
2000-05-01,159.00,162.00,48.75,52.63,14351800,37.79
2000-04-03,155.25,167.94,143.06,157.25,21992900,37.64
2000-03-01,133.50,164.88,126.25,155.63,25483700,37.25
2000-02-01,134.25,143.13,124.94,132.38,23404600,31.59
2000-01-03,153.00,154.94,133.06,134.00,22127500,31.98

To convert the comma-separated text file into a MySQL database table, we use the commands:

```
CREATE TABLE stocks.GE(id INT NOT NULL PRIMARY KEY AUTO_INCREMENT,
date VARCHAR(12) NOT NULL,
open FLOAT NOT NULL,
high FLOAT NOT NULL,
low FLOAT NOT NULL,
close FLOAT NOT NULL,
volume INT NOT NULL,
adj_close FLOAT NOT NULL);
```

```
INSERT INTO stocks.GE(date,open,high,low,close,volume,adj_close)VALUES
('2011-07-01',18.86,19.45,18.29,18.41,52463100,18.41),
('2011-06-01',19.47,19.60,17.97,18.86,53953900,18.86),
('2011-05-02',20.70,20.71,18.97,19.64,45910500,19.48),
('2011-04-01',20.14,20.85,19.51,20.45,56260900,20.28);
Etc.
```

The resulting MySQL database table "stock.GE" is shown in Appendix 14.8.

The following Php program (called "to_retrieve_column_1.php") has been used to extract the "date" and "adj close" values from the MySQL database table and output two text files "fpA.txt" and "fpB.txt"

```
<?php
//—http://localhost/new_sci2/to_retrieve_column_1.php
//*******
// To log in
$db_hostname = 'localhost';
$db_database = 'stocks';
$db_username = 'root1';
$db_password = 'xxxxxxxx';
// To connect to MySQL
$db_server = mysql_connect($db_hostname, $db_username, $db_password);
if (!$db_server) die("Unable to connect to MySQL: " . mysql_error());
// To select a database
mysql_select_db($db_database,$db_server)
        or die("Unable to select database: " . mysql_error());
// To query a database
$query = "SELECT * FROM GE";
$result = mysql_query($query,$db_server);
if (!$result) die ("Database access failed: " . mysql_error());
$rows=mysql_num_rows($result);
// To fetch results one row at a time
// To write the results to a file
$fpA=fopen("file_GE_A.txt","w");
$fpB=fopen("file_GE_B.txt","w");
for ($j = 0 ; $j < $rows ; ++$j)
{
        $row = mysql_fetch_row($result);
        echo 'id: ' .       $row[0] . '<br />';

        echo 'date: ' .     $row[1] . '<br />';
        fwrite($fpA,$row[1]);
        fwrite($fpA,"\n");
        echo 'open: ' .     $row[2] . '<br />';

        echo 'high: ' .             $row[3] . '<br />';

        echo 'low: ' .              $row[4] . '<br />';

        echo 'close: ' .            $row[5] . '<br />';

        echo 'volume: ' .           $row[6] . '<br />';

        echo 'adj_close: ' .                $row[7] . '<br /><br />';
```

```
            fwrite($fpB,$row[7]);
            fwrite($fpB,"\n");

}

fclose($fpA);
fclose($fpB);

// To close the database connection
mysql_close($db_server);
?>
```

The following Php program (called "to_cal_dates.php")has been used to convert the date format strings into number of days from a reference date:

```
<?php
//...http://localhost/new_sci2/to_cal_dates.php
//$now = time(); // or your date as well
$reference=strtotime("2011-07-01"); // usually the current date
$fpA_1=fopen("file_GE_A_1.txt","w");
$filename="file_GE_A.txt";
$fp=fopen($filename,"r")or die("Could not open $filename");
while(!feof($fp)){
   $line=fgets($fp,1024);
   if ($line==strtotime("0000-00-00")){
      break;
   }else{
   $previous = strtotime($line);
   $datediff = $reference - $previous; // some previous date before the reference
   echo floor($datediff/(60*60*24))."<br/>";
   fwrite($fpA_1,floor($datediff/(60*60*24)));
            fwrite($fpA_1,"\n");
            }
            }
?>
```

Then, finally, the Matlab ("GE_stock.m") and Python programs("GE_stock_py.py") for plotting the GE stock data are:

Matlab Program

```
% GE_stock
%
clear; help GE_stock;
fid1=fopen('file_GE_A_1.txt','r');
fid2=fopen('file_GE_B.txt','r');
A=fscanf(fid1,'%g',[1 inf]);
A=A';
B=fscanf(fid2,'%g',[1 inf]);
B=B';
fclose(fid1);
fclose(fid2);
[m,n]=size(A);
[mb,nb]=size(B);
x=zeros(m);
y=zeros(mb);
for i=1:m
x(i)=A(m-i+1);
end
for i=1:mb
y(i)=B(mb-i+1);
end
plot(x,y,'b-');
xlabel('Days from 2000-01-03');
ylabel('Adj. Close price USD');
title('GE Stock from 2000-01-03 to 2011-07-01');
grid on;
```

Python Program

```
from scitools.std import *
infile=open('file_GE_A_1.txt','r')
linesA=[]
for line in infile:
    linesA.append(float(line))
infile.close()
infile=open('file_GE_B.txt','r')
linesB=[]
for line in infile:
    linesB.append(float(line))
```

```
infile.close()
linesA.reverse()
linesB.reverse()

plot(linesA,linesB,'b-');
xlabel('Days from 2000-01-03');
ylabel('Adj. Close price USD');
title('GE Stock from 2000-01-03 to 2011-07-01');
hardcopy('GE_stock_plot.png')
```

In these Matlab and Python programs, the sequence of the data has been reversed. That is, from 2000-01-03 to 2011-07-01. The plots are shown in Appendix 14.8. All the computer files in this section have been included in computer_files 14.8.

14.9 Curve fitting example using global temperature anomaly data

Most of the scientific data used to input to a scientific program are in the form of simple text file format or in graphical plots. They are easy to read and understand by human, but usually not readily suitable as input to a scientific computer code. The graphical plots need to be digitalized with software, such as "GetData Graph Digitizer". Due to distortion of the graphical plot, adjustments of the data from the digitizer have to be made. The "Global Temperature Anomaly" data plots were digitalized this way but later a tabulated form of the data was also found, so the analysis in this section was based on the tabulated data from NASA. See http://en.wikipedia.org/wiki/Instrumental_temperature_record.

The tabulated data (NASA_temp_data.txt) is shown below:

```
1880   -0.28     *
1881   -0.21     *
1882   -0.26   -0.27
1883   -0.27   -0.27
1884   -0.32   -0.29
1885   -0.32   -0.31
1886   -0.29   -0.31
1887   -0.35   -0.28
1888   -0.27   -0.29
1889   -0.17   -0.29
1890   -0.39   -0.28
```

1891 -0.27 -0.30
1892 -0.32 -0.33
1893 -0.33 -0.30
1894 -0.33 -0.27
1895 -0.25 -0.23
1896 -0.14 -0.22
1897 -0.11 -0.18
1898 -0.26 -0.15
1899 -0.15 -0.15
1900 -0.08 -0.18
1901 -0.15 -0.19
1902 -0.24 -0.22
1903 -0.30 -0.26
1904 -0.34 -0.26
1905 -0.24 -0.29
1906 -0.19 -0.30
1907 -0.39 -0.30
1908 -0.33 -0.32
1909 -0.35 -0.35
1910 -0.33 -0.33
1911 -0.34 -0.33
1912 -0.32 -0.29
1913 -0.30 -0.24
1914 -0.15 -0.23
1915 -0.09 -0.25
1916 -0.30 -0.25
1917 -0.39 -0.26
1918 -0.33 -0.28
1919 -0.20 -0.25
1920 -0.19 -0.22
1921 -0.14 -0.20
1922 -0.26 -0.21
1923 -0.22 -0.20
1924 -0.22 -0.18
1925 -0.17 -0.16
1926 -0.02 -0.14
1927 -0.15 -0.15
1928 -0.13 -0.13
1929 -0.26 -0.13
1930 -0.08 -0.12
1931 -0.02 -0.13
1932 -0.08 -0.09

1933	-0.19	-0.10
1934	-0.07	-0.10
1935	-0.12	-0.07
1936	-0.05	-0.01
1937	0.07	0.00
1938	0.10	0.04
1939	0.01	0.06
1940	0.04	0.06
1941	0.10	0.05
1942	0.03	0.09
1943	0.09	0.09
1944	0.19	0.06
1945	0.06	0.06
1946	-0.05	0.03
1947	0.00	-0.02
1948	-0.04	-0.06
1949	-0.07	-0.06
1950	-0.16	-0.05
1951	-0.04	-0.02
1952	0.03	-0.03
1953	0.11	-0.02
1954	-0.10	-0.05
1955	-0.10	-0.04
1956	-0.17	-0.04
1957	0.08	-0.01
1958	0.08	0.01
1959	0.06	0.06
1960	-0.01	0.05
1961	0.07	0.05
1962	0.04	0.00
1963	0.08	-0.03
1964	-0.21	-0.05
1965	-0.11	-0.06
1966	-0.03	-0.08
1967	-0.01	-0.02
1968	-0.04	0.00
1969	0.08	-0.01
1970	0.03	-0.01
1971	-0.10	0.03
1972	0.00	0.00
1973	0.14	-0.02
1974	-0.08	-0.03

```
1975  -0.05   0.00
1976  -0.16  -0.03
1977   0.12   0.00
1978   0.01   0.05
1979   0.08   0.13
1980   0.19   0.12
1981   0.26   0.16
1982   0.04   0.16
1983   0.25   0.13
1984   0.09   0.11
1985   0.04   0.15
1986   0.12   0.17
1987   0.27   0.19
1988   0.31   0.25
1989   0.19   0.30
1990   0.36   0.27
1991   0.35   0.23
1992   0.13   0.24
1993   0.13   0.24
1994   0.23   0.23
1995   0.37   0.28
1996   0.29   0.37
1997   0.39   0.39
1998   0.56   0.38
1999   0.32   0.42
2000   0.33   0.45
2001   0.47   0.45
2002   0.56   0.48
2003   0.55   0.54
2004   0.48   0.55
2005   0.63   0.56
2006   0.55   0.53
2007   0.58   0.55
2008   0.44   0.55
2009   0.57     *
2010   0.63     *
```

The first column is the calendar year. The second column is the annual average temperature anomaly with reference to the average global temperature from 1951 to 1980, in degree C. The third column is the same but for the five-year average. The "*" means no data available. The third column was not used in the analysis. For Matlab analysis, the "*" symbols have to be replaced with actual numbers even though the third column was not used. The "*" was acceptable as is for Python analysis.

The Matlab program (to_plot_temp_anomaly_4.m) is as follows:

```
% to_plot_temp_anomaly_4
clear; help to_plot_temp_anomaly_4;
fid=fopen('NASA_temp_data.txt','r');
A=fscanf(fid,'%g %g',[3 inf]);
A=A';
fclose(fid);
[m,n]=size(A);
x=zeros(m);
y=zeros(m);
for i=1:m
x(i)=A(i,1);
y(i)=A(i,2);
end
%
p=polyfit(x,y,2);
fprintf('p= %12.4e %12.4e %12.4e\n',p(1),p(2),p(3));
xx=x(1):(x(m)-x(1))/200.0:x(m);
xx=xx';
mxx=size(xx);
yy=zeros(mxx);
for i=1:mxx
yy(i)=polyval(p,xx(i));
end
%
q=polyfit(x,y,3);
fprintf('q= %12.4e %12.4e %12.4e %12.4e\n',q(1),q(2),q(3),q(4));
xxx=x(1):(x(m)-x(1))/200.0:x(m);
xxx=xxx';
mxxx=size(xxx);
yyy=zeros(mxxx);
for i=1:mxxx
yyy(i)=polyval(q,xxx(i));
end
%
r=polyfit(x,y,4);
fprintf('r= %12.4e %12.4e %12.4e %12.4e %12.4e\n',r(1),r(2),r(3),r(4),r(5));
xxxx=x(1):(x(m)-x(1))/200.0:x(m);
```

```
xxxx=xxxx';
mxxxx=size(xxxx);
yyyy=zeros(mxxxx);
for i=1:mxxxx
yyyy(i)=polyval(r,xxxx(i));
end
%
s=polyfit(x,y,5);
fprintf('s= %12.4e %12.4e %12.4e %12.4e %12.4e %12.4e\n',s(1),s(2),s(3),s(4),s(5),s(6));
x5=x(1):(x(m)-x(1))/200.0:x(m);
x5=x5';
mx5=size(x5);
y5=zeros(mx5);
for i=1:mx5
y5(i)=polyval(s,x5(i));
end
%
fid=fopen('fitted_data_matlab.txt','w');
for i=1:mxx
fprintf(fid,'%g %g %g %g %g\n',xx(i),yy(i),yyy(i),yyyy(i),y5(i));
end
%
plot(x,y,'b*',xx,yy,'r-',xxx,yyy,'g-',xxxx,yyyy,'b-',x5,y5,'k-');
xlabel('Calendar Year');
ylabel('Temperature Anomaly(^oC)');
title('Global Temperature Anomaly');
axis([1880 2010 -0.5 0.6]);
grid on;
text(1890,0.5,'Blue * NASA data');
text(1890,0.45,'Red line = quadratic polynomial fit');
text(1890,0.4,'Green line= cubic polynomial fit');
text(1890,0.35,'Blue line= = 4th order polynomial fit');
text(1890,0.3,'Black line = 5th order polynomial fit');
```

The result is shown in Appendix 14-9A.

The Python program (to_plot_temp_anomaly_4A.py) is as follows:

```
from scitools.std import *
def extract_data(filename):
    infile = open(filename,'r')
```

```
    temprature={}
    i=0
    key={}
    for line in infile:
        words=line.split()
        year=float(words[0])
        temp=float(words[1])
        temperature[year]=temp
        key[i]=year
        i=i+1
    infile.close()
    return key,temperature
#
key={}
temperature={}
key,temperature=extract_data('NASA_temp_data.txt')

for i in range(len(key)):
    print '%g %g' % (key[i],temperature[key[i]])

x=zeros(len(key))
y=zeros(len(key))
for i in range(len(key)):
    x[i]=key[i]
    y[i]=temperature[key[i]]

#plot(x,y,'b*')

coeff2=polyfit(x,y,2)
p=poly1d(coeff2)
print p # print the polynomial expression
xx=linspace(x[0],x[len(x)-1],200)
yy=p(xx)
#plot(x,y,'b*',xx,yy,'r-')
#show()
coeff3=polyfit(x,y,3)
q=poly1d(coeff3)
print q # print the polynomial expression
xxx=linspace(x[0],x[len(x)-1],200)
yyy=q(xxx)
```

```
coeff4=polyfit(x,y,4)
r=poly1d(coeff4)
print r # print the polynomial expression
xxxx=linspace(x[0],x[len(x)-1],200)
yyyy=r(xxxx)

coeff5=polyfit(x,y,5)
s=poly1d(coeff5)
print s # print the polynomial expression
x5=linspace(x[0],x[len(x)-1],201)
y5=s(x5)
#
outfile=open('fitted_data_python.txt','w')
for i in range(len(xx)):
   outfile.write('%g %g %g %g %g' % (xx[i],yy[i],yyy[i],yyyy[i],y5[i]))
   outfile.write('\n')
outfile.close()
#
plot(x,y,'b+',xx,yy,'r-',xxx,yyy,'g-',xxxx,yyyy,'b-',x5,y5,'k-')
xlabel('Calendar Year')
ylabel('Temperature Anomaly(C)')
title('Global Temperature Anomaly')
legend('b+ NASA','r- 2nd','g- 3rd','b- 4th','k- 5th')
hardcopy('temp_anomaly_python.png')
show()
```

The result is as shown in Appendix 14-9B.

A Matlab program to compare the polynomial fits using Matlab with those using Python is given below:

```
% compare_matlab_python_4
clear; help compare_matlab_python_4;
%
fid=fopen('fitted_data_matlab.txt','r');
A=fscanf(fid,'%g %g %g %g %g',[5 inf]);
A=A';
fclose(fid);
fid1=fopen('fitted_data_python.txt','r');
```

```
B=fscanf(fid1,'%g %g %g %g %g',[5 inf]);
B=B';
fclose(fid1);
%
[mA,nA]=size(A);
[mB,nB]=size(B);
xm=zeros(mA);
ym2=zeros(mA);
ym3=zeros(mA);
ym4=zeros(mA);
ym5=zeros(mA);
xp=zeros(mB);
yp2=zeros(mB);
yp3=zeros(mB);
yp4=zeros(mB);
yp5=zeros(mB);
%
for i=1:mA
xm(i)=A(i,1);
ym2(i)=A(i,2);
ym3(i)=A(i,3);
ym4(i)=A(i,4);
ym5(i)=A(i,5);
end
for i=1:mB
xp(i)=B(i,1);
yp2(i)=B(i,2);
yp3(i)=B(i,3);
yp4(i)=B(i,4);
yp5(i)=B(i,5);
end
%
for i=1:mA
fprintf('%g %g %g %g %g\n',xm(i),ym2(i),ym3(i),ym4(i),ym5(i));
end
disp(' ');
pause;
for i=1:mB
fprintf('%g %g %g %g %g\n',xp(i),yp2(i),yp3(i),yp4(i),yp5(i));
end
%
pause;
```

```
plot(xm,ym2,'r-',xm,ym3,'g-',xm,ym4,'b-',xm,ym5,'k-');
xlabel('Calendar Year');
ylabel('Temperature Anomaly (C)');
title('Curve Fittings Using Matlab');
axis([1880 2010 -0.5 0.6]);
text(1900,0.5,'red=2nd order polynomial');
text(1900,0.4,'green=3rd order polynomial');
text(1900,0.3,'blue=4th order polynomial');
text(1900,0.2,'black=5th order polynomial');
text(1900,0.1,'solid line=Matlab');
text(1900,0.0,'dash line=Python');
grid on;
pause;
plot(xp,yp2,'r--',xp,yp3,'g--',xp,yp4,'b--',xp,yp5,'k--');
xlabel('Calendar Year');
ylabel('Temperature Anomaly (C)');
title('Curve Fittings Using Python');
axis([1880 2010 -0.5 0.6]);
text(1900,0.5,'red=2nd order polynomial');
text(1900,0.4,'green=3rd order polynomial');
text(1900,0.3,'blue=4th order polynomial');
text(1900,0.2,'black=5th order polynomial');
text(1900,0.1,'solid line=Matlab');
text(1900,0.0,'dash line=Python');
grid on;
pause;
plot(xm,ym2,'r-',xm,ym3,'g-',xm,ym4,'b-',xm,ym5,'k-',xp,yp2,'r-',xp,yp3,'g-',xp,yp4,'b-
',xp,yp5,'k-');
xlabel('Calendar Year');
ylabel('Temperature Anomaly (C)');
title('Comparison of Curve Fittings Using Matlab and Python');
axis([1880 2010 -0.5 0.6]);
text(1900,0.5,'red=2nd order polynomial');
text(1900,0.4,'green=3rd order polynomial');
text(1900,0.3,'blue=4th order polynomial');
text(1900,0.2,'black=5th order polynomial');
text(1900,0.1,'solid line=Matlab');
text(1900,0.0,'dash line=Python');
grid on;
```

The result of the comparison is shown in Appendix 14-9C.

There are a few observations:

(1) The results for quadratic polynomial fits are very different, but for higher order polynomial fits, the results appear to be similar.
(2) The fourth and the fifth order polynomial fits appear to be almost the same. The matrices used in the curve-fitting become ill-condition.
(3) We cannot use the coefficients of the polynomials as printed out from the computer output to generate the fitted curves because of round-off errors (due to the subtraction of large numbers such that the most significant portions of the numbers cancel out.)
(4) In curve-fitting with polynomials, in general, the magnitudes of the coefficients tend to increase as the order of the polynomials increases. However, with the example in this section, this rule is only partially true. Rather, the higher the order, the more scatter of the magnitude of the polynomials.

14.10 Boundary value problems

Boundary values problems of physics and engineering can be solved by computer with the traditional finite difference method. The conditions at the boundaries are always included in the numerical algorithm. This is true for one, two or three dimensional problems. For one-dimensional problems, there is an alternative method not to directly set up the finite difference equations. It is to use the "shooting" method, in which the one-dimensional boundary value problem is considered to be an initial value problem, using the Runge-Kutta formulas, and attempting to match the boundary condition on the other end. In Matlab, the function to do the "shooting" is called "bvp4c", which is available for Matlab versions 6 and higher. In Python, the corresponding function is "scikits-bvp_solver-0.3.0". Unfortunately, at the time of this writing, the "scikits_bvp_solver-0.3.0" is not available for Python 2.7.

In this section, we shall first solve a simple one-dimensional boundary value problem, neutron diffusion in a slab of water with constant uniform neutron source, and with zero neutron flux at the two boundaries. The problem can be solved analytically, but is solved first with finite difference method using Matlab and using Python. Then the problem is solved with "bvp4c" of Matlab., to compare with the results using finite difference method.

For the finite difference method, we shall consider a one-dimensional slab geometry with 50 equal segments of 1 cm each. (Width of slab=L). There are 51 nodal points labeled as 0,1,2,...,50. The equation to solve is:

$$-D\frac{d^2\phi}{dx^2}+\Sigma_a\phi(x)=S(x)$$

The finite difference equation is:

$$-D\left(\frac{\phi_{i+1}-2\phi_i+\phi_{i-1}}{\Delta^2}\right)+\Sigma_a\phi_i=S_i$$

where,

$$S_i \,\square\, S(x_i)$$

$$\square\,\square\,\frac{L}{N}$$

$$i\,\square\,1,2,3,\ldots$$

Therefore,

$$a_{i,i-1}\phi_{i-1}+a_{i,i}\phi_i+a_{i,i+1}\phi_{i+1}=S_i$$

$$i=1,2,\ldots,N-1$$

$$\phi_0=0$$

$$\phi_N=0$$

We can write the equation in matrix form:

$$A\Phi=S$$

where,

$$A=\begin{pmatrix} a_{1,1} & a_{1,2} & & & & \\ a_{2,1} & a_{2,2} & a_{2,3} & & & \\ & a_{3,2} & a_{3,3} & a_{3,4} & & \\ & & & & & \\ & & & & & \\ & & & & a_{N-1,N-2} & a_{N-1,N-1} \end{pmatrix}$$

$$\Phi = \begin{pmatrix} \phi_1 \\ \phi_2 \\ \\ \\ \\ \\ \phi_{N-1} \end{pmatrix}$$

$$S = \begin{pmatrix} S_1 \\ S_2 \\ \\ \\ \\ \\ S_{N-1} \end{pmatrix}$$

where,

$$a_{i,i} = \frac{2D}{\Delta^2} + \Sigma_a$$

$$i = 1, 2, ..., N-1$$

$$a_{i,i-1} = -\frac{D}{\Delta^2}$$

$$i = 2, 3, ..., N+1$$

$$a_{i,i+1} = -\frac{D}{\Delta^2}$$

$$i = 1, 2, ..., N$$

The above labeling for nodes is for Matlab. For Python, the integers are counted from 0 instead of 1:

We define:

$$B = \begin{pmatrix} b_{0,0} & b_{0,1} & & & & \\ b_{1,0} & b_{1,1} & b_{1,2} & & & \\ & b_{2,1} & b_{2,2} & b_{2,3} & & \\ & & & & & \\ & & & & & \\ & & & & b_{N-2,N-3} & b_{N-2,N-2} \end{pmatrix}$$

$$b_{0,0} = a_{1,1}$$

$$b_{0,1} = a_{1,2}$$

$$b_{i,i} = \frac{2D}{\Delta^2} + \Sigma_a$$

$$i = 0,1,...,N-2$$

$$b_{i,i-1} = -\frac{D}{\Delta^2}$$

$$i = 1,2,...,N-2$$

$$b_{i,i+1} = -\frac{D}{\Delta^2}$$

$$i = 0,1,...,N-3$$

Then, we have,

$$BF = Z$$

$$F = \begin{pmatrix} F_0 \\ F_1 \\ \\ \\ \\ F_{N-2} \end{pmatrix} = \begin{pmatrix} \phi_1 \\ \phi_2 \\ \\ \\ \\ \phi_{N-2} \end{pmatrix}$$

$$Z = \begin{pmatrix} Z_0 \\ Z_1 \\ \\ \\ \\ \\ Z_{N-2} \end{pmatrix} = \begin{pmatrix} S_1 \\ S_2 \\ \\ \\ \\ \\ S_{N-1} \end{pmatrix}$$

$$\phi_0 = 0$$
$$\phi_N = 0$$

We now set up the Matlab and the Python analyses for the case:

$$\Sigma_a = 0.022cm^{-1}$$
$$D = 0.18cm$$
$$S = 10^{10}\frac{n}{cm^3 \sec}$$
$$\phi --- \frac{n}{cm^2 \sec}$$

The Matlab script for the finite difference method is “neutron_diffusion.m”:

```
% neutron_diffusion
%
% slab geometry, water, constant source
% Part 1 - finite difference
%
N=50;  % number of meshes
del=1;  % mesh size in cm
D=0.18; % diffusion coefficient in cm
sig=0.022; % macroscopic cross section in cm^-1
% equation to solve  -D F" + sig F = S
% where F=neutron flux in neutrons/cm^2 per sec
% S=neutron source in neutrons/cm^3 per sec
%
S=zeros(N-1);
```

```
for i=1:N-1
S(i)=1.0e10;
end
xx=zeros(N-1);
F=zeros(N-1);  % interior nodes
F0=0; % flux at surface x=0 cm
FN=0; % flux at surface x=N*del=50 cm
A=zeros(N-1,N-1);
for i=2:N-1
A(i,i-1)=-D/(del^2);
end
for i=1:N-1
A(i,i)=2*D/(del^2)+sig;
end
for i=1:N-2
A(i,i+1)=-D/(del^2);
end
for i=1:N-1
xx(i)=i*del;
end
%
F=A\S;
phi=zeros(N+1); % neutron flux including end points
phi(1)=F0;
phi(N+1)=FN;
for i=2:N
phi(i)=F(i-1);
end
%
x=zeros(N+1);
x(N+1)=N*del;
for i=2:N
x(i)=xx(i-1);
end
%
plot(x,phi,'r-');
xlabel('x (cm)');
ylabel('neutron flux (n/cm^2 per sec)');
title('Neutron diffusion in water - finite difference');
text(15,3e11,'-D F" + sig F = S where');
text(15,2.5e11,'D=0.18,sig=0.022,S=1.0e10');
text(15,2e11,'with zero flux at x=0 and x=50');
```

```
%
for i=1:N+1
fprintf('%g %g\n',x(i),phi(i));
end
```

The Python script using finite difference method described above is "neutron_diffusion_py.py":

```
# neutron_diffusion_py
from numpy import *
from scitools.std import *
from numpy import matrix
from numpy import linalg
# slab geometry, water, constant source
# Part 1 -finite difference
#
N=50  # number of meshes
de=1  # mesh size in cm
D=0.18  # diffusion coefficient in cm
sig=0.022  # macroscopic cross section in cm**-1
# equation to solve  -D F" + sig F = S
# where F=neutron flux in neutrons/cm**2 per sec
# S=neutron source in neutrons/cm**3 per sec
#
Z=zeros(N-1)
for i in range(N-1):
   Z[i]=1.0e10

F=zeros(N-1)   # interior nodes
phi0=0   # flux at x=0 cm
phiN=0   # flux at x=N*de=50 cm
B=zeros([N-1,N-1])
for i in range(1,N-1):
   B[i][i-1]=-D/(de**2)
   print '%g %g' %(i,B[i][i-1])
for i in range(N-1):
   B[i][i]=2*D/(de**2)+sig
   print '%g %g' %(i,B[i][i])
for i in range(N-2):
   B[i][i+1]=-D/(de**2)
   print '%g %g' %(i,B[i][i+1])
```

```
F=linalg.solve(B,Z)  # Solve the linear equation system
phi=zeros(N+1)
phi[0]=phi0
phi[N]=phiN
for i in range(1,N):
   phi[i]=F[i-1]
#
x=zeros(N+1)
x[0]=0
x[N]=N
for i in range(1,N,1):
   x[i]=i
#
plot(x,phi,'r-')
xlabel('x (cm)')
ylabel('neutron flux (n/cm**2 per sec)')
title('Neutron diffusion in water-finite difference-Python')
legend('-D F" + sig F = S')
#
for i in range(0,N+1,1):
   print '%g %g' %(x[i],phi[i])
```

In order to use the “bvp4c” function to solve the above boundary value problem, we need to rewrite the second order ordinary differential equation for neutron diffusion as a set of two coupled first order differential equations in the same way as in ODE23 or ODE45, then just to plug into a more or less fixed format of Matlab script. There is little freedom to make changes from the fixed “format”, even the name of the functions. The initial guess of the solution in the statement “solinit” is important, because the boundary value problem can have no solution, one solution, or more than one solution, for a given pair of boundary conditions on both ends.

The first program “bvp4c_neutron.m” is for the full slab as in the finite difference programs above, in which, the neutron fluxes at both surfaces are zero. The second program “bvp4c_neutron_1.m” is for half of the slab taking advantage of symmetry, i.e., the boundary condition on one end is that the derivative of the neutron flux is zero. Note that we have to use completely new functions, “bvp5ode” instead of “bvp4ode”; “bp5bc” instead of “bvp4bc”in order to model the zero derivative of flux at one end of the slab. It will not be easy to extend this shooting method to two and three dimensional problems.

The Matlab programs are:

"bvp4c_neutron_diffusion.m" for full slab:

```
function bvp4
xlow=0;xhigh=50;
solinit=bvpinit(linspace(xlow,xhigh,51),[4.5e11 0]);
sol=bvp4c(@bvp4ode,@bvp4bc,solinit);
xint=linspace(xlow,xhigh);
Sxint=deval(sol,xint);
plot(xint,Sxint(1,:));
xlabel('x (cm)');
ylabel('neutron flux (n/cm^2 per sec)');
title('Neutron diffuion in water - using bvp4c');
%-----------------
function dydx=bvp4ode(x,y)
sig=0.022;
D=0.18;
S=1.0e10;
dydx=[y(2) sig*y(1)/D-S/D];
%-----------------
function res=bvp4bc(ya,yb)
res=[ya(1) yb(1)];
```

"bvp4c_neutron_diffusion_1.m" for half slab:

```
% bvp4c_neutron_1
%clear; %help bvp4c_neutron_1;
function bvp5
xlow=0;xhigh=25;
solinit=bvpinit(linspace(xlow,xhigh,26),[4.5e11 0]);
sol=bvp4c(@bvp5ode,@bvp5bc,solinit);
xint=linspace(xlow,xhigh);
Sxint=deval(sol,xint);
plot(xint,Sxint(1,:));
xlabel('x (cm)');
ylabel('neutron flux (n/cm^2 per sec)');
title('Neutron diffuion in water - using bvp4c');
%-----------------
function dydx=bvp5ode(x,y)
sig=0.022;
```

```
D=0.18;
S=1.0e10;
dydx=[y(2) sig*y(1)/D-S/D];
%-----------------
function res=bvp5bc(ya,yb)
res=[ya(2) yb(1)];
```

The Matlab and Python programs are included in the computer_files_14.10. the results of the analyses are shown in Appendix 14.10.

14.11 Particle in a box-Eigen value problem

This example is mathematically very similar to the example in Section 14.10. But this is an eigenvalue problem. We shall consider a particle in a rigid infinite potential well in one dimension. The following is the equation we want to solve subject to the boundary condition that the wave function vanishes at the boundaries.

$$-\frac{\hbar^2}{2m}\frac{d^2\psi}{dx^2} = E\psi$$

where

$$\hbar = \frac{h}{2\pi}$$

$$h = 6.63\times 10^{-34}\,joule\bullet\sec$$

$$m = 9.1\times 10^{-31}\,kg$$

We shall use finite difference method:

$$-\frac{\hbar^2}{2m}\frac{\psi_{i+1}-2\psi_i+\psi_{i-1}}{\Delta^2} = E\psi_i$$

where

$$\Delta = 0.02\times 10^{-10}\,meter$$

or

$$\left(\frac{-\hbar^2}{2m\Delta^2}\right)\psi_{i-1} + \left(\frac{\hbar^2}{m\Delta^2}\right)\psi_i + \left(\frac{-\hbar^2}{2m\Delta^2}\right)\psi_{i+1} = E\psi_i$$

$$i = 1, 2, \ldots, N-1$$

We have divided the width of the potential well (1 Angstrom) into 50 meshes, i.e., N=50. We re-write the above equation as:

$$a_{i,i-1}\psi_{i-1} + a_{i,i}\psi_i + a_{i,i+1}\psi_{i+1} = E\psi_i$$

$$for$$

$$i = 1, 2, ..., N-1$$

$$and$$

$$\psi_0 = 0$$

$$\psi_N = 0$$

where,

$$a_{i,i-1} = -\frac{\hbar^2}{2m\Delta^2}$$

$$for$$

$$i = 2, 3, ..., N-1$$

$$a_{i,i+1} = -\frac{\hbar^2}{2m\Delta^2}$$

$$for$$

$$i = 1, 2, ..., N-2$$

$$a_{i,i} = \frac{\hbar^2}{m\Delta^2}$$

$$for$$

$$i = 1, 2, ..., N-1$$

The above equations may be re-written in matrix form:

$$A\Psi = E\Psi$$

where

$$\Psi = \begin{pmatrix} \psi_1 \\ \psi_2 \\ \\ \\ \\ \\ \psi_{N-1} \end{pmatrix}$$

$$A = \begin{pmatrix} a_{1,1} & a_{1,2} & & & \\ a_{2,1} & a_{2,2} & a_{2,3} & & \\ & a_{3,2} & a_{3,3} & a_{3,4} & \\ & & & & \\ & & & & \\ & & & & a_{N-1,N-1} \end{pmatrix}$$

$$N = 50$$

The above matrix eigenvalue problem may be solved readily using the Matlab function "eig".

For Python which starts the counting from zero instead of from 1, we may re-write the above as

$$BF = EF$$

where

$$F = \begin{pmatrix} F_0 \\ F_1 \\ \\ \\ \\ \\ F_{N-2} \end{pmatrix} = \begin{pmatrix} \psi_1 \\ \psi_2 \\ \\ \\ \\ \\ \psi_{N-1} \end{pmatrix}$$

$$B = \begin{pmatrix} b_{0,0} & b_{0,1} & & & \\ b_{1,0} & b_{1,1} & b_{1,2} & & \\ & b_{2,1} & b_{2,2} & b_{2,3} & \\ & & & & \\ & & & & \\ & & & & b_{N-2,N-2} \end{pmatrix}$$

That is, the B matrix and the A matrix are the same, only the labeling are shifted. The Matlab program is shown below:

```
% particle_box
%
% Particle in a rigid 1-D box by
% finite difference
%
N=50;  % number of meshes
del=0.02e-10;  % mesh size in meter (N*del=1 Angstrom)
m=9.1e-31; % mass of the particle in kg
h=6.63e-34; % Planck's constant (joule sec)
hbar=h/(2*pi);
%
xx=zeros(N-1);
F=zeros(N-1);  % interior nodes
F0=0; % wave function at surface x=0 meter
FN=0; % wave function at surface x=N*del=1.0e-10 meter
```

```
A=zeros(N-1,N-1);
for i=2:N-1
A(i,i-1)=-hbar^2/(2*m*del^2);
end
for i=1:N-1
A(i,i)=hbar^2/(m*del^2);
end
for i=1:N-2
A(i,i+1)=-hbar^2/(2*m*del^2);
end
for i=1:N-1
xx(i)=i*del;
end
%
% To find the eigenvalues and eigen vectors
[V,D]=eig(A);
E=zeros(N-1);  % Energy in joules
EeV=zeros(N-1);  %Energy in eV
for i=1:N-1
E(i)=D(i,i);
EeV(i)=E(i)/1.602e-19;
end
% Sort the eigenvalues from small to large
[YEeV,I]=sort(EeV);
%
fprintf('The eigenvalues (in eV) are  ');
disp(' ');
for i=1:N-1
fprintf('%g %g\n',i,YEeV(i));
end
%
%____________________________________________________________
disp(' ');
%
fprintf('The eigenvector corresponding to eigenvalue %g\n',YEeV(1));
disp (' ');
for i=1:N-1
F(i)=V(i,I(1));
end
%
phi=zeros(N+1); % wave function including end points
phi(1)=F0;
```

```
phi(N+1)=FN;
for i=2:N
phi(i)=F(i-1);
end
%
x=zeros(N+1);
x(N+1)=N*del;
for i=2:N
x(i)=xx(i-1);
end
%
plot(x,phi,'r-');
xlabel('x (meter)');
ylabel('wave function');
title(['Eigenvector corresponding to eigenvalue=' num2str(YEeV(1)) ' eV']);
%axis([0 1.0e-10 -1 1]);
%
for i=1:N+1
fprintf('%g %g\n',x(i),phi(i));
end
%______________________________________________________________________
pause;
%______________________________________________________________________
disp(' ');
%
fprintf('The eigenvector corresponding to eigenvalue %g\n',YEeV(2));
disp (' ');
for i=1:N-1
F(i)=V(i,I(2));
end
%
phi=zeros(N+1); % wave function including end points
phi(1)=F0;
phi(N+1)=FN;
for i=2:N
phi(i)=F(i-1);
end
%
x=zeros(N+1);
x(N+1)=N*del;
for i=2:N
x(i)=xx(i-1);
```

```
end
%
plot(x,phi,'r-');
xlabel('x (meter)');
ylabel('wave function');
title(['Eigenvector corresponding to eigenvalue=' num2str(YEeV(2)) ' eV']);
%axis([0 1.0e-10 -1 1]);
%
for i=1:N+1
fprintf('%g %g\n',x(i),phi(i));
end
%________________________________________________________________
pause;
%________________________________________________________________
disp(' ');
%
fprintf('The eigenvector corresponding to eigenvalue %g\n',YEeV(3));
disp (' ');
for i=1:N-1
F(i)=V(i,I(3));
end
%
phi=zeros(N+1); % wave function including end points
phi(1)=F0;
phi(N+1)=FN;
for i=2:N
phi(i)=F(i-1);
end
%
x=zeros(N+1);
x(N+1)=N*del;
for i=2:N
x(i)=xx(i-1);
end
%
plot(x,phi,'r-');
xlabel('x (meter)');
ylabel('wave function');
title(['Eigenvector corresponding to eigenvalue=' num2str(YEeV(3)) ' eV']);
%axis([0 1.0e-10 -1 1]);
%
for i=1:N+1
```

```
fprintf('%g %g\n',x(i),phi(i));
end
%_______________________________________________________________
pause;
%_______________________________________________________________
disp(' ');
%
fprintf('The eigenvector corresponding to eigenvalue %g\n',YEeV(4));
disp (' ');
for i=1:N-1
F(i)=V(i,I(4));
end
%
phi=zeros(N+1); % wave function including end points
phi(1)=F0;
phi(N+1)=FN;
for i=2:N
phi(i)=F(i-1);
end
%
x=zeros(N+1);
x(N+1)=N*del;
for i=2:N
x(i)=xx(i-1);
end
%
plot(x,phi,'r-');
xlabel('x (meter)');
ylabel('wave function');
title(['Eigenvector corresponding to eigenvalue=' num2str(YEeV(4)) ' eV']);
%axis([0 1.0e-10 -1 1]);
%
for i=1:N+1
fprintf('%g %g\n',x(i),phi(i));
end
```

The corresponding Python program is shown below:

```
# particle_box_py
from numpy import *
```

```
from scitools.std import *
from numpy import matrix
from numpy import linalg
# Particle in a box by
# finite difference
#
N=50  # number of meshes
de=0.02e-10  # mesh size in meter (N*de=1 Angstrom)
m=9.1e-31  # mass of the particle in kg
h=6.63e-34  # Planck's constant (joule sec)
hbar=h/(2*pi)
#
F=zeros(N-1)   # interior nodes
phi0=0   # flux at x=0 meter
phiN=0   # flux at x=N*de=1.0e-10 meter
B=zeros([N-1,N-1])
for i in range(1,N-1):
   B[i][i-1]=-hbar**2/(2*m*de**2)
   print '%g %g' %(i,B[i][i-1])
for i in range(N-1):
   B[i][i]=hbar**2/(m*de**2)
   print '%g %g' %(i,B[i][i])
for i in range(N-2):
   B[i][i+1]=-hbar**2/(2*m*de**2)
   print '%g %g' %(i,B[i][i+1])
#
D,V=linalg.eig(B)
E=zeros(N-1)   # Energy in joules
EeV=zeros(N-1)  # energy in eV
print 'The eigenvalues EeV(i) are'
print '  '
for i in range(N-1):
   E[i]=D[i]
   EeV[i]=E[i]/1.602e-19
   print '%g %g' % (i,EeV[i])
#
# Sort the eigenvalues from small to large
YEeV=sorted(EeV)
print ' '
print 'The sorted eigenvalues YEeV[j] are'
print ' '
for j in range(N-1):
```

```
   print '%g %g' % (j,YEeV[j])
#________________________________________________________________
E_selected=YEeV[0]
for i in range(N-1):
   if E_selected==EeV[i]:
      J=i
#
phi=zeros(N+1)
phi[0]=phi0
phi[N]=phiN
for i in range(1,N):
   phi[i]=V[i-1][J]
#
x=zeros(N+1)
x[0]=0
x[N]=N*de
for i in range(1,N,1):
   x[i]=i*de
#
plot(x,phi,'r-')
xlabel('x (meter)')
ylabel('wave function')
title('Eigenvector corresponding to first energy level')
hardcopy('1st_level_python.png')
#
for i in range(0,N+1,1):
   print '%g %g' %(x[i],phi[i])
#________________________________________________________________
E_selected=YEeV[1]
for i in range(N-1):
   if E_selected==EeV[i]:
      J=i
#
phi=zeros(N+1)
phi[0]=phi0
phi[N]=phiN
for i in range(1,N):
   phi[i]=V[i-1][J]
#
x=zeros(N+1)
x[0]=0
x[N]=N*de
```

```
for i in range(1,N,1):
   x[i]=i*de
#
plot(x,phi,'r-')
xlabel('x (meter)')
ylabel('wave function')
title('Eigenvector corresponding to 2nd energy level')
hardcopy('2nd_level_python.png')
#
for i in range(0,N+1,1):
   print '%g %g' %(x[i],phi[i])
#______________________________________________________________
E_selected=YEeV[2]
for i in range(N-1):
   if E_selected==EeV[i]:
      J=i
#
phi=zeros(N+1)
phi[0]=phi0
phi[N]=phiN
for i in range(1,N):
   phi[i]=V[i-1][J]
#
x=zeros(N+1)
x[0]=0
x[N]=N*de
for i in range(1,N,1):
   x[i]=i*de
#
plot(x,phi,'r-')
xlabel('x (meter)')
ylabel('wave function')
title('Eigenvector corresponding to third energy level')
hardcopy('3rd_level_python.png')
#
for i in range(0,N+1,1):
   print '%g %g' %(x[i],phi[i])
#______________________________________________________________
E_selected=YEeV[3]
for i in range(N-1):
   if E_selected==EeV[i]:
      J=i
```

```
#
phi=zeros(N+1)
phi[0]=phi0
phi[N]=phiN
for i in range(1,N):
   phi[i]=V[i-1][J]
#
x=zeros(N+1)
x[0]=0
x[N]=N*de
for i in range(1,N,1):
   x[i]=i*de
#
plot(x,phi,'r-')
xlabel('x (meter)')
ylabel('wave function')
title('Eigenvector corresponding to fourth energy level')
hardcopy('4th_level_python.png')
#
for i in range(0,N+1,1):
   print '%g %g' %(x[i],phi[i])
#________________________________________________________________
```

The results of the first four lowest eigenvalues and their corresponding eigenvectors are shown in Appendix 14.11. The computer files are in computer_files_14.11.

Note that Matlab and Python may produce eigenvectors of opposite signs. This is acceptable because in an eigenvalue problem, the eigenvector appears on both sides of the equation, so both are acceptable. After all, the wave function is not a physically measurable quantity in quantum mechanics, only the square of the wave function has the interpretation as the probability density. So wave functions of either sign will predict the same probability density. In the computer program of Python, some plot statements may have been intentionally changed in order to make the plots look the same as those from Matlab. In reality, the sign of the wave function does not matter. Either sign is acceptable.

Appendices

APPENDIX 5.1

id	element	atomic_number	symbol	atomic_weight	absorption	scattering
1	Hydrogen	1	H	1.008	0.33	80
2	Deuterium	1	D	2.015	0.00046	5.4
3	Helium	2	He	4.003	0	0.8
4	Lithium	3	Li	6.94	70	1.4
5	Berylium	4	Be	9.01	0.009	7
6	Boron	5	B	10.82	750	4
7	Carbon	6	C	12.01	0.0045	4.8
8	Nitrogen	7	N	14.008	1.8	10
9	Oxygen	8	O	16	0.0002	4.2
10	Fluorine	9	F	19	0.009	4.1
11	Neon	10	Ne	20.18	2.8	2.4
12	Sodium	11	Na	22.997	0.5	4
13	Magnesium	12	Mg	24.32	0.06	3.6
14	Aluminum	13	Al	26.98	0.21	1.4
15	Silicon	14	Si	28.09	0.13	1.7
16	Phosphorus	15	P	30.98	0.2	5
17	Sulfur	16	S	32.07	0.49	1.1
18	Chlorine	17	Cl	35.457	31.6	0
19	Argon	18	Ar	39.94	0.62	1.5
20	Potassium	19	K	39.1	2	1.5
21	Scandium	21	Sc	45.1	23	0
22	Titanium	22	Ti	47.9	5.6	4
23	Vanadium	23	V	50.95	5.1	5
24	Chromium	24	Cr	52.01	2.9	3
25	Calcium	20	Ca	40.08	0.43	9
26	Manganese	25	Mn	54.93	13	2.3
27	Iron	26	Fe	55.85	2.4	11
28	Cobalt	27	Co	58.94	37	5
29	Nickel	28	Ni	58.69	4.5	17.5
30	Copper	29	Cu	63.54	3.6	7.2
31	Zinc	30	Zn	65.38	1.1	3.6
32	Lanthanum	57	La	138.92	8.9	18
33	Yttrium	39	Y	88.92	1.4	3
34	Neodymium	60	Nd	144.27	44	25
35	Cerium	58	Ce	140.13	0.7	9
36	Praseodymium	59	Pr	140.92	11	0
37						

	Gadolinium	64	Gd	156.9	44000	0
38	Dysprosium	66	Dy	162.46	1100	0
39	Erbium	68	Er	167.2	166	0
40	Samarium	62	Sm	150.43	6500	0
41	Ytterbium	70	Yb	173	36	12
42	Holmium	67	Ho	164.94	64	0
43	Terbium	65	Tb	159.2	44	0
44	Thulium	69	Tm	169.4	118	0
45	Lutetium	71	Lu	174.99	108	0
46	Promethium	61	Pm	145	0	0
47	Uranium	92	U	238.07	7.42	8.2
48	Thorium	90	Th	232.12	7	13
49	Europium	63	Eu	152	4500	0
50	Zirconium	40	Zr	91.22	0.18	8
51	Molybdenum	42	Mo	95.95	2.4	7

id	element	uses	oxide_price_USD_per_kg	atomic_number
1	Lanthanum	Batteries,Catalyst,Lasers	40	57
2	Yttrium	Lasers,Superconductors	50	39
3	Neodymium	Lasers,Magnets,Computers	60	60
4	Cerium	Catalyst,Fuel addititive,Optical polish	65	58
5	Praseodymium	Lasers,Magnets,Lighting,Alloys	75	59
6	Gadolinium	Lasers,Magnets,Computers,X-rays	150	64
7	Dysprosium	Lasers,Magnets,Cars	160	66
8	Erbium	Lasers,Alloys,Photography	165	68
9	Samarium	Lasers,Magnets,Neutron absorption	350	62
10	Ytterbium	Lasers,Alloys,Gamma rays	450	70
11	Holmium	Lasers,Magnets,Optics	750	67
12	Terbium	Lasers,Phosphors,Lighting	850	65
13	Europium	Lasers,Phosphors,Lighting	1200	63
14	Thulium	Lasers,X-rays	2500	69
15	Lutetium	Catalyst,Medicine	3500	71
16	Scandium	Lasers,Lighting,Aerospace	14000	21
17	Promethium	Nuclear batteries	No price	61

Appendix 5.2

Displaying a MySQL table Page 1 of 2

id	element	atomic_number	symbol	atomic_weight	absorption	scattering
1	Hydrogen	1	H	1.008	0.33	80
2	Deuterium	1	D	2.015	0.00046	5.4
3	Helium	2	He	4.003	0	0.8
4	Lithium	3	Li	6.94	70	1.4
5	Berylium	4	Be	9.01	0.009	7
6	Boron	5	B	10.82	750	4
7	Carbon	6	C	12.01	0.0045	4.8
8	Nitrogen	7	N	14.008	1.8	10
9	Oxygen	8	O	16	0.0002	4.2
10	Fluorine	9	F	19	0.009	4.1
11	Neon	10	Ne	20.18	2.8	2.4
12	Sodium	11	Na	22.997	0.5	4
13	Magnesium	12	Mg	24.32	0.06	3.6
14	Aluminum	13	Al	26.98	0.21	1.4
15	Silicon	14	Si	28.09	0.13	1.7
16	Phosphorus	15	P	30.98	0.2	5
17	Sulfur	16	S	32.07	0.49	1.1
18	Chlorine	17	Cl	35.457	31.6	0
19	Argon	18	Ar	39.94	0.62	1.5
20	Potassium	19	K	39.1	2	1.5
21	Scandium	21	Sc	45.1	23	0
22	Titanium	22	Ti	47.9	5.6	4
23	Vanadium	23	V	50.95	5.1	5
24	Chromium	24	Cr	52.01	2.9	3
25	Calcium	20	Ca	40.08	0.43	9
26	Manganese	25	Mn	54.93	13	2.3
27	Iron	26	Fe	55.85	2.4	11
28	Cobalt	27	Co	58.94	37	5
29	Nickel	28	Ni	58.69	4.5	17.5
30	Copper	29	Cu	63.54	3.6	7.2
31	Zinc	30	Zn	65.38	1.1	3.6
32	Lanthanum	57	La	138.92	8.9	18
33	Yttrium	39	Y	88.92	1.4	3
34	Neodymium	60	Nd	144.27	44	25
35	Cerium	58	Ce	140.13	0.7	9
36	Praseodymium	59	Pr	140.92	11	0
37						

http://localhost/new_sci2/to_print_basicdata1.php 8/9/2011

	Gadolinium	64	Gd	156.9	44000	0
38	Dysprosium	66	Dy	162.46	1100	0
39	Erbium	68	Er	167.2	166	0
40	Samarium	62	Sm	150.43	6500	0
41	Ytterbium	70	Yb	173	36	12
42	Holmium	67	Ho	164.94	64	0
43	Terbium	65	Tb	159.2	44	0
44	Thulium	69	Tm	169.4	118	0
45	Lutetium	71	Lu	174.99	108	0
46	Promethium	61	Pm	145	0	0
47	Uranium	92	U	238.07	7.42	8.2
48	Thorium	90	Th	232.12	7	13
49	Europium	63	Eu	152	4500	0
50	Zirconium	40	Zr	91.22	0.18	8
51	Molybdenum	42	Mo	95.95	2.4	7

id	date	open	high	low	close	volume	adj_close
1	2011-07-01	18.86	19.45	18.29	18.41	52463100	18.41
2	2011-06-01	19.47	19.6	17.97	18.86	53953900	18.86
3	2011-05-02	20.7	20.71	18.97	19.64	45910500	19.48
4	2011-04-01	20.14	20.85	19.51	20.45	56260900	20.28
5	2011-03-01	21.12	21.17	18.6	20.05	63914200	19.89
6	2011-02-01	20.38	21.65	20.08	20.92	52895600	20.75
7	2011-01-03	18.49	20.74	18.12	20.14	76413100	19.84
8	2010-12-01	16.03	18.49	16.03	18.29	57131500	18.02
9	2010-11-01	16.09	16.86	15.63	15.83	55387200	15.47
10	2010-10-01	16.4	17.49	15.88	16.02	64676100	15.66
11	2010-09-01	14.73	16.7	14.6	16.25	60450700	15.88
12	2010-08-02	16.32	16.54	14.25	14.48	60617900	14.05
13	2010-07-01	14.33	16.57	13.75	16.12	75597900	15.64
14	2010-06-01	16.24	16.51	14.27	14.42	83717300	13.99
15	2010-05-03	18.97	19.34	15.15	16.35	106550400	15.76
16	2010-04-01	18.27	19.7	18.18	18.86	82505100	18.18
17	2010-03-01	16.1	18.94	15.83	18.2	93006300	17.55
18	2010-02-01	16.2	17.03	15.25	16.06	77313200	15.48
19	2010-01-04	15.22	16.92	15.15	16.08	88647000	15.41
20	2009-12-01	16.27	16.49	15.13	15.13	62454500	14.5
21	2009-11-02	14.3	16.25	14.15	16.02	80429200	15.25
22	2009-10-01	16.31	16.87	14.15	14.26	103007100	13.57
23	2009-09-01	13.74	17.52	13.03	16.42	132466400	15.63
24	2009-08-03	13.65	14.88	13.16	13.9	86516200	13.15
25	2009-07-01	11.76	13.45	10.5	13.4	100768400	12.68
26	2009-06-01	13.82	13.99	11.25	11.72	87259400	11.09
27	2009-05-01	12.74	14.55	12.22	13.48	104569000	12.65
28	2009-04-01	9.91	12.81	9.8	12.65	133547800	11.87
29	2009-03-02	8.29	11.35	5.87	10.11	277426300	9.49
30	2009-02-02	12.03	12.9	8.4	8.51	194928800	7.99
31	2009-01-02	16.51	17.24	11.87	12.13	117846700	11.06
32	2008-12-01	16.36	19.3	15.35	16.2	98683700	14.77
33	2008-11-03	19.78	21.04	12.58	17.17	134841700	15.36
34	2008-10-01	24	25.75	17.27	19.51	164650600	17.45
35	2008-09-02	28.54	29.28	22.16	25.5	105769100	22.81

36	2008-08-01	28.43	30.39	27.76	28.1	43604700	24.8
37	2008-07-01	26.42	29.89	25.6	28.29	69943000	24.97
38	2008-06-02	30.75	31.14	26.15	26.69	75216900	23.56
39	2008-05-01	32.8	33.62	30.21	30.72	52851400	26.82
40	2008-04-01	37.36	38.52	31.55	32.7	64485500	28.55
41	2008-03-03	33.34	37.74	31.65	37.01	59927700	32.31
42	2008-02-01	35.59	36.3	33.09	33.14	44926300	28.93
43	2008-01-02	37.1	37.45	32.92	35.36	55123800	30.59
44	2007-12-03	38.2	38.2	36.07	37.07	42936400	32.07
45	2007-11-01	40.89	40.98	36.52	38.29	45181800	32.84
46	2007-10-01	41.28	42.15	39.4	41.16	32919400	35.31
47	2007-09-04	38.84	42.07	38.45	41.4	37426500	35.51
48	2007-08-01	38.6	40.46	36.2	38.87	46947200	33.12
49	2007-07-02	38.42	40.98	37.73	38.76	43667100	33.02
50	2007-06-01	37.68	39.77	36.65	38.28	43860200	32.62
51	2007-05-01	36.82	37.81	36.45	37.58	31562900	31.79
52	2007-04-02	35.36	37.24	34.55	36.86	41666000	31.18
53	2007-03-01	34.61	36	33.9	35.36	37497700	29.91
54	2007-02-01	36.18	36.5	34.5	34.91	34598700	29.53
55	2007-01-03	37.41	38.28	35.76	36.05	34343900	30.26
56	2006-12-01	35.38	38.49	34.96	37.21	33604700	31.23
57	2006-11-01	35.2	36.28	34.62	35.28	23114100	29.39
58	2006-10-02	35.4	36.48	34.92	35.11	26500400	29.25
59	2006-09-01	34.18	35.65	33.76	35.3	24034200	29.41
60	2006-08-01	32.65	34.44	32.2	34.06	18494400	28.17
61	2006-07-03	33.1	33.62	32.06	32.69	24910500	27.04
62	2006-06-01	34.3	34.92	32.78	32.96	27849600	27.26
63	2006-05-01	34.64	35.24	33.7	34.26	24209600	28.13
64	2006-04-03	34.79	34.99	33.07	34.59	26428700	28.4
65	2006-03-01	32.97	35	32.58	34.78	26519300	28.56
66	2006-02-01	32.66	33.75	32.21	32.87	26951100	26.99
67	2006-01-03	35.1	35.63	32.63	32.75	34947000	26.69
68	2005-12-01	35.85	36.26	34.95	35.05	22568500	28.56
69	2005-11-01	33.97	36.34	33.51	35.72	22225800	28.9
70	2005-10-03	33.6	34.5	32.67	33.91	23636600	27.44
71	2005-09-01	33.43	34.58	33	33.67	22843400	27.25
72	2005-08-01	34.57	34.62	32.85	33.61	19156900	27.02

73	2005-07-01	34.85	35.78	33.93	34.5	22692600	27.73
74	2005-06-01	36.48	37.13	34.15	34.65	24312400	27.85
75	2005-05-02	36.08	37.34	35.56	36.48	17054700	29.15
76	2005-04-01	36.18	36.6	35.02	36.2	21540700	28.92
77	2005-03-01	35.27	36.48	35.06	36.06	18737000	28.81
78	2005-02-01	36	36.61	35.05	35.2	17348000	28.12
79	2005-01-03	36.71	36.89	34.95	36.13	19883000	28.69
80	2004-12-01	35.36	37.75	35.27	36.5	18800400	28.98
81	2004-11-01	34.1	36.86	33.81	35.36	18420700	27.91
82	2004-10-01	33.7	34.4	32.65	34.12	16090400	26.93
83	2004-09-01	32.79	34.53	32.62	33.58	18122500	26.5
84	2004-08-02	32.65	33.35	31.42	32.79	15559200	25.73
85	2004-07-01	32.4	33.62	31.5	33.25	22230200	26.09
86	2004-06-01	31	33.49	30.82	32.4	28805300	25.42
87	2004-05-03	30.12	31.47	29.55	31.12	20702700	24.27
88	2004-04-01	30.42	31.85	29.8	29.95	32068200	23.36
89	2004-03-01	32.69	33.48	28.88	30.52	40261200	23.8
90	2004-02-02	33.69	33.99	32.35	32.52	18725500	25.36
91	2004-01-02	31	34.57	30.92	33.63	23093800	26.07
92	2003-12-01	29.2	31.29	28.78	30.98	20243900	24.02
93	2003-11-03	29.05	29.95	27.37	28.67	22067400	22.08
94	2003-10-01	29.81	31.3	28	29.01	21493200	22.34
95	2003-09-02	29.75	32.42	29.31	29.81	21533800	22.96
96	2003-08-01	28.2	30.39	27.18	29.57	16648400	22.63
97	2003-07-01	28.48	29.5	26.9	28.44	22288900	21.77
98	2003-06-02	29.42	31.66	28.53	28.68	20550900	21.95
99	2003-05-01	29.45	29.45	27.35	28.7	19460600	21.82
100	2003-04-01	25.55	29.78	25.5	29.45	21207800	22.39
101	2003-03-03	24.2	28	23.16	25.5	26107100	19.39
102	2003-02-03	23.35	24.2	21.3	24.05	23505800	18.29
103	2003-01-02	24.65	26.26	22.45	23.14	23240300	17.46
104	2002-12-02	27.98	27.98	24.1	24.35	20521100	18.37
105	2002-11-01	25.28	27.4	23.2	27.12	28840700	20.31
106	2002-10-01	24.75	27.21	21.4	25.25	34091600	18.91
107	2002-09-03	29.5	29.7	23.51	24.65	31835500	18.46
108	2002-08-01	32.1	32.98	28.27	30.15	26539000	22.42
109	2002-07-01	29.06	32.2	23.02	32.2	39648900	23.94

110	2002-06-03	31.14	31.4	27.42	29.05	29971600	21.6	
111	2002-05-01	31.75	33.45	30.4	31.14	23783100	23.01	
112	2002-04-01	37.05	37.8	30.15	31.55	31131400	23.31	
113	2002-03-01	39.1	41.84	36.83	37.4	25796800	27.63	
114	2002-02-01	36.9	39.65	34.72	38.5	25112400	28.45	
115	2002-01-02	40.3	41.34	34.49	37.15	24680100	27.32	
116	2001-12-03	38.4	41.39	36.21	40.08	23080100	29.48	
117	2001-11-01	36.25	41.78	36.05	38.5	16974400	28.19	
118	2001-10-01	37.3	39.49	36.04	36.41	19544800	26.66	
119	2001-09-04	40.9	42.17	28.5	37.2	42638800	27.24	
120	2001-08-01	43	43.53	39.84	40.9	16831300	29.81	
121	2001-07-02	48.92	50.2	42.99	43.5	20559200	31.71	
122	2001-06-01	48.99	52.61	46.26	49	29526100	35.6	
123	2001-05-01	48.05	53.55	47.51	49	16915500	35.6	
124	2001-04-02	41.52	50.01	39.04	48.53	22337500	35.26	
125	2001-03-01	45.5	46.6	36.42	41.86	30658800	30.41	
126	2001-02-01	46.5	48.45	45.02	46.5	20455600	33.66	
127	2001-01-02	46.75	48.75	42.63	45.98	24345500	33.29	
128	2000-12-01	50.88	56.19	47.19	47.94	17054700	34.71	
129	2000-11-01	54.75	55.25	47.94	49.56	14524300	35.76	
130	2000-10-02	58	59.94	49	54.81	20282300	39.55	
131	2000-09-01	59.25	60.06	55	57.81	12225400	41.71	
132	2000-08-01	51.94	60.5	51.19	58.63	11558800	42.21	
133	2000-07-03	52.5	54.75	49.5	51.69	13163300	37.21	
134	2000-06-01	52.06	54	47.94	53	12857500	38.05	
135	2000-05-01	159	162	48.75	52.63	14351800	37.79	
136	2000-04-03	155.25	167.94	143.06	157.25	21992900	37.64	
137	2000-03-01	133.5	164.88	126.25	155.63	25483700	37.25	
138	2000-02-01	134.25	143.13	124.94	132.38	23404600	31.59	
139	2000-01-03	153	154.94	133.06	134	22127500	31.98	

APPENDIX 5.3

id	element	atomic_number	symbol	atomic_weight	absorption	scattering
1	Hydrogen	1	H	1.008	0.33	80
2	Deuterium	1	D	2.015	0.00046	5.4
3	Helium	2	He	4.003	0	0.8
4	Lithium	3	Li	6.94	70	1.4
5	Berylium	4	Be	9.01	0.009	7
6	Boron	5	B	10.82	750	4
7	Carbon	6	C	12.01	0.0045	4.8
8	Nitrogen	7	N	14.008	1.8	10
9	Oxygen	8	O	16	0.0002	4.2
10	Fluorine	9	F	19	0.009	4.1
11	Neon	10	Ne	20.18	2.8	2.4
12	Sodium	11	Na	22.997	0.5	4
13	Magnesium	12	Mg	24.32	0.06	3.6
14	Aluminum	13	Al	26.98	0.21	1.4
15	Silicon	14	Si	28.09	0.13	1.7
16	Phosphorus	15	P	30.98	0.2	5
17	Sulfur	16	S	32.07	0.49	1.1
18	Chlorine	17	Cl	35.457	31.6	0
19	Argon	18	Ar	39.94	0.62	1.5
20	Potassium	19	K	39.1	2	1.5
21	Scandium	21	Sc	45.1	23	0
22	Titanium	22	Ti	47.9	5.6	4
23	Vanadium	23	V	50.95	5.1	5
24	Chromium	24	Cr	52.01	2.9	3
25	Calcium	20	Ca	40.08	0.43	9
26	Manganese	25	Mn	54.93	13	2.3
27	Iron	26	Fe	55.85	2.4	11
28	Cobalt	27	Co	58.94	37	5
29	Nickel	28	Ni	58.69	4.5	17.5
30	Copper	29	Cu	63.54	3.6	7.2
31	Zinc	30	Zn	65.38	1.1	3.6
32	Lanthanum	57	La	138.92	8.9	18
33	Yttrium	39	Y	88.92	1.4	3
34	Neodymium	60	Nd	144.27	44	25
35	Cerium	58	Ce	140.13	0.7	9
36	Praseodymium	59	Pr	140.92	11	0
37						

	Gadolinium	64	Gd	156.9	44000	0
38	Dysprosium	66	Dy	162.46	1100	0
39	Erbium	68	Er	167.2	166	0
40	Samarium	62	Sm	150.43	6500	0
41	Ytterbium	70	Yb	173	36	12
42	Holmium	67	Ho	164.94	64	0
43	Terbium	65	Tb	159.2	44	0
44	Thulium	69	Tm	169.4	118	0
45	Lutetium	71	Lu	174.99	108	0
46	Promethium	61	Pm	145	0	0
47	Uranium	92	U	238.07	7.42	8.2
48	Thorium	90	Th	232.12	7	13
49	Europium	63	Eu	152	4500	0
50	Zirconium	40	Zr	91.22	0.18	8
51	Molybdenum	42	Mo	95.95	2.4	7

element_symbol	uses
Sc	Lasers,Lighting,Aerospace
La	Batteries,Catalyst,Lasers
Y	Lasers,Superconductors
Nd	Lasers,Magnets,Computers
Ce	Catalyst,Fuel addititive,Optical polish
Pr	Lasers,Magnets,Lighting,Alloys
Gd	Lasers,Magnets,Computers,X-rays
Dy	Lasers,Magnets,Cars
Er	Lasers,Alloys,Photography
Sm	Lasers,Magnets,Neutron absorption
Yb	Lasers,Alloys,Gamma rays
Ho	Lasers,Magnets,Optics
Tb	Lasers,Phosphors,Lighting
Tm	Lasers,X-rays
Lu	Catalyst,Medicine
Pm	Nuclear batteries
Eu	Lasers,Phosphors,Lighting

id	element	atomic_number	symbol	atomic_weight	absorption	scattering	total
1	Hydrogen	1	H	1.008	0.33	80	80.33
2	Deuterium	1	D	2.015	0.00046	5.4	5.40046
3	Helium	2	He	4.003	0	0.8	0.8
4	Lithium	3	Li	6.94	70	1.4	71.4
5	Berylium	4	Be	9.01	0.009	7	7.009
6	Boron	5	B	10.82	750	4	754
7	Carbon	6	C	12.01	0.0045	4.8	4.8045
8	Nitrogen	7	N	14.008	1.8	10	11.8
9	Oxygen	8	O	16	0.0002	4.2	4.2002
10	Fluorine	9	F	19	0.009	4.1	4.109
11	Neon	10	Ne	20.18	2.8	2.4	5.2
12	Sodium	11	Na	22.997	0.5	4	4.5
13	Magnesium	12	Mg	24.32	0.06	3.6	3.66
14	Aluminum	13	Al	26.98	0.21	1.4	1.61
15	Silicon	14	Si	28.09	0.13	1.7	1.83
16	Phosphorus	15	P	30.98	0.2	5	5.2
17	Sulfur	16	S	32.07	0.49	1.1	1.59
18	Chlorine	17	Cl	35.457	31.6	0	31.6
19	Argon	18	Ar	39.94	0.62	1.5	2.12
20	Potassium	19	K	39.1	2	1.5	3.5
21	Scandium	21	Sc	45.1	23	0	23
22	Titanium	22	Ti	47.9	5.6	4	9.6
23	Vanadium	23	V	50.95	5.1	5	10.1
24	Chromium	24	Cr	52.01	2.9	3	5.9
25	Calcium	20	Ca	40.08	0.43	9	9.43
26	Manganese	25	Mn	54.93	13	2.3	15.3
27	Iron	26	Fe	55.85	2.4	11	13.4
28	Cobalt	27	Co	58.94	37	5	42
29	Nickel	28	Ni	58.69	4.5	17.5	22
30	Copper	29	Cu	63.54	3.6	7.2	10.8
31	Zinc	30	Zn	65.38	1.1	3.6	4.7
32	Lanthanum	57	La	138.92	8.9	18	26.9
33	Yttrium	39	Y	88.92	1.4	3	4.4
34	Neodymium	60	Nd	144.27	44	25	69
35	Cerium	58	Ce	140.13	0.7	9	9.7
36	Praseodymium	59	Pr	140.92	11	0	11
37							

	Gadolinium	64	Gd	156.9	44000	0	44000
38	Dysprosium	66	Dy	162.46	1100	0	1100
39	Erbium	68	Er	167.2	166	0	166
40	Samarium	62	Sm	150.43	6500	0	6500
41	Ytterbium	70	Yb	173	36	12	48
42	Holmium	67	Ho	164.94	64	0	64
43	Terbium	65	Tb	159.2	44	0	44
44	Thulium	69	Tm	169.4	118	0	118
45	Lutetium	71	Lu	174.99	108	0	108
46	Promethium	61	Pm	145	0	0	0
47	Uranium	92	U	238.07	7.42	8.2	15.62
48	Thorium	90	Th	232.12	7	13	20
49	Europium	63	Eu	152	4500	0	4500
50	Zirconium	40	Zr	91.22	0.18	8	8.18
51	Molybdenum	42	Mo	95.95	2.4	7	9.4

id	element	uses	oxide_price_USD_per_kg	atomic_number
1	Lanthanum	Batteries,Catalyst,Lasers	40	57
2	Yttrium	Lasers,Superconductors	50	39
3	Neodymium	Lasers,Magnets,Computers	60	60
4	Cerium	Catalyst,Fuel addititive,Optical polish	65	58
5	Praseodymium	Lasers,Magnets,Lighting,Alloys	75	59
6	Gadolinium	Lasers,Magnets,Computers,X-rays	150	64
7	Dysprosium	Lasers,Magnets,Cars	160	66
8	Erbium	Lasers,Alloys,Photography	165	68
9	Samarium	Lasers,Magnets,Neutron absorption	350	62
10	Ytterbium	Lasers,Alloys,Gamma rays	450	70
11	Holmium	Lasers,Magnets,Optics	750	67
12	Terbium	Lasers,Phosphors,Lighting	850	65
13	Europium	Lasers,Phosphors,Lighting	1200	63
14	Thulium	Lasers,X-rays	2500	69
15	Lutetium	Catalyst,Medicine	3500	71
16	Scandium	Lasers,Lighting,Aerospace	14000	21
17	Promethium	Nuclear batteries	No price	61

Appendix 5.4

Element

Atomic_Number

Symbol

Atomic_Weight

Absorption

Scattering

ADD RECORD

Element Hydrogen
Atomic_Number 1
Symbol H
Atomic_Weight 1.008
Absorption 0.33
Scattering 80

DELETE RECORD

Element Deuterium
Atomic_Number 1
Symbol D
Atomic_Weight 2.015
Absorption 0.00046
Scattering 5.4

DELETE RECORD

Element Helium
Atomic_Number 2
Symbol He
Atomic_Weight 4.003
Absorption 0
Scattering 0.8

DELETE RECORD

Element Lithium
Atomic_Number 3
Symbol Li
Atomic_Weight 6.94
Absorption 70
Scattering 1.4

DELETE RECORD

Element Berylium
Atomic_Number 4
Symbol Be
Atomic_Weight 9.01
Absorption 0.009
Scattering 7

DELETE RECORD

Element Boron
Atomic_Number 5
Symbol B
Atomic_Weight 10.82

```
Absorption     750
Scattering     4
          DELETE RECORD

Element   Carbon
Atomic_Number    6
Symbol C
Atomic_Weight     12.01
Absorption     0.0045
Scattering     4.8
          DELETE RECORD

Element   Nitrogen
Atomic_Number    7
Symbol N
Atomic_Weight     14.008
Absorption     1.8
Scattering     10
          DELETE RECORD

Element   Oxygen
Atomic_Number    8
Symbol O
Atomic_Weight     16
Absorption     0.0002
Scattering     4.2
          DELETE RECORD

Element   Fluorine
Atomic_Number    9
Symbol F
Atomic_Weight     19
Absorption     0.009
Scattering     4.1
          DELETE RECORD

Element   Neon
Atomic_Number    10
Symbol Ne
Atomic_Weight     20.18
Absorption     2.8
Scattering     2.4
          DELETE RECORD

Element   Sodium
Atomic_Number    11
Symbol Na
Atomic_Weight     22.997
Absorption     0.5
Scattering     4
          DELETE RECORD

Element   Magnesium
Atomic_Number    12
Symbol Mg
```

```
Atomic_Weight     24.32
Absorption     0.06
Scattering     3.6
```
DELETE RECORD

```
Element   Aluminum
Atomic_Number    13
Symbol Al
Atomic_Weight     26.98
Absorption     0.21
Scattering     1.4
```
DELETE RECORD

```
Element   Silicon
Atomic_Number    14
Symbol Si
Atomic_Weight     28.09
Absorption     0.13
Scattering     1.7
```
DELETE RECORD

```
Element   Phosphorus
Atomic_Number    15
Symbol P
Atomic_Weight     30.98
Absorption     0.2
Scattering     5
```
DELETE RECORD

```
Element   Sulfur
Atomic_Number    16
Symbol S
Atomic_Weight     32.07
Absorption     0.49
Scattering     1.1
```
DELETE RECORD

```
Element   Chlorine
Atomic_Number    17
Symbol Cl
Atomic_Weight     35.457
Absorption     31.6
Scattering     0
```
DELETE RECORD

```
Element   Argon
Atomic_Number    18
Symbol Ar
Atomic_Weight     39.94
Absorption     0.62
Scattering     1.5
```
DELETE RECORD

```
Element   Potassium
Atomic_Number    19
```

Symbol K
Atomic_Weight 39.1
Absorption 2
Scattering 1.5
DELETE RECORD

Element Scandium
Atomic_Number 21
Symbol Sc
Atomic_Weight 45.1
Absorption 23
Scattering 0
DELETE RECORD

Element Titanium
Atomic_Number 22
Symbol Ti
Atomic_Weight 47.9
Absorption 5.6
Scattering 4,
DELETE RECORD

Element Vanadium
Atomic_Number 23
Symbol V
Atomic_Weight 50.95
Absorption 5.1
Scattering 5
DELETE RECORD

Element Chromium
Atomic_Number 24
Symbol Cr
Atomic_Weight 52.01
Absorption 2.9
Scattering 3
DELETE RECORD

Element Calcium
Atomic_Number 20
Symbol Ca
Atomic_Weight 40.08
Absorption 0.43
Scattering 9
DELETE RECORD

Element Manganese
Atomic_Number 25
Symbol Mn
Atomic_Weight 54.93
Absorption 13
Scattering 2.3
DELETE RECORD

Element Iron

Atomic_Number 26
Symbol Fe
Atomic_Weight 55.85
Absorption 2.4
Scattering 11
DELETE RECORD

Element Cobalt
Atomic_Number 27
Symbol Co
Atomic_Weight 58.94
Absorption 37
Scattering 5
DELETE RECORD

Element Nickel
Atomic_Number 28
Symbol Ni
Atomic_Weight 58.69
Absorption 4.5
Scattering 17.5
DELETE RECORD

Element Copper
Atomic_Number 29
Symbol Cu
Atomic_Weight 63.54
Absorption 3.6
Scattering 7.2
DELETE RECORD

Element Zinc
Atomic_Number 30
Symbol Zn
Atomic_Weight 65.38
Absorption 1.1
Scattering 3.6
DELETE RECORD

Element Lanthanum
Atomic_Number 57
Symbol La
Atomic_Weight 138.92
Absorption 8.9
Scattering 18
DELETE RECORD

Element Yttrium
Atomic_Number 39
Symbol Y
Atomic_Weight 88.92
Absorption 1.4
Scattering 3
DELETE RECORD

```
Element    Neodymium
Atomic_Number     60
Symbol Nd
Atomic_Weight      144.27
Absorption      44
Scattering      25
```

DELETE RECORD

```
Element    Cerium
Atomic_Number     58
Symbol Ce
Atomic_Weight      140.13
Absorption      0.7
Scattering      9
```

DELETE RECORD

```
Element    Praseodymium
Atomic_Number     59
Symbol Pr
Atomic_Weight      140.92
Absorption      11
Scattering      0
```

DELETE RECORD

```
Element    Gadolinium
Atomic_Number     64
Symbol Gd
Atomic_Weight      156.9
Absorption      44000
Scattering      0
```

DELETE RECORD

```
Element    Dysprosium
Atomic_Number     66
Symbol Dy
Atomic_Weight      162.46
Absorption      1100
Scattering      0
```

DELETE RECORD

```
Element    Erbium
Atomic_Number     68
Symbol Er
Atomic_Weight      167.2
Absorption      166
Scattering      0
```

DELETE RECORD

```
Element    Samarium
Atomic_Number     62
Symbol Sm
Atomic_Weight      150.43
Absorption      6500
Scattering      0
```

DELETE RECORD

```
Element    Ytterbium
Atomic_Number     70
Symbol Yb
Atomic_Weight      173
Absorption      36
Scattering      12
```

DELETE RECORD

```
Element    Holmium
Atomic_Number     67
Symbol Ho
Atomic_Weight      164.94
Absorption      64
Scattering      0
```

DELETE RECORD

```
Element    Terbium
Atomic_Number     65
Symbol Tb
Atomic_Weight      159.2
Absorption      44
Scattering      0
```

DELETE RECORD

```
Element    Thulium
Atomic_Number     69
Symbol Tm
Atomic_Weight      169.4
Absorption      118
Scattering      0
```

DELETE RECORD

```
Element    Lutetium
Atomic_Number     71
Symbol Lu
Atomic_Weight      174.99
Absorption      108
Scattering      0
```

DELETE RECORD

```
Element    Promethium
Atomic_Number     61
Symbol Pm
Atomic_Weight      145
Absorption      0
Scattering      0
```

DELETE RECORD

```
Element    Uranium
Atomic_Number     92
Symbol U
Atomic_Weight      238.07
Absorption      7.42
Scattering      8.2
```

DELETE RECORD

```
Element    Thorium
Atomic_Number     90
Symbol Th
Atomic_Weight      232.12
Absorption      7
Scattering      13
```

DELETE RECORD

```
Element    Europium
Atomic_Number     63
Symbol Eu
Atomic_Weight      152
Absorption      4500
Scattering      0
```

DELETE RECORD

```
Element    Zirconium
Atomic_Number     40
Symbol Zr
Atomic_Weight      91.22
Absorption      0.18
Scattering      8
```

DELETE RECORD

```
Element    Molybdenum
Atomic_Number     42
Symbol Mo
Atomic_Weight      95.95
Absorption      2.4
Scattering      7
```

DELETE RECORD

```
Element    Hafnium
Atomic_Number     72
Symbol Hf
Atomic_Weight      178.6
Absorption      115
Scattering      0
```

DELETE RECORD

Appendix 9.3

steamTable


```
<Steam_table>

<temperature>
<t>450</t>
<p>422.1</p>
<vf>0.019433</vf>
<vg>1.1011</vg>
<uf>428.6</uf>
<ug>1119.5</ug>
</temperature>

<temperature>
<t>475</t>
<p>539.3</p>
<vf>0.019901</vf>
<vg>0.8594</vg>
<uf>456.6</uf>
<ug>1119.2</ug>
</temperature>

<temperature>
<t>500</t>
<p>680.0</p>
<vf>0.02043</vf>
<vg>0.6761</vg>
<uf>485.1</uf>
<ug>1117.4</ug>
</temperature>

<temperature>
<t>525</t>
<p>847.1</p>
<vf>0.02104</vf>
<vg>0.5350</vg>
<uf>514.5</uf>
<ug>1113.9</ug>
</temperature>

<temperature>
<t>550</t>
<p>1044.0</p>
<vf>0.02175</vf>
<vg>0.4249</vg>
<uf>544.9</uf>
<ug>1108.6</ug>
</temperature>

<temperature>
<t>575</t>
<p>1274.0</p>
<vf>0.02259</vf>
<vg>0.3378</vg>
<uf>576.5</uf>
<ug>1100.8</ug>
</temperature>

<temperature>
<t>600</t>
<p>1541.0</p>
<vf>0.02363</vf>
<vg>0.2677</vg>
<uf>609.9</uf>
```


Page 1

```
<ug>1090.0</ug>
</temperature>

<temperature>
<t>625</t>
<p>1849.7</p>
<vf>0.02494</vf>
<vg>0.2103</vg>
<uf>645.7</uf>
<ug>1075.1</ug>
</temperature>

<temperature>
<t>650</t>
<p>2205.0</p>
<vf>0.02673</vf>
<vg>0.16206</vg>
<uf>685.0</uf>
<ug>1053.7</ug>
</temperature>

<temperature>
<t>675</t>
<p>2616.0</p>
<vf>0.02951</vf>
<vg>0.11952</vg>
<uf>731.0</uf>
<ug>1020.3</ug>
</temperature>

<temperature>
<t>700</t>
<p>3090.0</p>
<vf>0.03666</vf>
<vg>0.07438</vg>
<uf>801.7</uf>
<ug>947.7</ug>
</temperature>
</Steam_table>
```

Appendix 10.1

id	element	atomic_number	symbol	atomic_weight	absorption	scattering
1	Hydrogen	1	H	1.008	0.33	80
2	Deuterium	1	D	2.015	0.00046	5.4
3	Helium	2	He	4.003	0	0.8
4	Lithium	3	Li	6.94	70	1.4
5	Berylium	4	Be	9.01	0.009	7
6	Boron	5	B	10.82	750	4
7	Carbon	6	C	12.01	0.0045	4.8
8	Nitrogen	7	N	14.008	1.8	10
9	Oxygen	8	O	16	0.0002	4.2
10	Fluorine	9	F	19	0.009	4.1
11	Neon	10	Ne	20.18	2.8	2.4
12	Sodium	11	Na	22.997	0.5	4
13	Magnesium	12	Mg	24.32	0.06	3.6
14	Aluminum	13	Al	26.98	0.21	1.4
15	Silicon	14	Si	28.09	0.13	1.7
16	Phosphorus	15	P	30.98	0.2	5
17	Sulfur	16	S	32.07	0.49	1.1
18	Chlorine	17	Cl	35.457	31.6	0
19	Argon	18	Ar	39.94	0.62	1.5
20	Potassium	19	K	39.1	2	1.5
21	Scandium	21	Sc	45.1	23	0
22	Titanium	22	Ti	47.9	5.6	4
23	Vanadium	23	V	50.95	5.1	5
24	Chromium	24	Cr	52.01	2.9	3
25	Calcium	20	Ca	40.08	0.43	9
26	Manganese	25	Mn	54.93	13	2.3
27	Iron	26	Fe	55.85	2.4	11
28	Cobalt	27	Co	58.94	37	5
29	Nickel	28	Ni	58.69	4.5	17.5
30	Copper	29	Cu	63.54	3.6	7.2
31	Zinc	30	Zn	65.38	1.1	3.6
32	Lanthanum	57	La	138.92	8.9	18
33	Yttrium	39	Y	88.92	1.4	3
34	Neodymium	60	Nd	144.27	44	25
35	Cerium	58	Ce	140.13	0.7	9

36	Praseodymium	59	Pr	140.92	11	0
37	Gadolinium	64	Gd	156.9	44000	0
38	Dysprosium	66	Dy	162.46	1100	0
39	Erbium	68	Er	167.2	166	0
40	Samarium	62	Sm	150.43	6500	0
41	Ytterbium	70	Yb	173	36	12
42	Holmium	67	Ho	164.94	64	0
43	Terbium	65	Tb	159.2	44	0
44	Europium	63	Eu	152	4500	0
45	Thulium	69	Tm	169.4	118	0
46	Lutetium	71	Lu	174.99	108	0
47	Promethium	61	Pm	145	0	0
48	Uranium	92	U	238.07	7.42	8.2
50	Thorium	90	Th	232.12	7	13

```
<?xml version="1.0" ?>
<Big_array>
  <subarray>
    <id>1</id>
    <element>Hydrogen</element>
    <atomic_number>1</atomic_number>
    <symbol>H</symbol>
    <atomic_weight>1.008</atomic_weight>
    <absorption>0.33</absorption>
    <scattering>80</scattering>
  </subarray>
  <subarray>
    <id>2</id>
    <element>Deuterium</element>
    <atomic_number>1</atomic_number>
    <symbol>D</symbol>
    <atomic_weight>2.015</atomic_weight>
    <absorption>0.00046</absorption>
    <scattering>5.4</scattering>
  </subarray>
  <subarray>
    <id>3</id>
    <element>Helium</element>
    <atomic_number>2</atomic_number>
    <symbol>He</symbol>
    <atomic_weight>4.003</atomic_weight>
    <absorption>0.0</absorption>
    <scattering>0.8</scattering>
  </subarray>
  <subarray>
    <id>4</id>
    <element>Lithium</element>
    <atomic_number>3</atomic_number>
    <symbol>Li</symbol>
    <atomic_weight>6.94</atomic_weight>
    <absorption>70</absorption>
    <scattering>1.4</scattering>
  </subarray>
  <subarray>
    <id>5</id>
    <element>Berylium</element>
    <atomic_number>4</atomic_number>
    <symbol>Be</symbol>
    <atomic_weight>9.01</atomic_weight>
    <absorption>0.009</absorption>
    <scattering>7</scattering>
  </subarray>
  <subarray>
    <id>6</id>
    <element>Boron</element>
    <atomic_number>5</atomic_number>
    <symbol>B</symbol>
```

```
    <atomic_weight>10.82</atomic_weight>
    <absorption>750</absorption>
    <scattering>4</scattering>
  </subarray>
- <subarray>
    <id>7</id>
    <element>Carbon</element>
    <atomic_number>6</atomic_number>
    <symbol>C</symbol>
    <atomic_weight>12.01</atomic_weight>
    <absorption>0.0045</absorption>
    <scattering>4.8</scattering>
  </subarray>
- <subarray>
    <id>8</id>
    <element>Nitrogen</element>
    <atomic_number>7</atomic_number>
    <symbol>N</symbol>
    <atomic_weight>14.008</atomic_weight>
    <absorption>1.8</absorption>
    <scattering>10</scattering>
  </subarray>
- <subarray>
    <id>9</id>
    <element>Oxygen</element>
    <atomic_number>8</atomic_number>
    <symbol>O</symbol>
    <atomic_weight>16</atomic_weight>
    <absorption>0.0002</absorption>
    <scattering>4.2</scattering>
  </subarray>
- <subarray>
    <id>10</id>
    <element>Fluorine</element>
    <atomic_number>9</atomic_number>
    <symbol>F</symbol>
    <atomic_weight>19</atomic_weight>
    <absorption>0.009</absorption>
    <scattering>4.1</scattering>
  </subarray>
- <subarray>
    <id>11</id>
    <element>Neon</element>
    <atomic_number>10</atomic_number>
    <symbol>Ne</symbol>
    <atomic_weight>20.18</atomic_weight>
    <absorption>2.8</absorption>
    <scattering>2.4</scattering>
  </subarray>
- <subarray>
    <id>12</id>
    <element>Sodium</element>
```

```
    <atomic_number>11</atomic_number>
    <symbol>Na</symbol>
    <atomic_weight>22.997</atomic_weight>
    <absorption>0.5</absorption>
    <scattering>4</scattering>
  </subarray>
- <subarray>
    <id>13</id>
    <element>Magnesium</element>
    <atomic_number>12</atomic_number>
    <symbol>Mg</symbol>
    <atomic_weight>24.32</atomic_weight>
    <absorption>0.06</absorption>
    <scattering>3.6</scattering>
  </subarray>
- <subarray>
    <id>14</id>
    <element>Aluminum</element>
    <atomic_number>13</atomic_number>
    <symbol>Al</symbol>
    <atomic_weight>26.98</atomic_weight>
    <absorption>0.21</absorption>
    <scattering>1.4</scattering>
  </subarray>
- <subarray>
    <id>15</id>
    <element>Silicon</element>
    <atomic_number>14</atomic_number>
    <symbol>Si</symbol>
    <atomic_weight>28.09</atomic_weight>
    <absorption>0.13</absorption>
    <scattering>1.7</scattering>
  </subarray>
- <subarray>
    <id>16</id>
    <element>Phosphorus</element>
    <atomic_number>15</atomic_number>
    <symbol>P</symbol>
    <atomic_weight>30.98</atomic_weight>
    <absorption>0.2</absorption>
    <scattering>5</scattering>
  </subarray>
- <subarray>
    <id>17</id>
    <element>Sulfur</element>
    <atomic_number>16</atomic_number>
    <symbol>S</symbol>
    <atomic_weight>32.07</atomic_weight>
    <absorption>0.49</absorption>
    <scattering>1.1</scattering>
  </subarray>
- <subarray>
```

<id>**18**</id>
<element>**Chlorine**</element>
<atomic_number>**17**</atomic_number>
<symbol>**Cl**</symbol>
<atomic_weight>**35.457**</atomic_weight>
<absorption>**31.6**</absorption>
<scattering>**0**</scattering>
</subarray>
- <subarray>
<id>**19**</id>
<element>**Argon**</element>
<atomic_number>**18**</atomic_number>
<symbol>**Ar**</symbol>
<atomic_weight>**39.94**</atomic_weight>
<absorption>**0.62**</absorption>
<scattering>**1.5**</scattering>
</subarray>
- <subarray>
<id>**20**</id>
<element>**Potassium**</element>
<atomic_number>**19**</atomic_number>
<symbol>**K**</symbol>
<atomic_weight>**39.1**</atomic_weight>
<absorption>**2**</absorption>
<scattering>**1.5**</scattering>
</subarray>
- <subarray>
<id>**21**</id>
<element>**Scandium**</element>
<atomic_number>**21**</atomic_number>
<symbol>**Sc**</symbol>
<atomic_weight>**45.1**</atomic_weight>
<absorption>**23**</absorption>
<scattering>**0**</scattering>
</subarray>
- <subarray>
<id>**22**</id>
<element>**Titanium**</element>
<atomic_number>**22**</atomic_number>
<symbol>**Ti**</symbol>
<atomic_weight>**47.9**</atomic_weight>
<absorption>**5.6**</absorption>
<scattering>**4**</scattering>
</subarray>
- <subarray>
<id>**23**</id>
<element>**Vanadium**</element>
<atomic_number>**23**</atomic_number>
<symbol>**V**</symbol>
<atomic_weight>**50.95**</atomic_weight>
<absorption>**5.1**</absorption>
<scattering>**5**</scattering>

```
</subarray>
<subarray>
  <id>24</id>
  <element>Chromium</element>
  <atomic_number>24</atomic_number>
  <symbol>Cr</symbol>
  <atomic_weight>52.01</atomic_weight>
  <absorption>2.9</absorption>
  <scattering>3</scattering>
</subarray>
<subarray>
  <id>25</id>
  <element>Calcium</element>
  <atomic_number>20</atomic_number>
  <symbol>Ca</symbol>
  <atomic_weight>40.08</atomic_weight>
  <absorption>0.43</absorption>
  <scattering>9</scattering>
</subarray>
<subarray>
  <id>26</id>
  <element>Manganese</element>
  <atomic_number>25</atomic_number>
  <symbol>Mn</symbol>
  <atomic_weight>54.93</atomic_weight>
  <absorption>13</absorption>
  <scattering>2.3</scattering>
</subarray>
<subarray>
  <id>27</id>
  <element>Iron</element>
  <atomic_number>26</atomic_number>
  <symbol>Fe</symbol>
  <atomic_weight>55.85</atomic_weight>
  <absorption>2.4</absorption>
  <scattering>11</scattering>
</subarray>
<subarray>
  <id>28</id>
  <element>Cobalt</element>
  <atomic_number>27</atomic_number>
  <symbol>Co</symbol>
  <atomic_weight>58.94</atomic_weight>
  <absorption>37</absorption>
  <scattering>5</scattering>
</subarray>
<subarray>
  <id>29</id>
  <element>Nickel</element>
  <atomic_number>28</atomic_number>
  <symbol>Ni</symbol>
  <atomic_weight>58.69</atomic_weight>
```

<absorption>**4.5**</absorption>
<scattering>**17.5**</scattering>
</subarray>
- <subarray>
<id>**30**</id>
<element>**Copper**</element>
<atomic_number>**29**</atomic_number>
<symbol>**Cu**</symbol>
<atomic_weight>**63.54**</atomic_weight>
<absorption>**3.6**</absorption>
<scattering>**7.2**</scattering>
</subarray>
- <subarray>
<id>**31**</id>
<element>**Zinc**</element>
<atomic_number>**30**</atomic_number>
<symbol>**Zn**</symbol>
<atomic_weight>**65.38**</atomic_weight>
<absorption>**1.1**</absorption>
<scattering>**3.6**</scattering>
</subarray>
- <subarray>
<id>**32**</id>
<element>**Lanthanum**</element>
<atomic_number>**57**</atomic_number>
<symbol>**La**</symbol>
<atomic_weight>**138.92**</atomic_weight>
<absorption>**8.9**</absorption>
<scattering>**18**</scattering>
</subarray>
- <subarray>
<id>**33**</id>
<element>**Yttrium**</element>
<atomic_number>**39**</atomic_number>
<symbol>**Y**</symbol>
<atomic_weight>**88.92**</atomic_weight>
<absorption>**1.4**</absorption>
<scattering>**3**</scattering>
</subarray>
- <subarray>
<id>**34**</id>
<element>**Neodymium**</element>
<atomic_number>**60**</atomic_number>
<symbol>**Nd**</symbol>
<atomic_weight>**144.27**</atomic_weight>
<absorption>**44**</absorption>
<scattering>**25**</scattering>
</subarray>
- <subarray>
<id>**35**</id>
<element>**Cerium**</element>
<atomic_number>**58**</atomic_number>

```
    <symbol>Ce</symbol>
    <atomic_weight>140.13</atomic_weight>
    <absorption>0.7</absorption>
    <scattering>9</scattering>
  </subarray>
- <subarray>
    <id>36</id>
    <element>Praseodymium</element>
    <atomic_number>59</atomic_number>
    <symbol>Pr</symbol>
    <atomic_weight>140.92</atomic_weight>
    <absorption>11</absorption>
    <scattering>0</scattering>
  </subarray>
- <subarray>
    <id>37</id>
    <element>Gadolinium</element>
    <atomic_number>64</atomic_number>
    <symbol>Gd</symbol>
    <atomic_weight>156.9</atomic_weight>
    <absorption>44000</absorption>
    <scattering>0</scattering>
  </subarray>
- <subarray>
    <id>38</id>
    <element>Dysprosium</element>
    <atomic_number>66</atomic_number>
    <symbol>Dy</symbol>
    <atomic_weight>162.46</atomic_weight>
    <absorption>1100</absorption>
    <scattering>0</scattering>
  </subarray>
- <subarray>
    <id>39</id>
    <element>Erbium</element>
    <atomic_number>68</atomic_number>
    <symbol>Er</symbol>
    <atomic_weight>167.2</atomic_weight>
    <absorption>166</absorption>
    <scattering>0</scattering>
  </subarray>
- <subarray>
    <id>40</id>
    <element>Samarium</element>
    <atomic_number>62</atomic_number>
    <symbol>Sm</symbol>
    <atomic_weight>150.43</atomic_weight>
    <absorption>6500</absorption>
    <scattering>0</scattering>
  </subarray>
- <subarray>
    <id>41</id>
```

```
    <element>Ytterbium</element>
    <atomic_number>70</atomic_number>
    <symbol>Yb</symbol>
    <atomic_weight>173</atomic_weight>
    <absorption>36</absorption>
    <scattering>12</scattering>
  </subarray>
- <subarray>
    <id>42</id>
    <element>Holmium</element>
    <atomic_number>67</atomic_number>
    <symbol>Ho</symbol>
    <atomic_weight>164.94</atomic_weight>
    <absorption>64</absorption>
    <scattering>0</scattering>
  </subarray>
- <subarray>
    <id>43</id>
    <element>Terbium</element>
    <atomic_number>65</atomic_number>
    <symbol>Tb</symbol>
    <atomic_weight>159.2</atomic_weight>
    <absorption>44</absorption>
    <scattering>0</scattering>
  </subarray>
- <subarray>
    <id>44</id>
    <element>Europium</element>
    <atomic_number>63</atomic_number>
    <symbol>Eu</symbol>
    <atomic_weight>152</atomic_weight>
    <absorption>4500</absorption>
    <scattering>0</scattering>
  </subarray>
- <subarray>
    <id>45</id>
    <element>Thulium</element>
    <atomic_number>69</atomic_number>
    <symbol>Tm</symbol>
    <atomic_weight>169.4</atomic_weight>
    <absorption>118</absorption>
    <scattering>0</scattering>
  </subarray>
- <subarray>
    <id>46</id>
    <element>Lutetium</element>
    <atomic_number>71</atomic_number>
    <symbol>Lu</symbol>
    <atomic_weight>174.99</atomic_weight>
    <absorption>108</absorption>
    <scattering>0</scattering>
  </subarray>
```

```
- <subarray>
    <id>47</id>
    <element>Promethium</element>
    <atomic_number>61</atomic_number>
    <symbol>Pm</symbol>
    <atomic_weight>145</atomic_weight>
    <absorption>0</absorption>
    <scattering>0</scattering>
  </subarray>
- <subarray>
    <id>48</id>
    <element>Uranium</element>
    <atomic_number>92</atomic_number>
    <symbol>U</symbol>
    <atomic_weight>238.07</atomic_weight>
    <absorption>7.42</absorption>
    <scattering>8.2</scattering>
  </subarray>
- <subarray>
    <id>50</id>
    <element>Thorium</element>
    <atomic_number>90</atomic_number>
    <symbol>Th</symbol>
    <atomic_weight>232.12</atomic_weight>
    <absorption>7</absorption>
    <scattering>13</scattering>
  </subarray>
</Big_array>
```

```
silver 1.59e-8
copper 1.68e-8
annealed copper 1.72e-8
gold 2.44e-8
aluminum 2.82e-8
calcium 3.36e-8
tungsten 5.6e-8
zinc 5.9e-8
nickel 6.99e-8
lithium 9.28e-8
iron 1.0e-7
platium 1.06e-7
tin 1.09e-7
lead 2.2e-7
titanium 4.20e-7
manganese 4.82e-7
constantan 4.9e-7
stainless steel 6.897e-7
mercury 9.8e-7
nichrome 1.10e-6
amorphous carbon 8.0e-4
germanium 4.6e-1
silicon 6.4e2
fused quartz 7.5e17
teflon 1.0e24
```

```
<?xml version="1.0" ?>
- <Big_array>
  - <table>
      <copper>1.68e-08</copper>
      <constantan>4.9e-07</constantan>
      <gold>2.44e-08</gold>
      <germanium>0.46</germanium>
      <titanium>4.2e-07</titanium>
      <zinc>5.9e-08</zinc>
      <mercury>9.8e-07</mercury>
      <lead>2.2e-07</lead>
      <amorphous_carbon>0.0008</amorphous_carbon>
      <platium>1.06e-07</platium>
      <tin>1.09e-07</tin>
      <annealed_copper>1.72e-08</annealed_copper>
      <lithium>9.28e-08</lithium>
      <nichrome>1.1e-06</nichrome>
      <teflon>1e+24</teflon>
      <nickel>6.99e-08</nickel>
      <fused_quartz>7.5e+17</fused_quartz>
      <tungsten>5.6e-08</tungsten>
      <silver>1.59e-08</silver>
      <aluminum>2.82e-08</aluminum>
      <stainless_steel>6.897e-07</stainless_steel>
      <manganese>4.82e-07</manganese>
      <silicon>640.0</silicon>
      <calcium>3.36e-08</calcium>
      <iron>1e-07</iron>
    </table>
  </Big_array>
```

Appendix 10.2

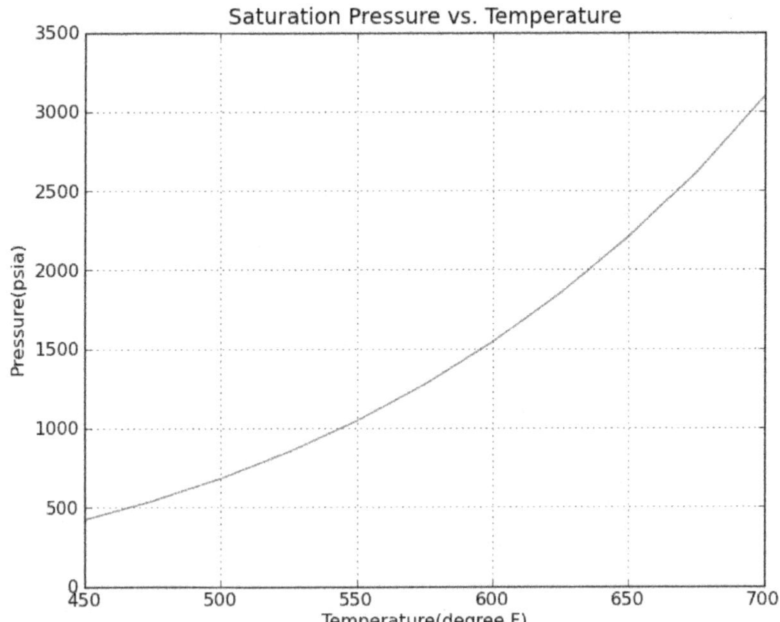

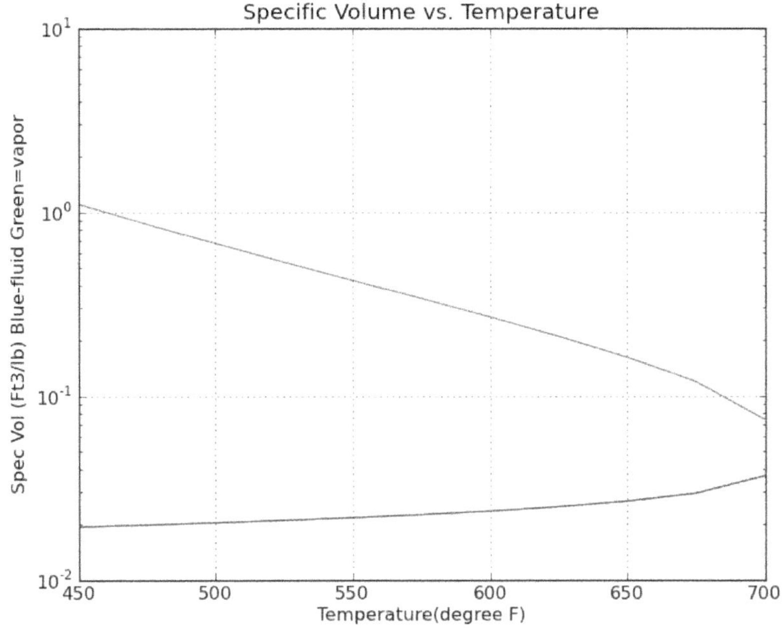
Specific Volume vs. Temperature
Spec Vol (Ft3/lb) Blue-fluid Green=vapor
Temperature(degree F)

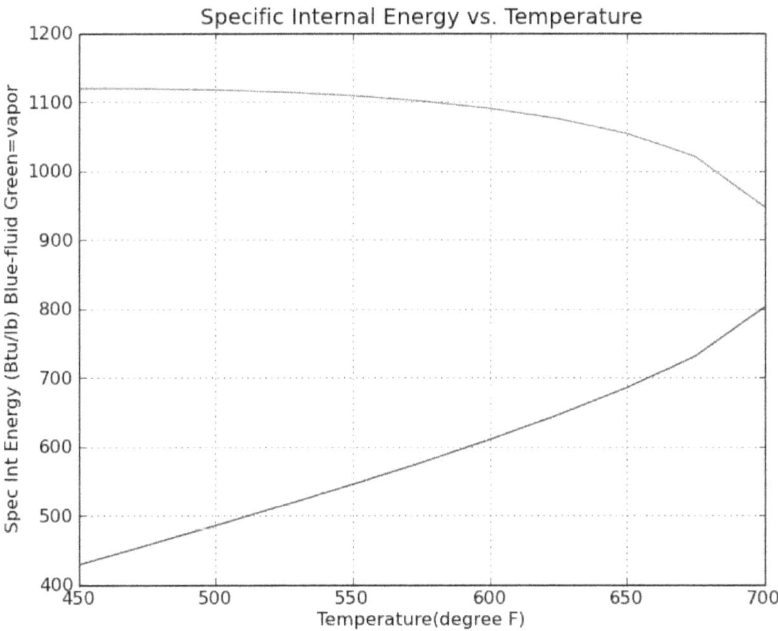
Specific Internal Energy vs. Temperature
Spec Int Energy (Btu/lb) Blue-fluid Green=vapor
Temperature(degree F)

Appendix 14.1

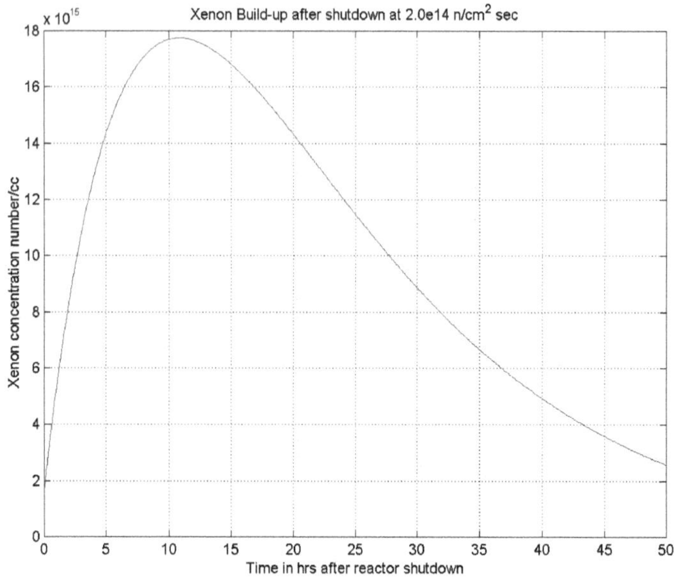

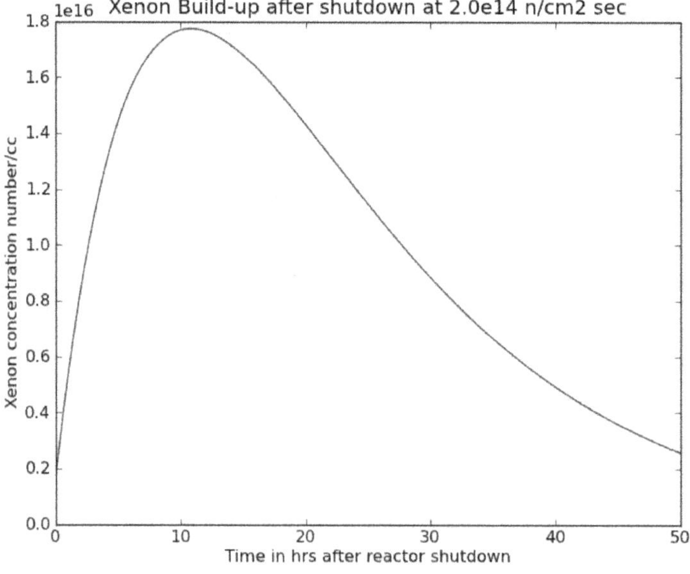

Appendix 14.2

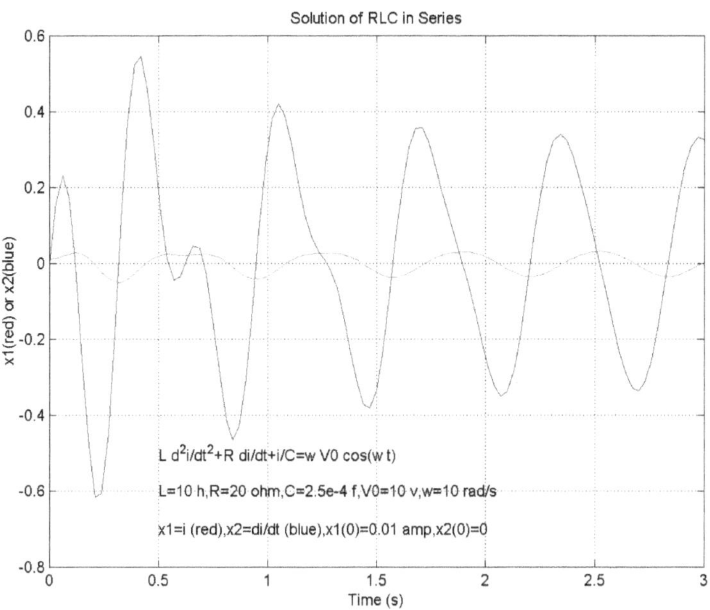

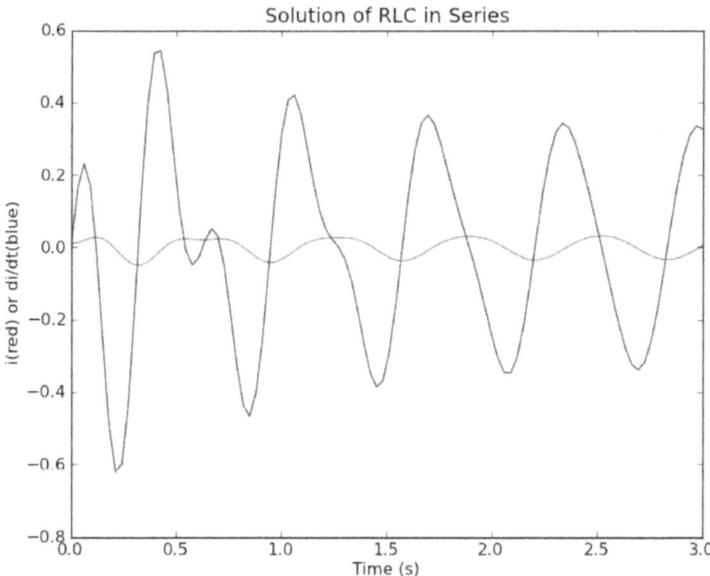

Appendix 14.3A

id	P	A	B	C	D	E	F
1	14.696	0.009782	0.0082997	0.0072076	0.0063694	0.0057059	0.0051676
2	50	0.033239	0.028208	0.0245	0.021653	0.019399	0.01757
3	150	0.099372	0.084372	0.07331	0.064812	0.058078	0.05261
4	400	0.26273	0.22334	0.194225	0.171831	0.154072	0.139633
5	600	0.39146	0.33308	0.28986	0.25658	0.23016	0.20867
6	900	0.58139	0.49537	0.43154	0.3823	0.34317	0.31129
7	1500	0.95064	0.81207	0.7088	0.62897	0.56528	0.51328
8	2500	1.53741	1.31845	1.15427	1.02659	0.92442	0.84071
9	4000	2.3598	2.0341	1.78789	1.59503	1.44	1.31248

APPENDIX 14.3B

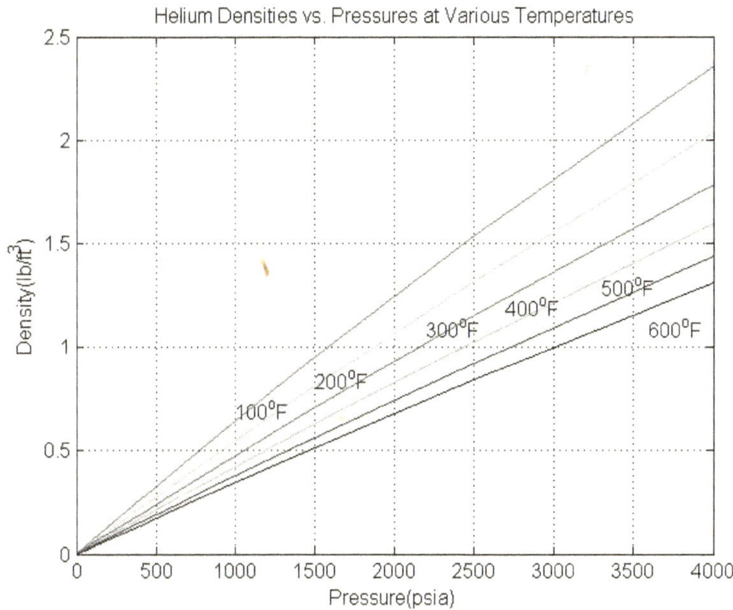

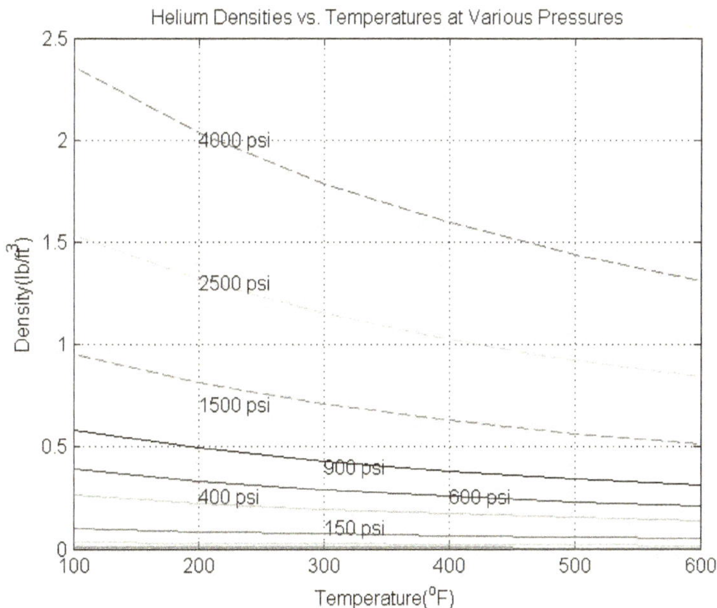

Appendix 14.3C

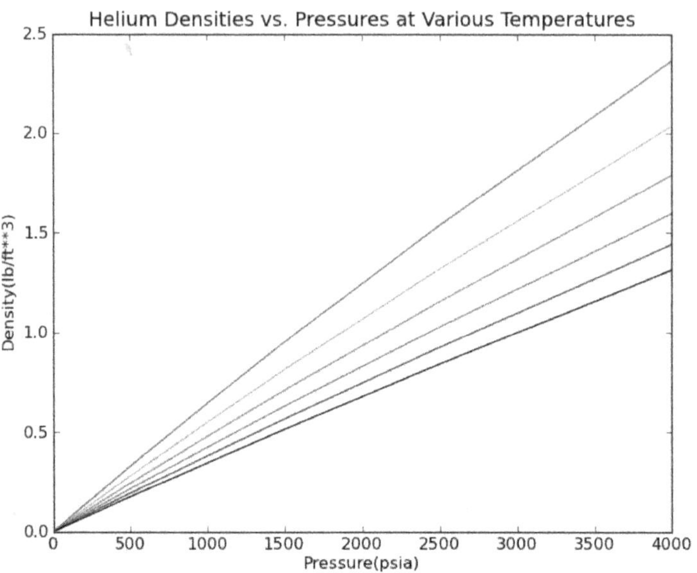

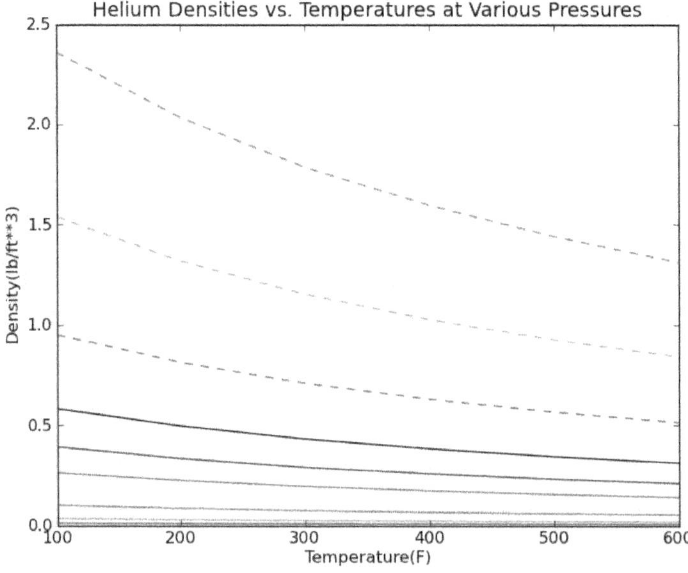

Appendix 14.3D

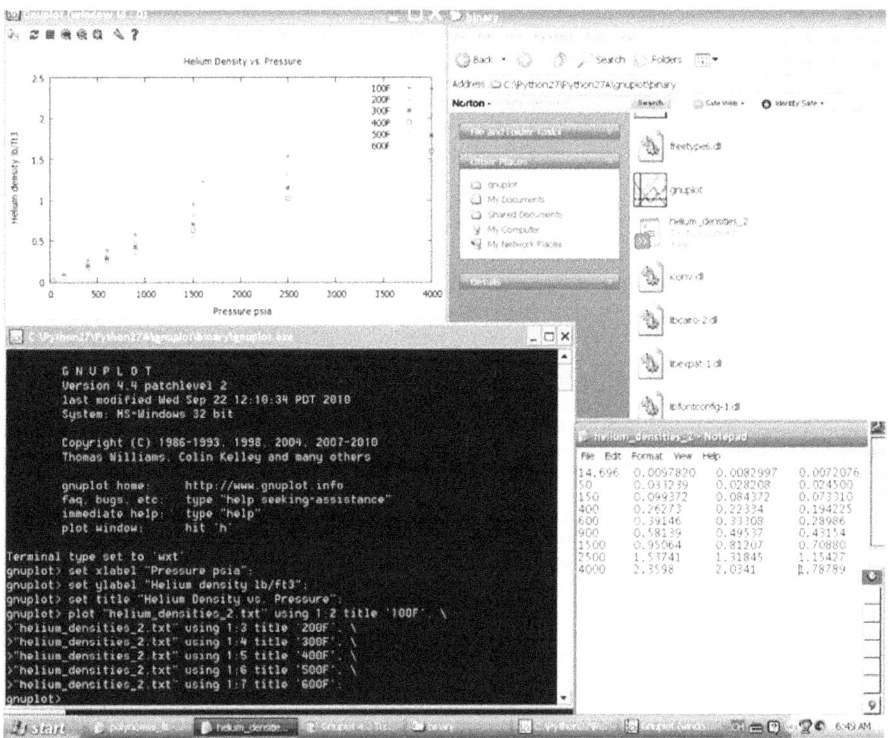

Appendix 14.4A

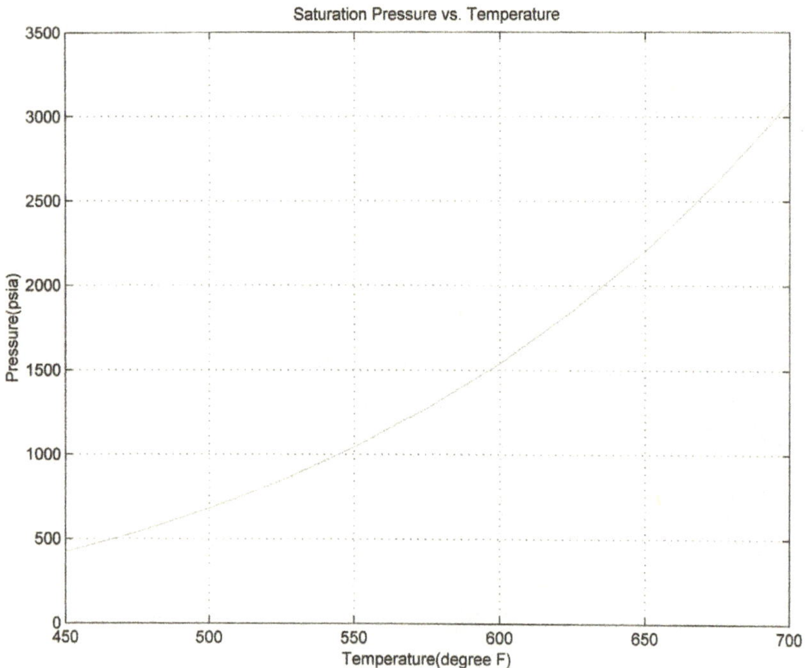

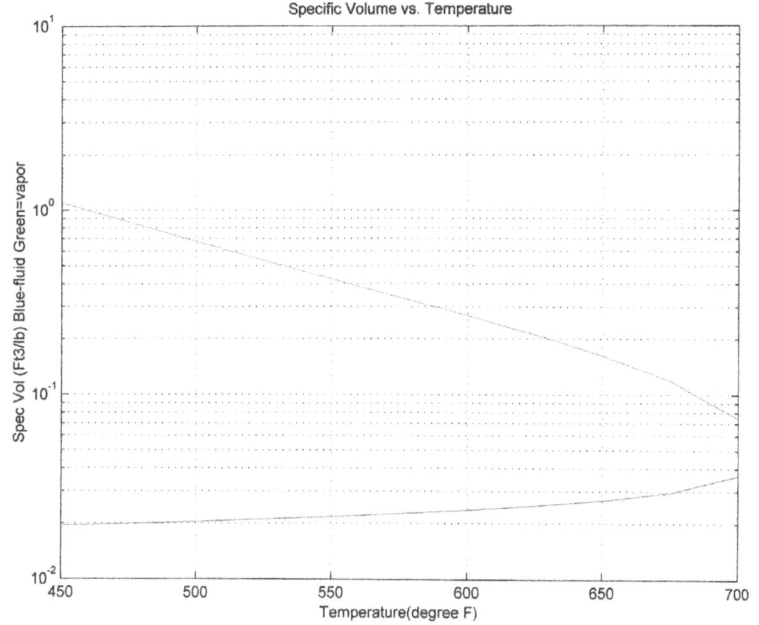
Specific Volume vs. Temperature
Spec Vol (Ft3/lb) Blue-fluid Green=vapor
10^1
10^0
10^{-1}
10^{-2}
450
500
550
600
650
700
Temperature(degree F)

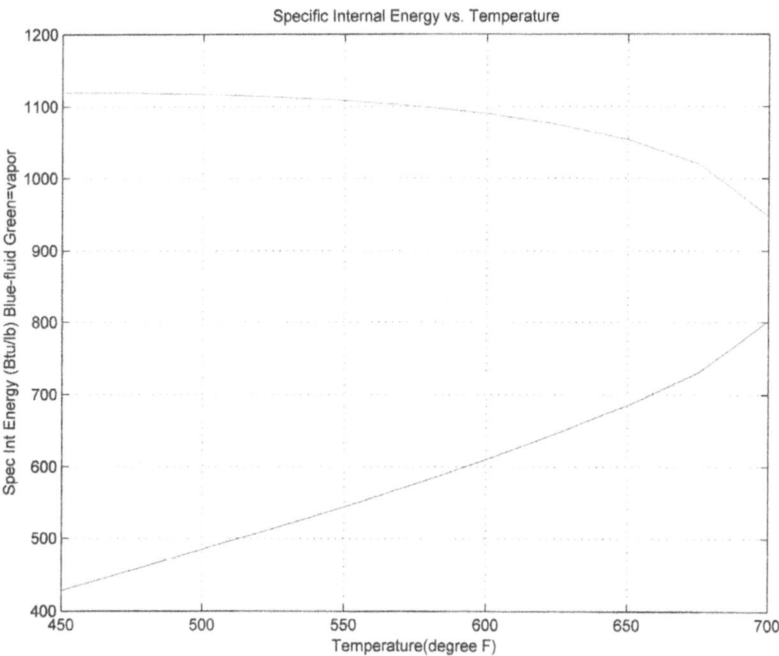
Specific Internal Energy vs. Temperature
Spec Int Energy (Btu/lb) Blue-fluid Green=vapor
1200
1100
1000
900
800
700
600
500
400
450
500
550
600
650
700
Temperature(degree F)

Appendix 14.4B

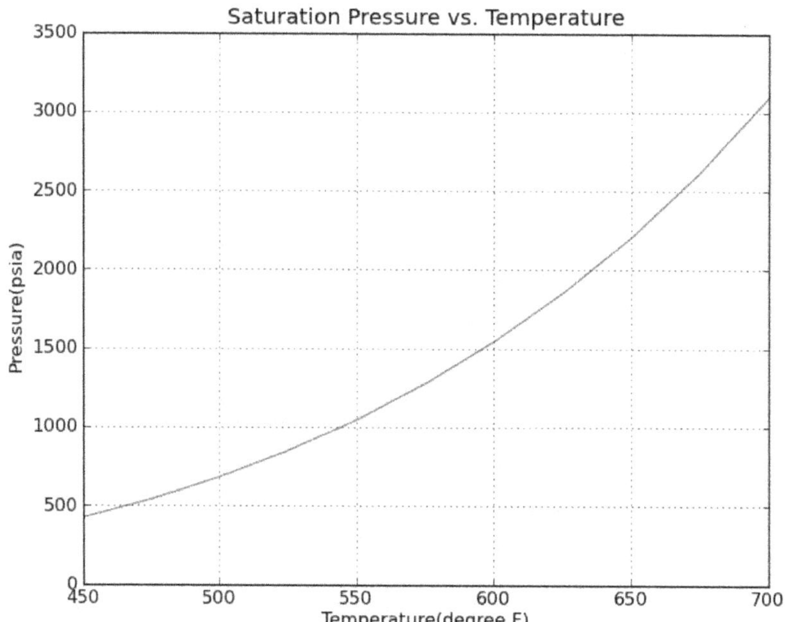

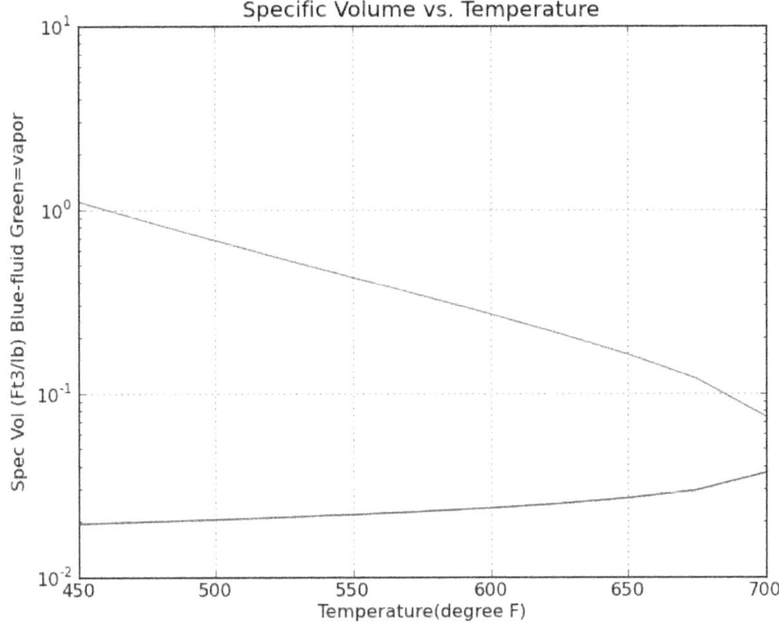
Specific Volume vs. Temperature
Spec Vol (Ft3/lb) Blue-fluid Green=vapor
Temperature(degree F)
10^{1}
10^{0}
10^{-1}
10^{-2}
450
500
550
600
650
700

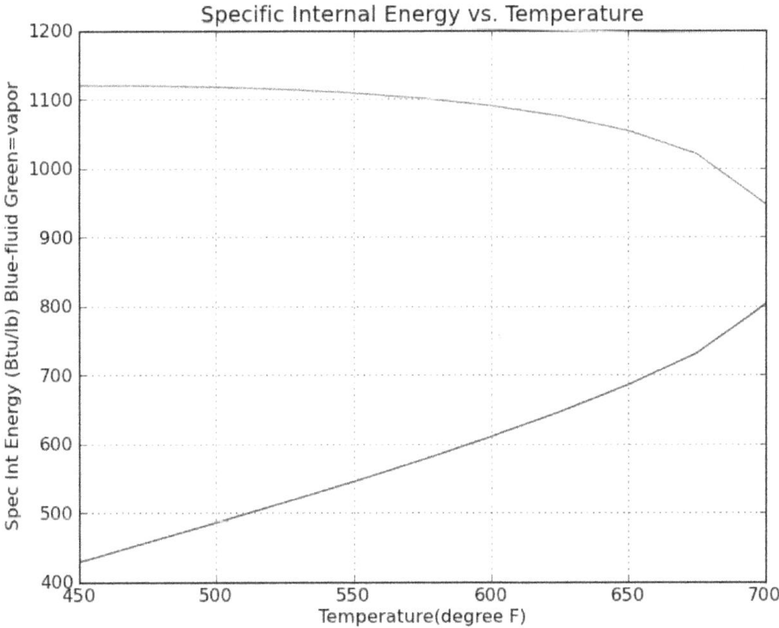
Specific Internal Energy vs. Temperature
Spec Int Energy (Btu/lb) Blue-fluid Green=vapor
Temperature(degree F)
1200
1100
1000
900
800
700
600
500
400
450
500
550
600
650
700

Appendix 14.5

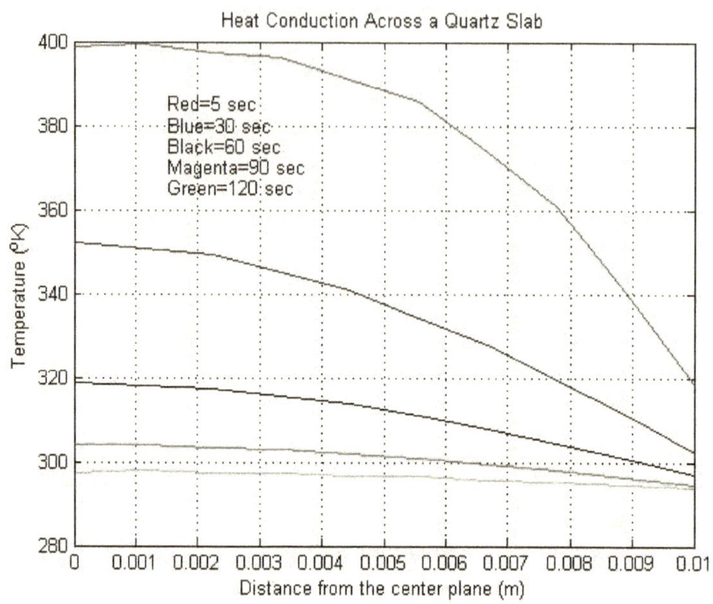

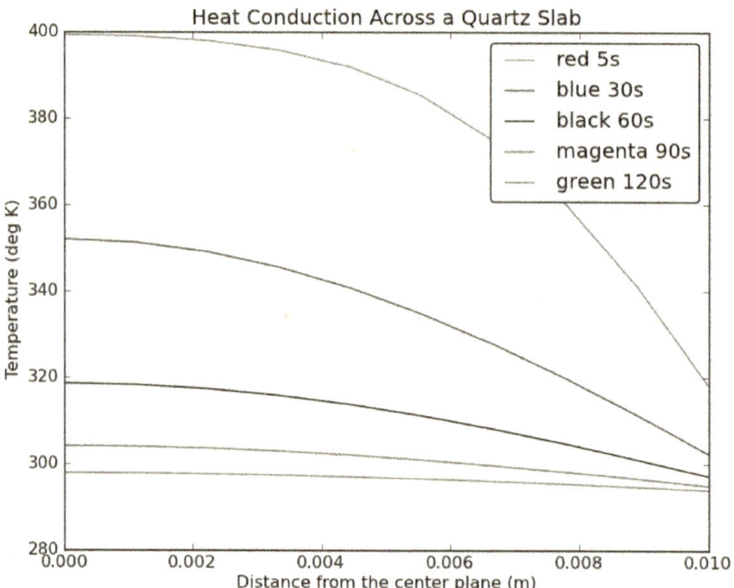

Appendix 14.6

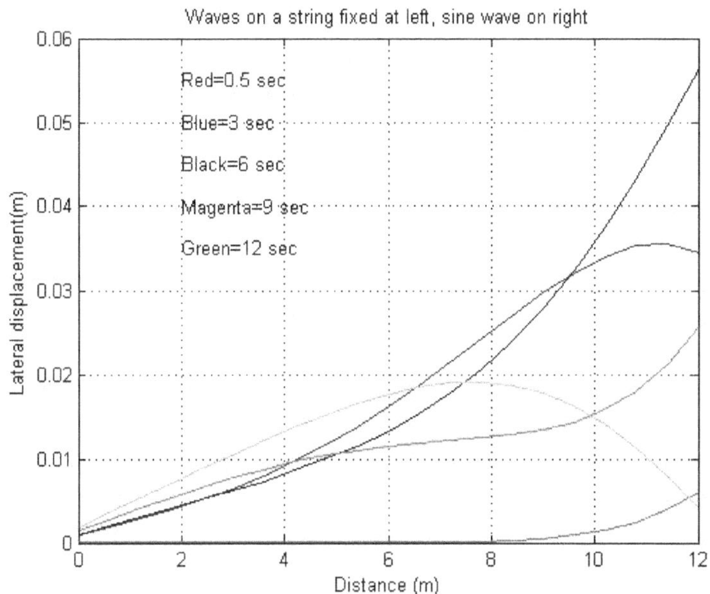

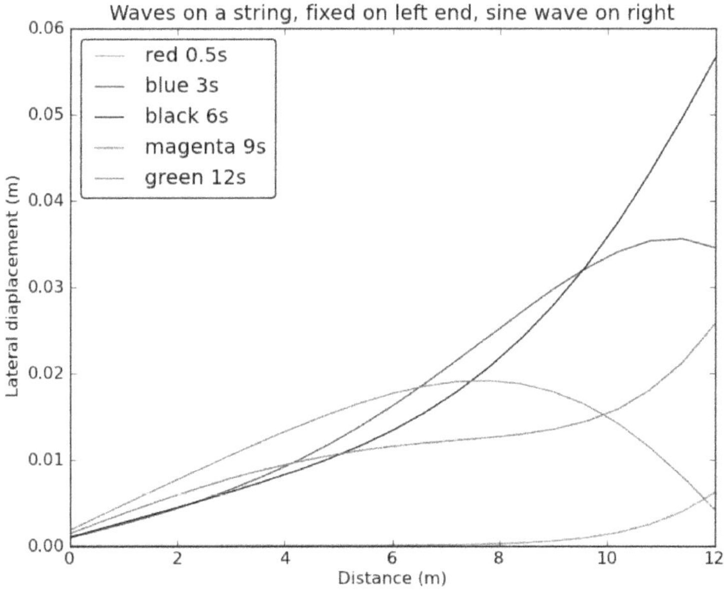

Appendix 14.7

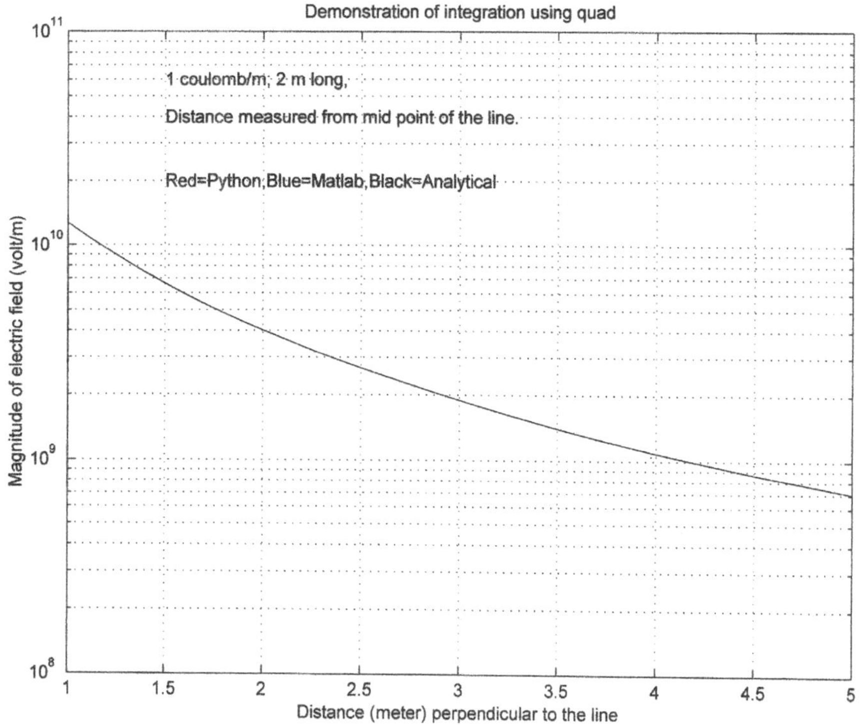

Appendix 14.8

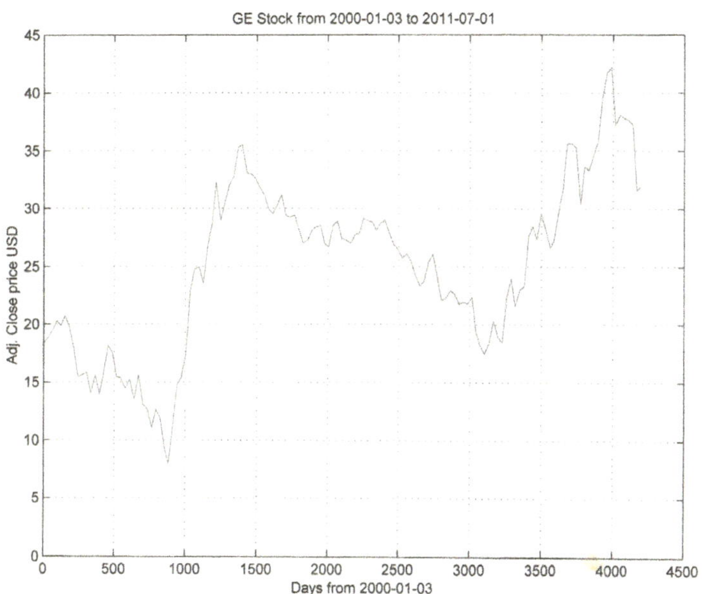

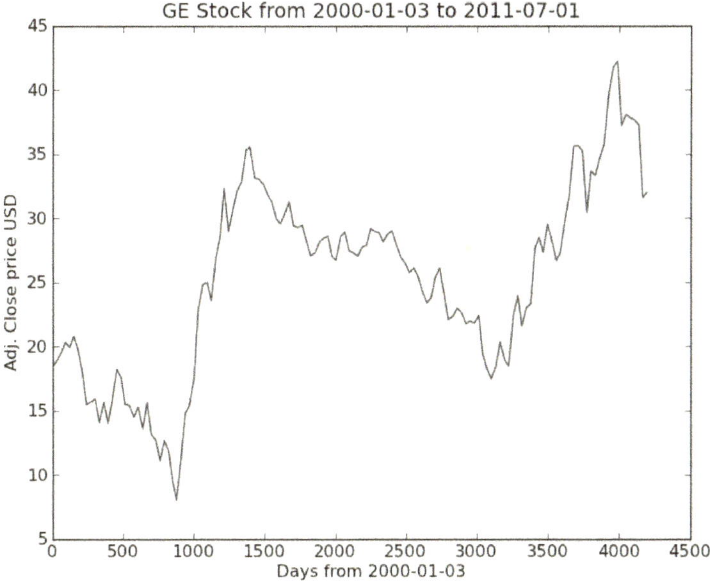

id	date	open	high	low	close	volume	adj_close
1	2011-07-01	18.86	19.45	18.29	18.41	52463100	18.41
2	2011-06-01	19.47	19.6	17.97	18.86	53953900	18.86
3	2011-05-02	20.7	20.71	18.97	19.64	45910500	19.48
4	2011-04-01	20.14	20.85	19.51	20.45	56260900	20.28
5	2011-03-01	21.12	21.17	18.6	20.05	63914200	19.89
6	2011-02-01	20.38	21.65	20.08	20.92	52895600	20.75
7	2011-01-03	18.49	20.74	18.12	20.14	76413100	19.84
8	2010-12-01	16.03	18.49	16.03	18.29	57131500	18.02
9	2010-11-01	16.09	16.86	15.63	15.83	55387200	15.47
10	2010-10-01	16.4	17.49	15.88	16.02	64676100	15.66
11	2010-09-01	14.73	16.7	14.6	16.25	60450700	15.88
12	2010-08-02	16.32	16.54	14.25	14.48	60617900	14.05
13	2010-07-01	14.33	16.57	13.75	16.12	75597900	15.64
14	2010-06-01	16.24	16.51	14.27	14.42	83717300	13.99
15	2010-05-03	18.97	19.34	15.15	16.35	106550400	15.76
16	2010-04-01	18.27	19.7	18.18	18.86	82505100	18.18
17	2010-03-01	16.1	18.94	15.83	18.2	93006300	17.55
18	2010-02-01	16.2	17.03	15.25	16.06	77313200	15.48
19	2010-01-04	15.22	16.92	15.15	16.08	88647000	15.41
20	2009-12-01	16.27	16.49	15.13	15.13	62454500	14.5
21	2009-11-02	14.3	16.25	14.15	16.02	80429200	15.25
22	2009-10-01	16.31	16.87	14.15	14.26	103007100	13.57
23	2009-09-01	13.74	17.52	13.03	16.42	132466400	15.63
24	2009-08-03	13.65	14.88	13.16	13.9	86516200	13.15
25	2009-07-01	11.76	13.45	10.5	13.4	100768400	12.68
26	2009-06-01	13.82	13.99	11.25	11.72	87259400	11.09
27	2009-05-01	12.74	14.55	12.22	13.48	104569000	12.65
28	2009-04-01	9.91	12.81	9.8	12.65	133547800	11.87
29	2009-03-02	8.29	11.35	5.87	10.11	277426300	9.49
30	2009-02-02	12.03	12.9	8.4	8.51	194928800	7.99
31	2009-01-02	16.51	17.24	11.87	12.13	117846700	11.06
32	2008-12-01	16.36	19.3	15.35	16.2	98683700	14.77
33	2008-11-03	19.78	21.04	12.58	17.17	134841700	15.36
34	2008-10-01	24	25.75	17.27	19.51	164650600	17.45
35	2008-09-02	28.54	29.28	22.16	25.5	105769100	22.81

36	2008-08-01	28.43	30.39	27.76	28.1	43604700	24.8
37	2008-07-01	26.42	29.89	25.6	28.29	69943000	24.97
38	2008-06-02	30.75	31.14	26.15	26.69	75216900	23.56
39	2008-05-01	32.8	33.62	30.21	30.72	52851400	26.82
40	2008-04-01	37.36	38.52	31.55	32.7	64485500	28.55
41	2008-03-03	33.34	37.74	31.65	37.01	59927700	32.31
42	2008-02-01	35.59	36.3	33.09	33.14	44926300	28.93
43	2008-01-02	37.1	37.45	32.92	35.36	55123800	30.59
44	2007-12-03	38.2	38.2	36.07	37.07	42936400	32.07
45	2007-11-01	40.89	40.98	36.52	38.29	45181800	32.84
46	2007-10-01	41.28	42.15	39.4	41.16	32919400	35.31
47	2007-09-04	38.84	42.07	38.45	41.4	37426500	35.51
48	2007-08-01	38.6	40.46	36.2	38.87	46947200	33.12
49	2007-07-02	38.42	40.98	37.73	38.76	43667100	33.02
50	2007-06-01	37.68	39.77	36.65	38.28	43860200	32.62
51	2007-05-01	36.82	37.81	36.45	37.58	31562900	31.79
52	2007-04-02	35.36	37.24	34.55	36.86	41666000	31.18
53	2007-03-01	34.61	36	33.9	35.36	37497700	29.91
54	2007-02-01	36.18	36.5	34.5	34.91	34598700	29.53
55	2007-01-03	37.41	38.28	35.76	36.05	34343900	30.26
56	2006-12-01	35.38	38.49	34.96	37.21	33604700	31.23
57	2006-11-01	35.2	36.28	34.62	35.28	23114100	29.39
58	2006-10-02	35.4	36.48	34.92	35.11	26500400	29.25
59	2006-09-01	34.18	35.65	33.76	35.3	24034200	29.41
60	2006-08-01	32.65	34.44	32.2	34.06	18494400	28.17
61	2006-07-03	33.1	33.62	32.06	32.69	24910500	27.04
62	2006-06-01	34.3	34.92	32.78	32.96	27849600	27.26
63	2006-05-01	34.64	35.24	33.7	34.26	24209600	28.13
64	2006-04-03	34.79	34.99	33.07	34.59	26428700	28.4
65	2006-03-01	32.97	35	32.58	34.78	26519300	28.56
66	2006-02-01	32.66	33.75	32.21	32.87	26951100	26.99
67	2006-01-03	35.1	35.63	32.63	32.75	34947000	26.69
68	2005-12-01	35.85	36.26	34.95	35.05	22568500	28.56
69	2005-11-01	33.97	36.34	33.51	35.72	22225800	28.9
70	2005-10-03	33.6	34.5	32.67	33.91	23636600	27.44
71	2005-09-01	33.43	34.58	33	33.67	22843400	27.25
72	2005-08-01	34.57	34.62	32.85	33.61	19156900	27.02

73	2005-07-01	34.85	35.78	33.93	34.5	22692600	27.73
74	2005-06-01	36.48	37.13	34.15	34.65	24312400	27.85
75	2005-05-02	36.08	37.34	35.56	36.48	17054700	29.15
76	2005-04-01	36.18	36.6	35.02	36.2	21540700	28.92
77	2005-03-01	35.27	36.48	35.06	36.06	18737000	28.81
78	2005-02-01	36	36.61	35.05	35.2	17348000	28.12
79	2005-01-03	36.71	36.89	34.95	36.13	19883000	28.69
80	2004-12-01	35.36	37.75	35.27	36.5	18800400	28.98
81	2004-11-01	34.1	36.86	33.81	35.36	18420700	27.91
82	2004-10-01	33.7	34.4	32.65	34.12	16090400	26.93
83	2004-09-01	32.79	34.53	32.62	33.58	18122500	26.5
84	2004-08-02	32.65	33.35	31.42	32.79	15559200	25.73
85	2004-07-01	32.4	33.62	31.5	33.25	22230200	26.09
86	2004-06-01	31	33.49	30.82	32.4	28805300	25.42
87	2004-05-03	30.12	31.47	29.55	31.12	20702700	24.27
88	2004-04-01	30.42	31.85	29.8	29.95	32068200	23.36
89	2004-03-01	32.69	33.48	28.88	30.52	40261200	23.8
90	2004-02-02	33.69	33.99	32.35	32.52	18725500	25.36
91	2004-01-02	31	34.57	30.92	33.63	23093800	26.07
92	2003-12-01	29.2	31.29	28.78	30.98	20243900	24.02
93	2003-11-03	29.05	29.95	27.37	28.67	22067400	22.08
94	2003-10-01	29.81	31.3	28	29.01	21493200	22.34
95	2003-09-02	29.75	32.42	29.31	29.81	21533800	22.96
96	2003-08-01	28.2	30.39	27.18	29.57	16648400	22.63
97	2003-07-01	28.48	29.5	26.9	28.44	22288900	21.77
98	2003-06-02	29.42	31.66	28.53	28.68	20550900	21.95
99	2003-05-01	29.45	29.45	27.35	28.7	19460600	21.82
100	2003-04-01	25.55	29.78	25.5	29.45	21207800	22.39
101	2003-03-03	24.2	28	23.16	25.5	26107100	19.39
102	2003-02-03	23.35	24.2	21.3	24.05	23505800	18.29
103	2003-01-02	24.65	26.26	22.45	23.14	23240300	17.46
104	2002-12-02	27.98	27.98	24.1	24.35	20521100	18.37
105	2002-11-01	25.28	27.4	23.2	27.12	28840700	20.31
106	2002-10-01	24.75	27.21	21.4	25.25	34091600	18.91
107	2002-09-03	29.5	29.7	23.51	24.65	31835500	18.46
108	2002-08-01	32.1	32.98	28.27	30.15	26539000	22.42
109	2002-07-01	29.06	32.2	23.02	32.2	39648900	23.94

110	2002-06-03	31.14	31.4	27.42	29.05	29971600	21.6
111	2002-05-01	31.75	33.45	30.4	31.14	23783100	23.01
112	2002-04-01	37.05	37.8	30.15	31.55	31131400	23.31
113	2002-03-01	39.1	41.84	36.83	37.4	25796800	27.63
114	2002-02-01	36.9	39.65	34.72	38.5	25112400	28.45
115	2002-01-02	40.3	41.34	34.49	37.15	24680100	27.32
116	2001-12-03	38.4	41.39	36.21	40.08	23080100	29.48
117	2001-11-01	36.25	41.78	36.05	38.5	16974400	28.19
118	2001-10-01	37.3	39.49	36.04	36.41	19544800	26.66
119	2001-09-04	40.9	42.17	28.5	37.2	42638800	27.24
120	2001-08-01	43	43.53	39.84	40.9	16831300	29.81
121	2001-07-02	48.92	50.2	42.99	43.5	20559200	31.71
122	2001-06-01	48.99	52.61	46.26	49	29526100	35.6
123	2001-05-01	48.05	53.55	47.51	49	16915500	35.6
124	2001-04-02	41.52	50.01	39.04	48.53	22337500	35.26
125	2001-03-01	45.5	46.6	36.42	41.86	30658800	30.41
126	2001-02-01	46.5	48.45	45.02	46.5	20455600	33.66
127	2001-01-02	46.75	48.75	42.63	45.98	24345500	33.29
128	2000-12-01	50.88	56.19	47.19	47.94	17054700	34.71
129	2000-11-01	54.75	55.25	47.94	49.56	14524300	35.76
130	2000-10-02	58	59.94	49	54.81	20282300	39.55
131	2000-09-01	59.25	60.06	55	57.81	12225400	41.71
132	2000-08-01	51.94	60.5	51.19	58.63	11558800	42.21
133	2000-07-03	52.5	54.75	49.5	51.69	13163300	37.21
134	2000-06-01	52.06	54	47.94	53	12857500	38.05
135	2000-05-01	159	162	48.75	52.63	14351800	37.79
136	2000-04-03	155.25	167.94	143.06	157.25	21992900	37.64
137	2000-03-01	133.5	164.88	126.25	155.63	25483700	37.25
138	2000-02-01	134.25	143.13	124.94	132.38	23404600	31.59
139	2000-01-03	153	154.94	133.06	134	22127500	31.98

Appendix 14.9A

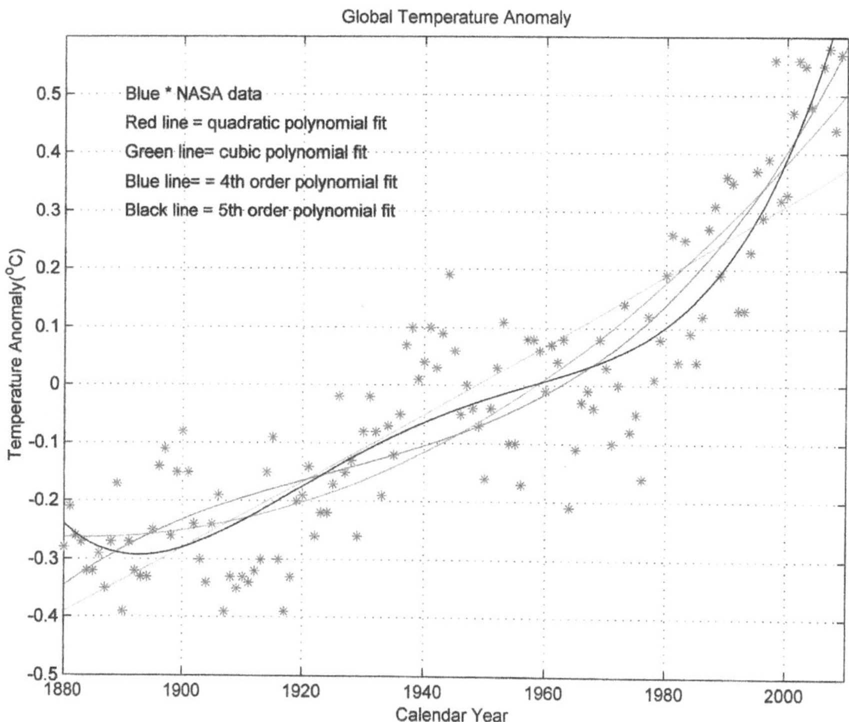

Appendix 14.9B

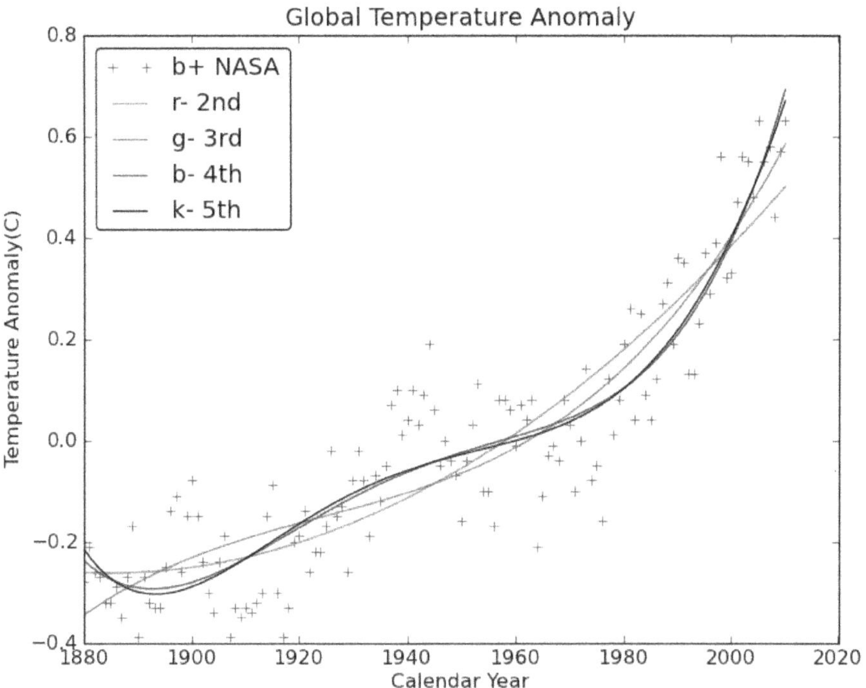

Appendix 14.9C

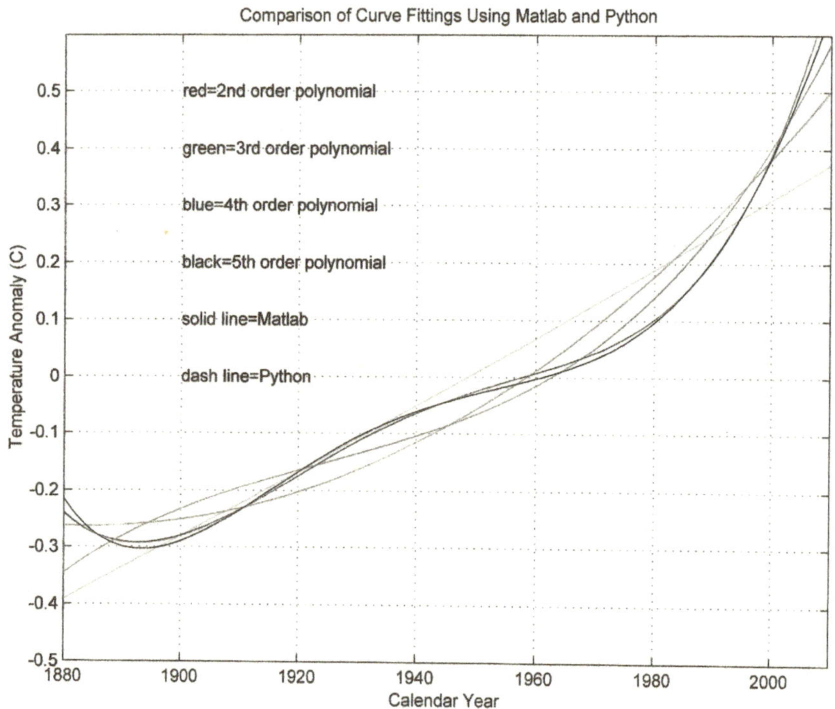

Appendix 14.10

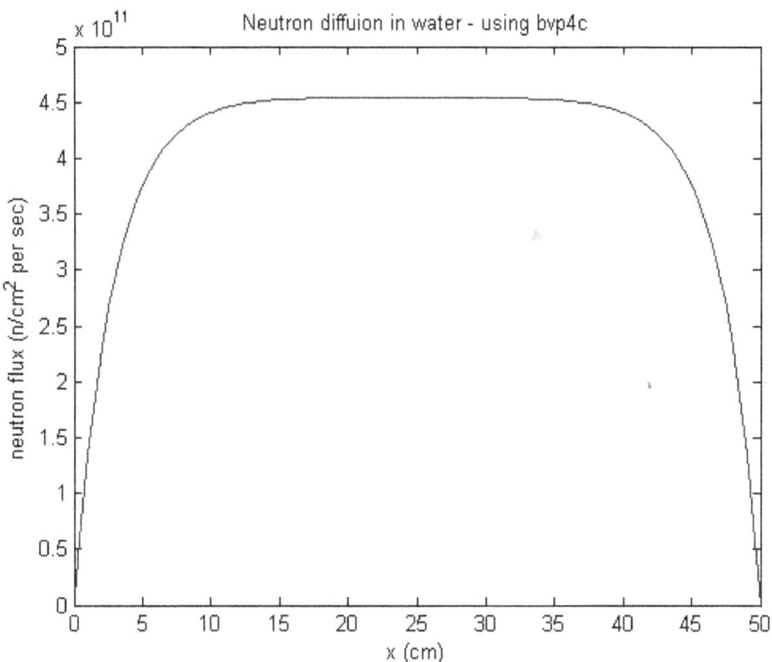

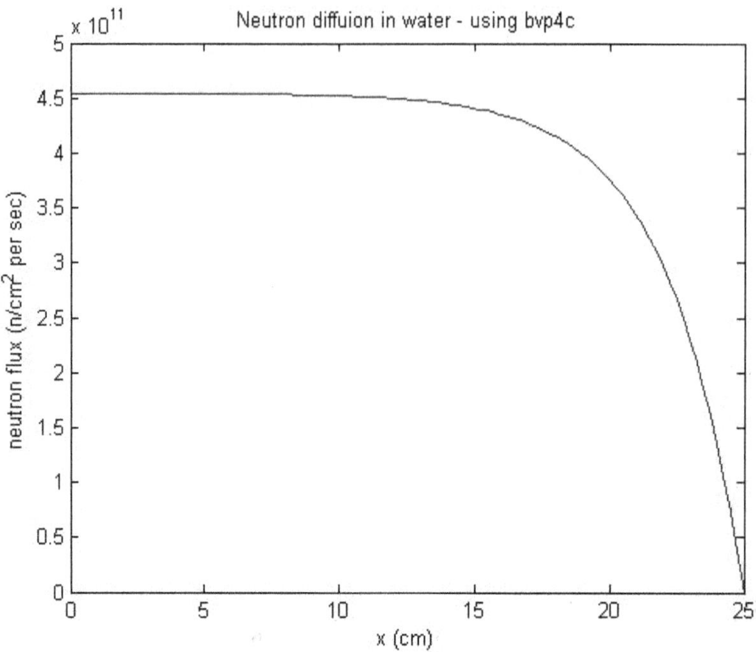
Neutron diffuion in water - using bvp4c
x 10^11
neutron flux (n/cm2 per sec)
x (cm)

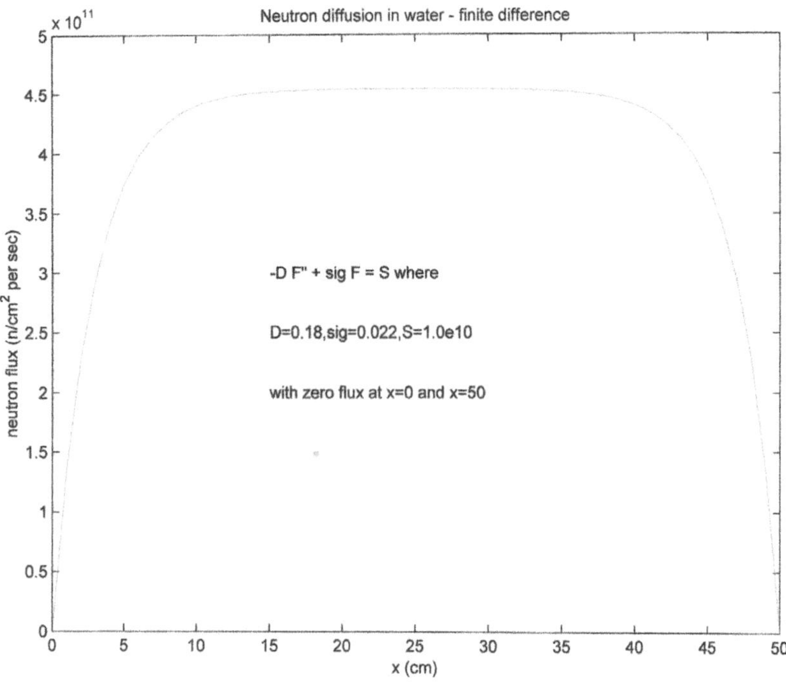
Neutron diffusion in water - finite difference
x 10^11
neutron flux (n/cm2 per sec)
-D F" + sig F = S where
D=0.18,sig=0.022,S=1.0e10
with zero flux at x=0 and x=50
x (cm)

Appendix 14.11

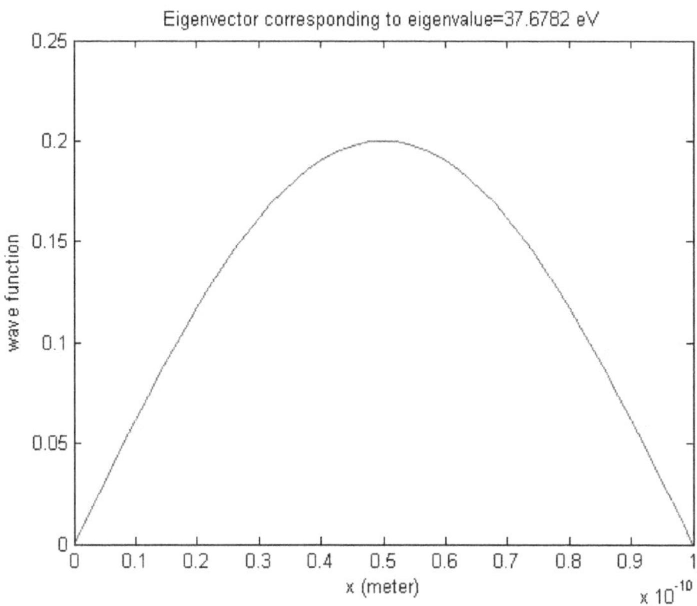

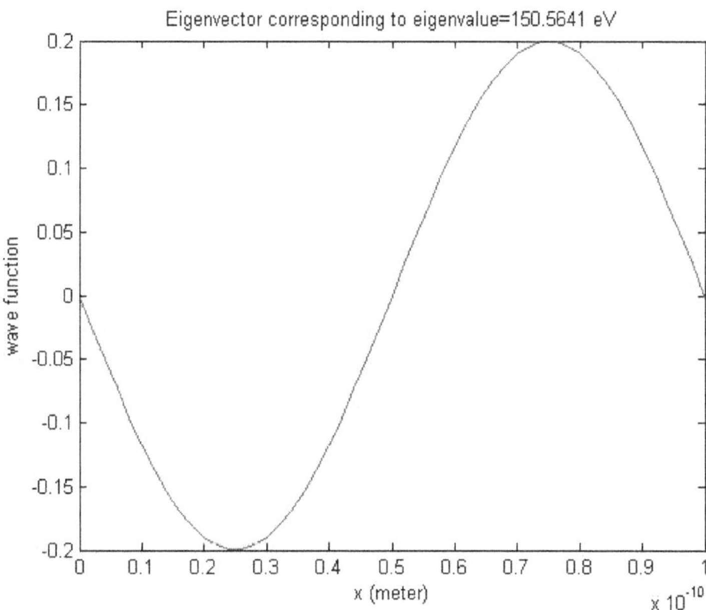

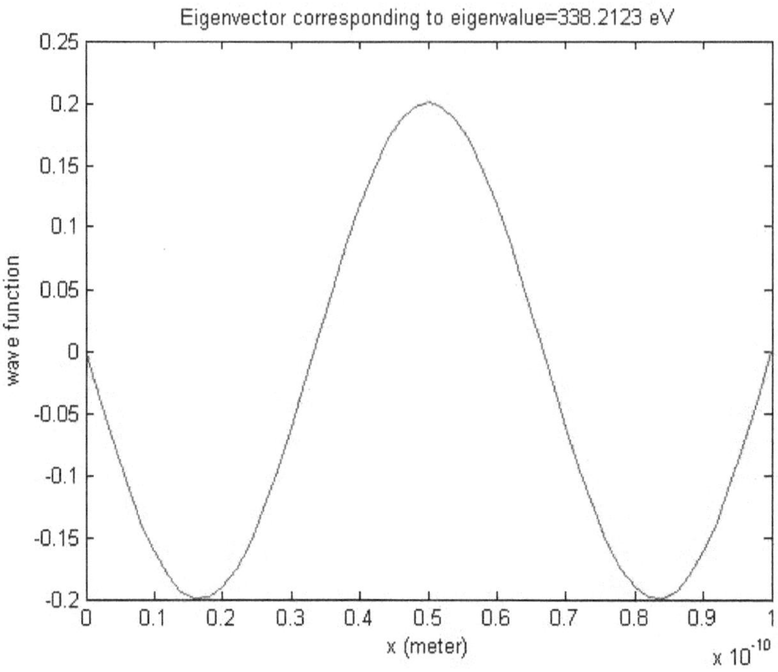
Eigenvector corresponding to eigenvalue=338.2123 eV
0.25
0.2
0.15
0.1
0.05
0
-0.05
-0.1
-0.15
-0.2
wave function
0
0.1
0.2
0.3
0.4
0.5
0.6
0.7
0.8
0.9
1
x (meter)
x 10^{-10}

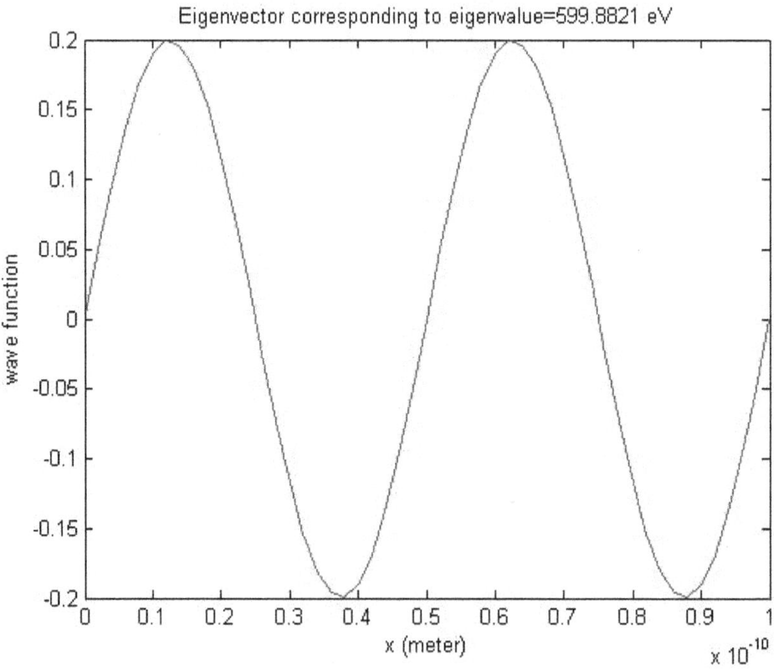
Eigenvector corresponding to eigenvalue=599.8821 eV
0.2
0.15
0.1
0.05
0
-0.05
-0.1
-0.15
-0.2
wave function
0
0.1
0.2
0.3
0.4
0.5
0.6
0.7
0.8
0.9
1
x (meter)
x 10^{-10}

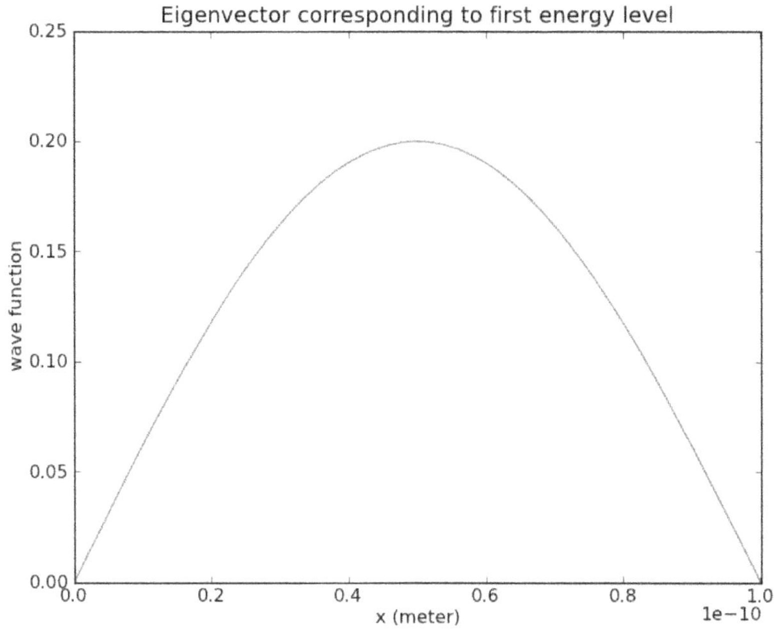
Eigenvector corresponding to first energy level
wave function
x (meter)
1e−10
0.25
0.20
0.15
0.10
0.05
0.00
0.0
0.2
0.4
0.6
0.8
1.0

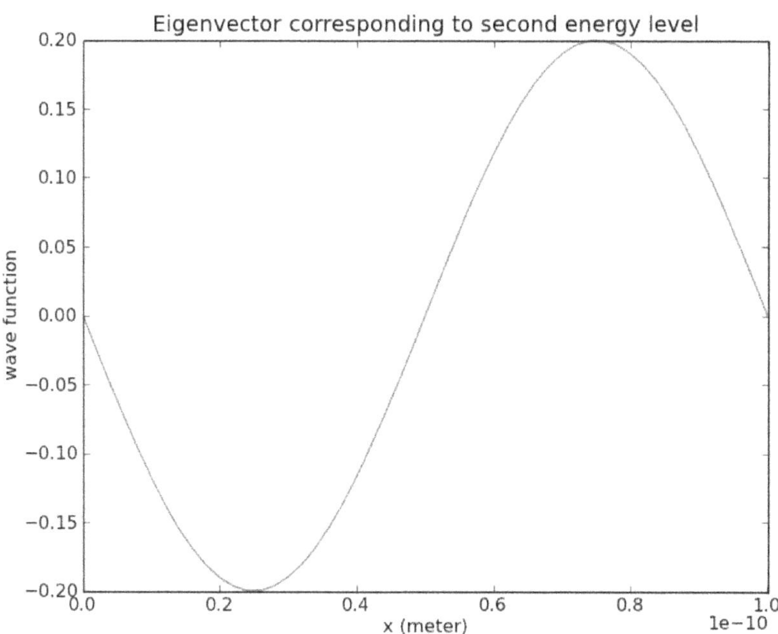
Eigenvector corresponding to second energy level
wave function
x (meter)
1e−10
0.20
0.15
0.10
0.05
0.00
−0.05
−0.10
−0.15
−0.20
0.0
0.2
0.4
0.6
0.8
1.0

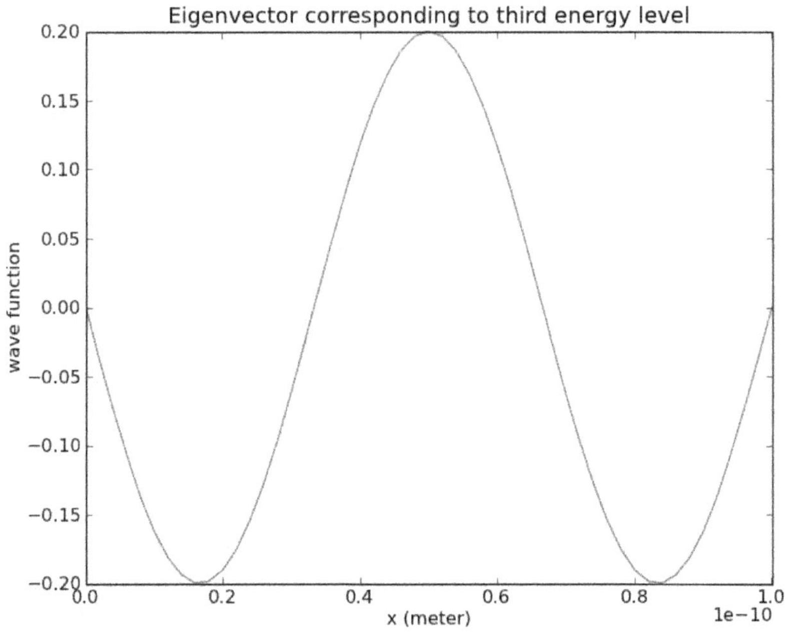
Eigenvector corresponding to third energy level
0.20
0.15
0.10
0.05
0.00
−0.05
−0.10
−0.15
−0.20
wave function
0.0
0.2
0.4
0.6
0.8
1.0
1e−10
x (meter)

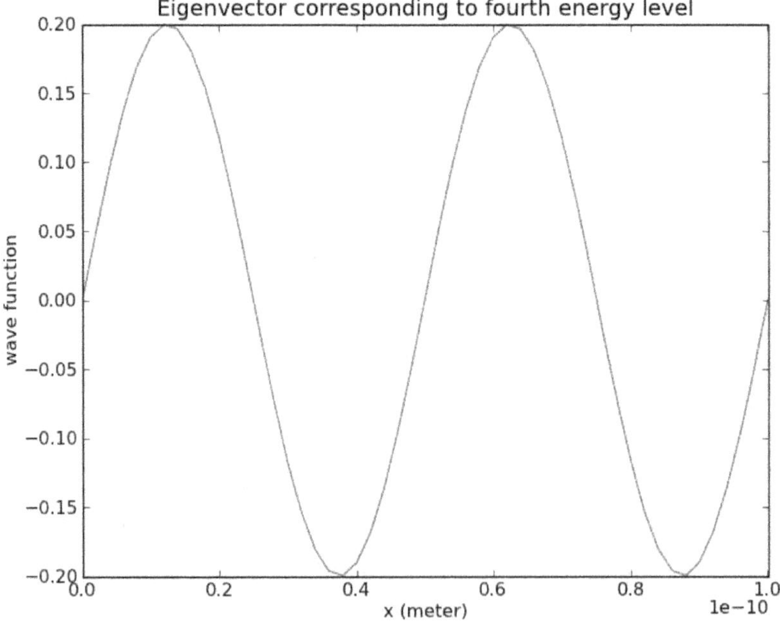
Eigenvector corresponding to fourth energy level
0.20
0.15
0.10
0.05
0.00
−0.05
−0.10
−0.15
−0.20
wave function
0.0
0.2
0.4
0.6
0.8
1.0
1e−10
x (meter)

Index

List of Computer Files

computer_files_3.1
- Scitools
- MySQL-python-1.2.3.win32-py2.7

computer_files_3.2
- gnuplot

computer_files_4.1
- xmltree
- libmysql.dll
- mysql.dll
- python.m.txt

computer_files_5.1
- basicdata1.sql.txt
- mysql_commands.txt
- mysql_commands_1.txt
- rare_earth.sql.txt
- rare_earth_1.sql.txt
- to_create_rare_earth.php.txt
- to_insert_in_basicdata1.php.txt
- to_print_basicdata1.php.txt

computer_files_5.2
- basicdata1.sql.txt
- file_basicdata1A.txt
- file_basicdata1B.txt
- file_basicdata1C.txt
- file_basicdata1D.txt
- file_GE_A.txt
- file_GE_B.txt
- GE.sql.txt
- to_retrieve_basicdata1.php.txt
- to_retrieve_basicdata1A.php.txt
- to_retrieve_basicdata1B.php.txt
- to_retrieve_column.php.txt
- to_retrieve_column_1.php.txt

computer_files_5.3
- basicdata1.sql.txt
- basicdata2.sql.txt
- basicdata3.sql.txt
- file_basicdata1C.txt
- file_basicdata1D.txt
- rare_earth_1.sql.txt

to_add_2_columns.php.txt
to_print_basicdata2.php.txt
to_print_basicdata3.php.txt
computer_files_5.4
mysmartysite
basicdata5.sql.txt
to_insert_in_basicdata5.php.txt
to_insert_in_basicdata5.tpl.txt
computer_files_6.1
basicdata1.sql.txt
basicdata4.sql.txt
create_basicdata4_commands.txt
perl2mysql_1.pl.txt
perl2mysql_2.pl.txt
rare_earth.sql.txt
computer_files_7.1
basicdata1.sql.txt
measurement.sql.txt
MySQL-python-1.2.3.win32-py2.7
output_measurement.txt
to_create_measurement.py.txt
to_insert_measurement.py.txt
to_parse_measurement.py.txt
to_retrieve_basicdata1.py.txt
computer_files_8.1
GE.sql.txt
GE_stock_mysql.txt
libmysql.dll
mysql.dll
mysql.m.txt
computer_files_8.2
create_insert_fetch.txt
create_steam_table4.m.txt
fetch_steam_table4.m.txt
insert_steam_table4.m.txt
steam_table4.jpg
steam_table4.sql.txt
computer_files_9.1
GE.xml
str_to_array_GE.php.txt
str_to_xml_GE.php.txt
table_GE_to_str.php.txt

test_file_GE.txt
computer_files_9.2
array_to_xml;_1.php.txt
material_property_1.xml
computer_files_9.3
steamtable3rev.php.txt
computer_files_9.4
steamTable.xml
steamTable_xml_dump.php.txt
steamTable_xml_dump1.php.txt
computer_files_9.5
steamTable.xml
steamTable_1.xml
to_use_DOM_steam.php.txt
to_use_DOM_steam_mod.php.txt
computer_files_10.1
basicdata1-py.xml
create_basicdata1.py.txt
create_resistivities.py.txt
resistivities.txt
resistivities_py.xml
computer_files_10.2
basicdata1_py.xml
parse_basicdata1_py.py.txt
parse_steam_table_1.py.txt
steamTable.xml
computer_files_11.1
RLC.xml
xmlDOM_write_RLC.pl.txt
computer_files_11.2
resistivities_py.xml
RLC.xml
steamTable.xml
xmlDOM_read_res.pl.txt
xmlDOM_read_RLC.pl.txt
xmlDOM_read_ST.pl.txt
computer_files_12.1
xmltree
basicdata1_ml.xml
xmldemo1x.m.txt
computer_files_12.2
xmltree

basicdata1_ml.xml
xmldemo2x.m.txt
xmldemo2xA.m.txt
computer_files_13.1
command_window_13_1.txt
hello.pl.txt
hello_perl.pl.txt
table_of_squares.pl.txt
table_of_squares_1.pl.txt
computer_files_13.2
command_window_13.2.txt
Fibonacci.py.txt
python.m.txt
sqd.py.txt
sqd_1.py.txt
computer_files_13.3
eigen_A.m.txt
eigen_values_vectorsA.txt
phpTofile.txt
result_php_2_ml.txt
testphpmatlab_eigen_A.php.txt
computer_files_13.4
Matlab_from_Perl.pl.txt
Matlab_from_Perl_A.pl.txt
Matlab_from_Perl_B.pl.txt
Matlab_from_Perl_C.pl.txt
Matlab_from_Perl_D.pl.txt
Matlab_from_Perl_E.pl.txt
Matlab_from_Perl_F.pl.txt
Matlab_from_Perl_G.pl.txt
computer_files_14.1
xenon_ode_2.m.txt
xenon_ode_2.py.txt
computer_files_14.2
rlc.m
RLC_Matlab_test.m.txt
RLC_Matlab_test.py.txt
computer_files_14.3
curve_plot_hilium.m.txt
curve_plot_hilium.py.txt
file_helium_A.txt
file_helium_B.txt

- file_helium_C.txt
- file_helium_D.txt
- file_helium_E.txt
- file_helium_F.txt
- file_helium_P.txt
- to_print_helium.php.txt
- to_retrieve_helium.php.txt

computer_files_14.4
- file_p.txt
- file_t.txt
- file_uf.txt
- file_ug.txt
- file_vf.txt
- file_vg.txt
- Steam_Table.m.txt
- Steam_Table_py.py.txt
- steamTable.xml
- steamTable_xml_dump2.php.txt

computer_files_14.5
- heat.m.txt
- heat_slab.m.txt
- heat_slab_2.py.txt

computer_files_14.6
- wave.m.txt
- wave_on_a_string.py.txt
- wave_string.m.txt

computer_files_14.7
- E_field.txt
- E_field_matlab.txt
- electric_field_2.m.txt
- electric_field_comp.m.txt
- integrand1.m.txt
- test_integrate14.py.txt

computer_files_14.8
- file_GE_A.txt
- file_GE_A_1.txt
- file_GE_B.txt
- GE.sql.txt
- GE_stock.m.txt
- GE_stock_py.py.txt
- stocks_commands.txt
- table_wordpad.txt

- to_cal_dates.php.txt
- to_retrieve_column_1.php.txt

computer_files_14.9

- compare_matlab_python_4.m.txt
- fitted_data_matlab.txt
- fitted_data_python.txt
- NASA_temp_data.txt
- to_plot_temp_anomaly_4.m.txt
- to_plot_temp_anomaly_4A.py.txt

computer_files_14.10

- bvp4c_neutron.m.txt
- bvp4c_neutron_1.m.txt
- neutron_diffusion.m.txt
- neutron_diffusion_py.py.txt

computer_files_14.11

- particle_box.m.txt
- particle_box_py.py.txt

www.ingramcontent.com/pod-product-compliance
Lightning Source LLC
Chambersburg PA
CBHW051224050326
40689CB00007B/795
* 9 7 8 1 4 6 5 3 6 4 4 3 2 *